Han-chan's Dream

This book was born not so long ago but very far away as *Han-chan's Dream*, and renamed because, as unique a character as this cat was, I wanted his felinity to be clear from the main title. Still, when you peg your notes to a certain name year after year, that name assumes a reality of its own. In my mind, this book was, is, and will always be *Han-chan's Dream,* a title adopted because observing the most highly intelligent cat I ever knew deny an imperfect reality by convincing himself it was only a bad dream first made me deeply aware of the complexity that dreaming brings to our conscious as well as unconscious lives. The picture holds my dream, not Han-chan's. I would stop writing and do nothing but flip-out – create hypershort 2 to 100 frame animation – if the folk with money only had the imagination to produce the hardware and software for the quick and easy applications needed to spark a graphic revolution. – rdg

その模様から名づけられた姿半白とその心のよさを筆者と共に理解して半ちゃんを愛した洋子の二人の思い出に捧げます

半ちゃんの夢

Every day these invisible dreams pass us on the street, or rise from beneath our feet, or look out upon us from beneath a bush. Loren Eiseley *The Night Country*

♪ *Invisible Dreams?* Eiseley found an unfinished field-mouse nest in a large flower pot by his front door, noted the field nearby had been denuded for a development project and imagined a mouse refugee had tried to create her dream-burrow, albeit in an unsuitable place. *All animals pursue ideals; we would make and live that of which we dream.* Most of us, like our genes, is potential not actual. The greater part of our lives dwells within. This is as true for mice as men. (*It so happens I helped get *Night Country* translated into Japanese and had the honor of writing the afterword at the request of the translators.)

♪ *The Cat on an Open Book.* A cat tries to get into your cranium either by lying exactly where yours did before you got up, or occupying the focus of your attention, *i.e.,* projected head-space. Han-chan, whose brain-heavy head was *not* disproportionately large, demonstrates the latter, a dog-eared (I am afraid I failed to detail the page corners) Japanese-English dictionary that competed with him for my attention.

The isbn # for this book, minus hyphens, to assist with web searches is: 9780984092321

考え過ぎの猫半ちゃんに学んだ事
The Cat Who Thought Too Much

HAN-CHAN

an essay into felinity

by

◆ robin d. gill ◆

paraverse press

Logophile Lafcadio Hearn once wrote,
*"Words will eventually have their rights
recognized by the people."* — Our radically
creative nonfiction sets them free to play and grow
in a garden of fanciful thought far from the well-crafted,
beautiful but empty journalism & utterly boring personal
'reality' narratives taught to a generation of Usanian writers,
but close to the playful Aubrey, Borges, Chesterton, Darwin (Erasmus),
Lucretius, Montaigne, Newcastle (Duchess of ~), Ôta, Plutarch, Rabelais,
Sterne, Twain, Wilde, . . . *etc.*. With one work published under two covers
(*Octopussy, Dry Kidney & Blue Spots*; *The Woman Without a Hole*), counting
our books is hard, but this should be our *thirteenth*, perfect for the subject, cats.
As you will see, it expands upon Hearn by bringing Felinese, which is to say
the cat's meow (or *niao*, in Japanese) & tail into the purview of literature.

©
2010
paraverse press
all rights reserved

But, please quote freely, so long as you cite
this book & take care to check the *Errata*
at **http://www.paraverse.org**

As aleays, we invite the LC to help us catalog, meanwhile
please enjoy our Publisher's Cataloging-in-Publication:

The Cat Who Thought Too Much
An Essay Into Felinity (aka Han-chan's Dream)
written and illustrated by
robin d. gill

ISBN # 0-9840923-2-3 (pbk)
13-digit: 978-0-9840923-2-1

1. Cats – felix domesticus. 2. Non-fiction literature – essay. 3. Animal behavior.
4. Animal intelligence. 5. Animal feelings. 6. Animal language. 7. Animal stories.
8. Pets – cats. 9. Philosophy? 10. Art – (if you so think). 11. Tanuki (raccoon fox).

I. gill, robin d. (also, Robin Gill, 1951~)

20101, January
Printed by Lightning Source
in the United States and United Kingdom.
Distributed by Ingram, Baker & Taylor, etc..
Available from Amazon, Barnes & Noble & elsewhere.

For more information, please visit our web site, www.paraverse.org.
For further questions, write us at info at paraverse dot org (rarely read
at present for it is slow), uncoolwabin at hotmail dot com (better), or
whatever e-mail address is suggested at the site. If that does not
work, try a social net-working site. *Forget snail-mail. At this*
time, your poor author-publisher *is* a snail (or boll weevil).

Contents~

Preface: On the title that was not to be   000
Why Han-chan's Dream did not become !

Foreword: How to write about a cat.   009
Why cats cannot walk in straight lines, nor I write in them.

The animal that kneads the world   017
Mirror, mirror on the wall, who is the most infantile of all?

Do cats love?   029
Do bears pee in the woods? A far from solitary animal.

How Han-chan almost killed a man   045
Or, mothers are brave even when they are male.

The sleeping cat or, rather, cats!   059
A pictorial essay on what cats do best, often together.

The very thought of it.   081
Imagination at work, or shaking off snow before going out.

Conversing with cats: easier in japanese?   099
Why some tongues give one a leg up with mastering Felinese.

Smiling with closed eyes   123
The shy animal, or naturally far from Ecotopia

Han-chan's greatest battle   137
On the way self-delusion can save your life.

Are cats the most or least false animal?   147
Differing interpretations of multiple contradictory messages.

Growing up tom and queen   161
The long hard road to sex, reproduction and castration.

Do cats save face?   175
What is it that Japanese call "What's Michael(ing)"?

Beauty: is it relative or . . . is it the cat?   185
Primates, horses, dogs . . . interspecies face (& muscle) value

Han-chan's dream   203
How cats deal with tragedy, a hypothesis.

Is the cat the best mouse trap?   215
Don't forget mousing snakes & snaking chickens!

The battle with the blue boss   225
A brave mother cat & a truly devious, or wise, snake.

Seeing Snakes Everywhere   233
Betting too much or, where paranoia meets perception

The more they die, the higher they fly   239
How and why cats play with their prey

When cats bring us things   259
The Last Year Killed Twice, illustrated.

A little red mouse   271
Are we keeping the right pet?

The Third-generation Tanuki   283
Cats, racoon foxes & a new theory of domestication.

Afterword   293
Finding felinity in an unexpected place.

Bibliography   298

People *index*   300

Concepts *index*   302

Illustrations *index*   305

(More, in color, at paraverse dot org)

Other Books Published To Date   306
Back Cover Illustration   310

FOREWORD

> *"How, then, with me, writing of this Leviathan? Unconsciously my chirography expands into placard capitals. Give me a condor's quill! Give me Vesuvius' crater for an inkstand!"* – Herman Melville 1851 *Moby Dick* (ch.104, *"The Fossil Whale"*)

How to write about a cat

With natural grace? Here I sit cussing up a storm, half-happy to be out in the country where no one can hear me and half-wishing someone could, imagining a call to the police, my subsequent arrest and incarceration getting me into the *"News of the Weird." A writer taken to the funny farm after he was driven crazy by his computer* would embarrass the hell out of the corporation responsible for the maleficent software. *No, not me!* I, who wrote my first seven books in a foreign language, Japanese, because longhand (one letter per box) felt more comfortable than typing, am far from graceful punching keys in my native tongue.

And, after ninety years living with cats – an average of five cats at a time for eighteen years – I wonder if *grace* is what it's all about, anyway. The more I learn about individual cats, the less inclined I am to hazard a definition of cathood. When it comes to pronouncing upon the nature of felinity, you might say the cat has my tongue. A bolder soul than I, Vicki Hearne, says she *can* tell us *"what it is about cats"*, thanks to Koshka, who is "somewhat clumsy", a trait which happily allows her "to work out fairly easily what he is up to." To wit:

> "He is like all cats in his relationship to straight lines. If he is on the windowsill in the living room and I put down a bowl of food on the floor in the kitchen, he selects a route to the bowl that takes him over the sofa and the bookcase and makes it look like a natural route . . . . it is

profoundly important to him that he avoid the stupidities of straight lines." – *Adam's Task*

This charming hyperbole makes Koshka sound like eighteenth century English advocate of the style of landscape called natural (at the time, this meant *Chinese*, as opposed to Italian and French), Joseph Spence:

> Nature never plants by the line. ... As to angles, I have such a mortal aversion to them, that was I to choose a motto for myself as a pretender to gardening, it should be, *'Mutat quadrata rotundis.'* I should almost prefer serpentizing walks to straight ones, and round off the corners of groves instead of pointing them.

Hearne is not naive. She knows all too well "the standard explanation for a great deal of cat behavior" refers "to mechanisms that are a function of the kind of predator a cat is." A good example of this may be found in *The Domestic Cat* when the editors, Turner and Bateson, rationalize their subjects doing far worse than pigeons at "pressing a lever to obtain food on a regular schedule" as follows:

> This should not be taken as evidence that cats are stupid, however. Cats eat intelligent prey such as mice under natural conditions rather than immobile objects, such as seeds. The cat must not only discover the places where prey are most commonly found, it must also avoid becoming too regular itself, lest its own movements are predicted by its potential prey. That is a complex job and may explain why . . . .

Kind words and facts, correct as far as they go. The problem is the conclusion: *cats are contrary because they are so programmed by nature.* That is what Hearne challenges when she questions the value of reducing the behavior of "any thoughtful species" to physical explanation. It is "as if a child's first experiments with fingerpaints gave us an emblem that 'explained' Michelangelo." I would go even further. The only thoughtful species *ever,* I repeat, *ever* to act for biological reasons is our own. Some people may fuck to make kids, but *no* cat fucks to make kittens. *No* cat eats for nutrition. And, *no* cat plays for hunting practice or to expend excess energy.

The idea of an *instinct for irregular behavior* to improve one's hunting chances is interesting, even if it doesn't explain *why* cats do what they do (by which I mean what is on their *mind*, rather than what is in their *genes*). The most convincing explanation of how irregularity may work for catching individual animals did not wait for the modern behavioralist. It comes from Mark Twain, who discovered it while learning to ride, or as he put it in his essay by that name, "Taming the Bicycle."

> "If you try to run over the dog he knows how to calculate, but if you are trying to miss him he does not know how to calculate, and is liable to jump the wrong way every time. It was always so in my experience. Even when I could not hit a wagon I could hit a dog that came to see me practice. They all liked to see me practice, and they all came, for there was little going on in our neighborhood to entertain a dog."

Chasing prey is one thing. *Finding* prey another. It requires regularity, syncopating with the time prey is more likely to appear, or easier to catch. If anything is written into the cat's mind it is the same universal grammar we (all animals) share; and the default setting is "regularity." The need for occasional irregularity would rather be *learned* – as human children must learn *not* to say "catched." A cat would quickly *learn* that using the same cover at the same time of day against the same local birds failed to achieve anything. Why "quickly"? Because any cat with half-a-brain would already have discovered that using the same trick time and time again simply does not work while playing games of ambush with its mother and siblings.

If cats don't go straight, I think it is because they are not given to tuning out the world. This is partly because they are opportunists: they hunt as they go. The entire world – excluding hostile territory, which may mean most of it – is their Happy Hunting Ground. The cat may or may not walk without object. Either way, the journey *is* their destination or, rather, destinations. Unless there is some intimidating animal, usually a fellow cat or human, they wish to avoid provoking, they interact with their surroundings using all five senses; in other words, they allow *things* a say in their navigation. Naturally, this takes them all over the place.

And, it is partly because cats love the world. They are materialists in the literal sense defined by Alan Watts in his little remembered book I consider his only masterpiece: *Do Things Matter?* Fond of their surroundings, these supposedly erratic creatures are more than anything else, *creatures of habit.* Every cat has its loves: trees, chair legs, boulders, verandas, window sills, rugs (lookouts, claw-scratch-spots, body-rub objects, cooling-down places, warming-up places, knead-inducers, odor-collectors) etcetera. You cannot love a big thing like the world but by loving parts of it, and some more than others.

So, when a cat criss-crosses a room, it is not avoiding "the stupidities of straight lines," but meeting its loves. It treads well-worn lover's paths, invisible grooves; and its genius is in its ability to retain and renew its love, rubbing softly against the chair leg as if it were the first time, every time.

The level of Hearne's explanation is fundamentally correct. It respects the real cat, the sweet or cranky, simple or complex individual cat all who have lived with cats know. *Koshka acts according to his own wishes*. Yet, it is silly to ascribe Koshka's action to *an aversion* for the straight. It is not philosophy or aesthetics that makes cats walk a crooked path. Neither does it reflect a perverse nature. Cats are no more so than women so called by men who could not have their way with them. It is love: *amor res mundalum.*

That *love for the world*, the love that even a sour-puss knows, is the most important thing cats can teach us. What about *dignity* and *independence*? Give me a break! We humans – especially those in the United States between Canada and Mexico, are already too damn cocky.

Koshka "selects a route to the bowl that takes him over the sofa and the bookcase and makes it look like a natural one" writes Hearne. *Of course* it looks natural. It *is* natural for Koshka. The route is channeled in his heart. That is not to say that Koshka has but one way to cross the room. The channel he takes is actually a number of channels arranged in serial, i.e. a medley. I would call it *improvisation* (Those who do it know that musical improvisation is mostly an impromptu collage of familiar sequences of sound, rather than the unadulterated creativity the term suggests to an outsider). Who would play fast and straight to get over a song! Why *does* the cat cross the room? Why do we make love? Why is a cat crossing the room any less natural than a chicken crossing the road?

Voila : the animal that is in love with the world

I said I wouldn't – or, couldn't – dare a definition; but I hardly begin and it's *"Move over Vicki Hearne!"* I will do it again, too, not because I believe myself but because generalizing, which, poetically written, becomes aphorism, captures ideas otherwise lost in the clutter of words. This is not to say *The Cat Who Thought Too Much* lacks first-hand observation, just that, we shall spend some time clearing the thicket of pre-existent cats-are-this-and-that claims to better make out the snark of felinity. Quotes abound, both to diversify the style (a single voice is a short-coming of the essay) and, because ideas are polished by bouncing them off those of others, and, sometimes, the process of echo-location helps me to find my mind, as well.

> I Am now beginning to get fairly into my work; and by the help of a vegitable diet, with a few of the cold seeds, I make no doubt but I shall be able to go on with my uncle Toby's story, and my own, in a tolerable straight line. Now,
>
> Inv. T. S.   Scul. T. S.
> These were the four lines I moved in through my first, second, third, and fourth volumes.——In the fifth volume I have been very good,——the precise line I have described in it being this:

The above is a plot line from *Tristam Shandy* (1759-67) put here in 1995. Laurence Sterne's style has something akin to a cat's line of progress and, I am afraid, mine. As I futilely held out for a publisher willing to offset this book with my color illustrations, I ended up using it in two other books. First, in the introduction of a book of haiku about sea cucumbers *Rise, Ye Sea Slugs!* (2003) and second in a book on composite translation and word play called *A Dolphin in the Woods* (2009). With respect to the sea slugs, literally called "海鼠 sea rat" in Japanese, it just so happens the literary term *namako-tai*, or "sea cucumber style" (in a word, *Holothurian*), meaning an amorphous escriture, was first invented and applied by Soseki, the man with the moustache and unruly hair featured on a 1000 yen note, in reference to his famous serial novel *I Am a Cat* (1905-6).

cat tails

1. *Does It Matter?* Most people in the so-called materialistic West, says Watt, *hate* material, i.e., the matter of *mater* earth, as can be seen in their stainless steel and plastic kitchens. In *De Profundis*, Wilde had written in a more obviously spiritual vein that "We call ours a utilitarian age, and we do not know the uses of a single thing. We have forgotten that water can cleanse, and fire purify, and that the Earth is mother to us all."(1905) Watts improves upon this sad truth with concrete examples of how to appreciate elemental things.

2. *Improvisational Creativity: How Much?* I have exaggerated cat creativity and ours. Just as most humans use a surprisingly small number of the potential positions available for love-making, most cats only improvise at first and soon settle down to a small number of routes, which might better be called *grooves*. When many cats live together, these operate like private shipping lanes to prevent collisions. Some old cats may have only one groove. Ah, but look how delicately he or she walks it!

3. *Tristam Shandy.* If you are a native speaker of English and haven't read – or, if such a *koshkaesque* plot bothers you, *tried* to read – this post-modern novel written about three hundred years ago by Laurence Sterne, shame on you! Why, there are at least two Japanese translations! It is no wonder Japanese are appreciative. Murasaki Shikibu's *Tale of Genji* (c1005) includes a chapter-heading with a blank page and a variety of meta-literary musings (eg. her criticism of bias in stepmother stories), which make what may be the world's oldest novel a post-modern one.

♪ ***The Sketch of Han-chan*** on the next page is at the head of a letter I never mailed. I decided to keep it. It is addressed to a famous haiku poet. My unappropriate (as Kaneko was very old and I was not) haiku is translated above it:

*only the ears
of the old cat perk up
this fine spring day.*

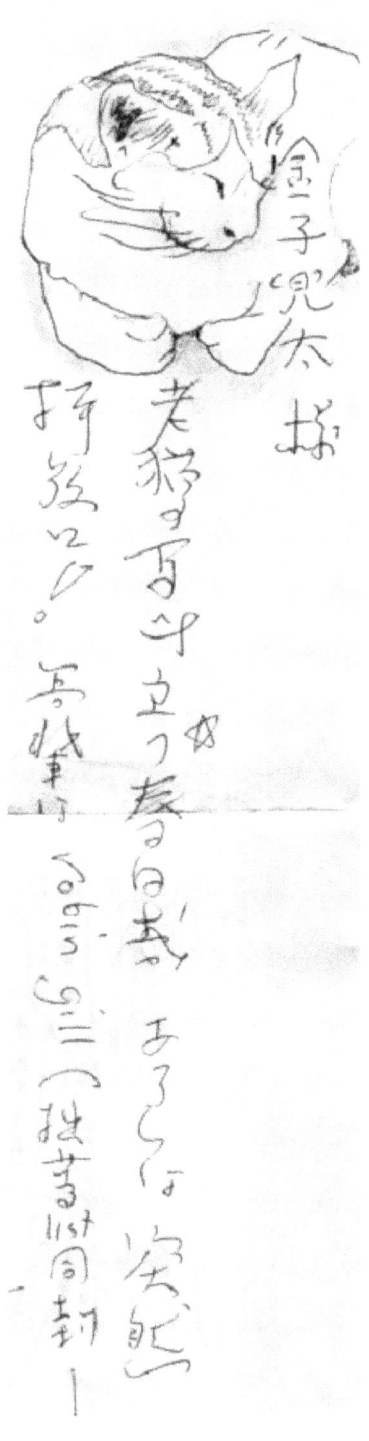

another measure of neoteny
Kneading *the* World

> good instance of useless muscular tricks accompanying emotion. – when horses fighting, they put down ears, when 'turning round to kick' kicking they do same. although it is then quite useless – **Cats kneading when old, like kittens at the breast** now if horns were to grow on horses, yet they must continue to put down ears when kicking. . . . Why does dog put down ears when, when pleased. – is it opposite movement to drawing them close to head, when going to fight . . . – Charles Darwin (bold font in original, italics mine: *Notebook M* 146e)

the boast

We, the only populous member of the great apes, are also the happiest, for we are *homo-ludens,* the young at heart. The kitten, as Ogden Nash reminds us in a rare rhyme on "that," all too soon becomes a *cat*, jaded and aloof (i.e., hopelessly adult), while the child, still learning how to walk, has only begun to learn the game of life. Oh, playful species, the Fountain of Youth has been found and it is us!

Boasts about the juvenile nature of our species, delinquent about growing up and proud of it, were all too common in the twentieth century. The message accompanying such boasts – that we had better design our society to accommodate this or we are going to be in big trouble! – was understandable, coming after a couple hundred years of confining man (beginning with occidental males and spreading over much of the globe) to black and white tubular clothing and the gray-flannel mindset to match that suit; and, if a belief in the peculiar neoteny of our species can, by naturalizing play, give moral support to the delightfully childish element in our culture on the one side while warning us about our irresponsible tendency to discount the future and act like juveniles on the other, I am all for it. But ninety-plus cat-years of experience gives me reason to doubt the validity of the claim.

nursing time

Like the more controversial trait of *intelligence*, there is no single measure of *neoteny*. True, we humans take a long time to learn to walk. A cat has learned to rat by the time a man-child has begun to crawl, and bore a litter of kittens, themselves running, before we have even found our feet. Even considering our different life calendars, we are notoriously neotenous when it comes to basic motor functions (walking, running, climbing, swimming, throwing, etc.). To be helpless is, indeed, human.

But what if we look at the *retention* of infantile behavior into adulthood? I have never seen a child nurse past age three and never read of one doing it past five or so. I have seen cats nursing who were over a year old on many occasions, and can recall my favorite, Han-chan, butting in at age three. If seven of our years is equivalent to one of a cat's . . . .

Actually, the year game is more complex, for the sexes differ. If a female turns into a mother in a year, hardly seven by human count, she is the opposite of neotenous. *She* is precocious. On the other hand, if her brother cannot really join the mating game until he is three, *he* is clearly neotenous.

Nursing by young cats from a previous litter can begin *before* their mother gives birth to a subsequent one and may serve to hasten it and/or warm up the tits. (Along this line, my sister Prudence once made a brilliant observation about thumb-sucking: done in the womb, it begins as a *preparation for nursing*, and only becomes regressive behavior *post facto,* or rather, *post partum!*) And, if the cat's mother gives them half a chance to do it, the older sibling's nursing continues later. If litters were always culled down to a choice one or two kittens, I would not be surprised if nursing *never* stopped.

kneading: from milk to metaphysical

Nursing-related mannerisms are even more telling. Few *adult* humans suck their thumbs – unless it is accidentally hammered, or otherwise injured – but most cats can be found doing *their* simulations, no matter their age. They knead their front legs, or sometimes, just the paws, as *if* they were working away at their mother's breast. This, for readers not fortunate enough to have shared close quarters with a cat, is what Darwin's note refers to.

Humans have nothing comparable to a cat's kneading – or "milk-treading" to use Desmond Morris's term – because we do not need to actively milk our mothers. Nevertheless, human thumb-sucking and cat kneading are behaviorally more similar than other nursing-related behavior involving the tongue, which we will discuss in a moment.

Like thumb-sucking, kneading is usually done *on something*. Sometimes that something is the soft breast or belly of their owner who cannot help but feel motherized by it. After reading one author who declares that cats bring us game because they think of us as *incompetent kittens*, how refreshing to see the tables turn when another tells us this kneading means the cat is treating us as *foster mothers*. I say, we have a strange role-playing game going on here! Speaking of which, I once saw a cat suck a woman's tit as it kneaded on prime time television in Japan. Tits on prime time were not exceptional in late 20c Japan, but that video was. Usually the recipient of feline kneading in Japan is something else: the owner's upper-back and shoulders. It happens that *kata-kori* (stiff-shoulders) is *the* popular complaint in this country where people boast uniquely poor posture, called *nekoze,* or . . . "cat-back."

The kneading is not confined to bodies. A cat may knead the ground, a pillow, a table top, you name it! With one of my cats in Japan, it was seasonal. She would seek out and knead a fluffy alpaca rug as soon as the weather began to chill in the early fall. I noticed my mother's cat, a very different breed, do the same sort of thing as soon as the first cold-front hit tropical Key Biscayne. And, when I said that kneading is *usually* done on something, it was because many cats knead the air and tongue-out in their dreams, and one of my cats, Kuro'ko-chan, mistress of the silent meow, more often than not laid on her back kneading the air!

tongue-out

Unlike thumb-sucking, the tongue does not stick out when a cat is insecure or lonely. Like purring – kittens and their mothers purr continuously when nursing (perhaps it facilitates milk-flow) – tongue-out shows *contentment*; but, unlike purring, the tongue may come out on its own. The tip, curled slightly up on the sides as if nursing, often accompanies a pleasant dream. Purring, like a dog's tail-wagging, shows specific appreciation, or approbation, for being allowed to lie with you, being rubbed under the neck, or in the case of my sweetest cat, Kuro'ko, simply from being looked at. The triggering mechanism for the tongue-out is harder to grasp. When the temperature is just right, the cat full, and all is well with the world, suddenly, it's there: a pink, long-lasting embodied sigh of contentment!

All of this may seem terribly passé – the passé is always terribly so – to cat owners; but only thirty years ago – before I had cats of my own – I vaguely recall asking someone whether the cat in his studio was *sick* because his tongue was hanging out! Please keep in mind that I am writing for those who know cats *and* those who don't. And, it is a fact that even in Japan, where this trait of cats is well enough known to be used to express a happy human in comic books and, occasionally, advertisements, a surprising number of people have no idea what it means. If not all people can read human emotions, illiteracy with respect to other species is probably the rule rather than the exception.

The meaning of a cat's tongue-out must be learned by a human because we have nothing like it. Women in many cultures readily flick or stick out their tongues when in a good spirits, but this literally inviting behavior is only momentary and, as far as I know, less natural for not happening as they doze off, i.e., when they loose conscious control as it may with a cat. It is more a wink of the mouth than a nursing-related behavior. Kissing is closer, but conscious and the cultural variation so great it would take a whole book just to describe it. Japanese, who called it "mouth-sucking" are usually pictured with both tongues out of mouth, while English smack lips like chimpanzees and French (if Frenching is French) use their tongues as racoon fishing for minnows in the dark. If humans were like cats, we would all part and purse our lips as if we were sucking *whenever* we relax. *We do not.*

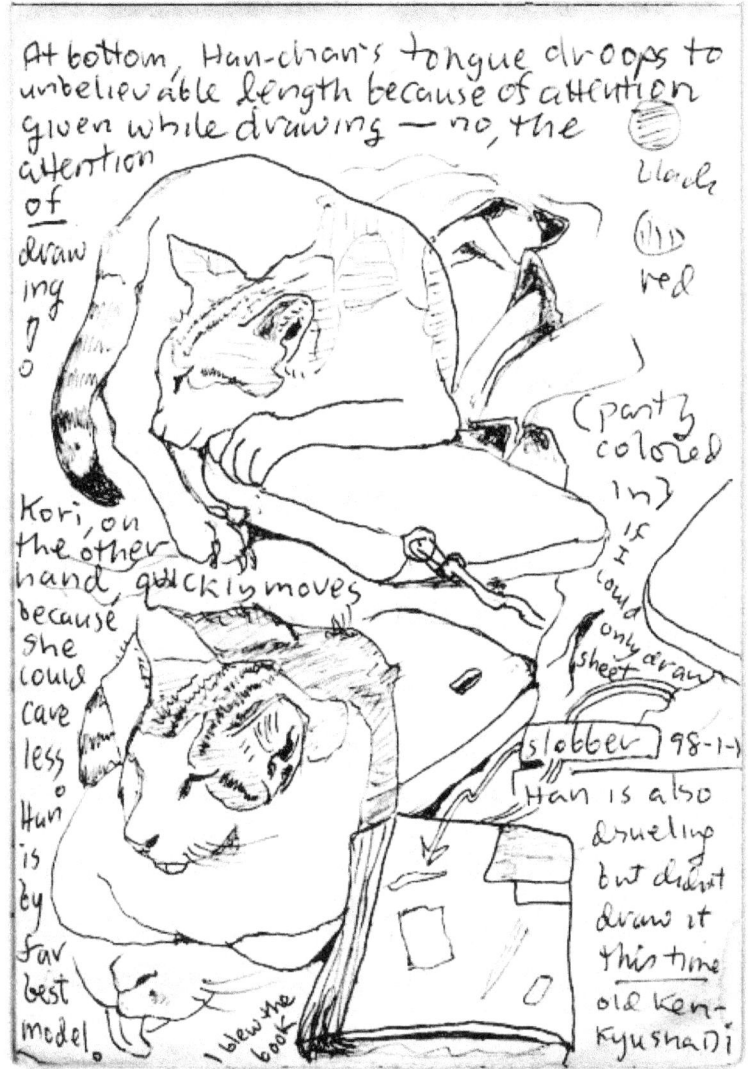

Kori-chan, on top, has taken possession of a small electric heater that is depicted many times in the Sleeping Cats chapter, pages 59-80. In this chapter, we are concerned with the bottom part of this picture. Han-chan was delirious with pleasure when I gazed at him straight-on to draw and he would purr with his tongue hanging lower and lower. He did not mind but did not equally like to pose for a sidelong portrait as seen in the *Smiling with Closed Eyes* picture on pages 123 and 136.

kneading vs. tongue-out

Kneading and tongue-out rarely occur together as they do when nursing. The emotions they express are somewhat different. I have not managed to trace their divergence as kittens grow into cats but can describe their end states.

While kneading someone is a measure of affection, and may be done in a relaxed manner, it is often performed when a cat is anxious about something or feeling lonely. Originally combined with sucking, it was a means toward an end, satisfying rather than satisfaction itself. But such is life, feline or human, that, with the passage of time, a means of satisfaction may itself come to satisfy. Sometimes, it even seems a way to work off nervous energy, a substitute for the savage rite, the sharpening of nails all cat owners have come to marvel at and, if the cat does it in the wrong place (or casts a ferocious glance at the owner), fear. More rarely, the nails come out and pull back what is pushed, and we prefer to be kneaded less!

Tongue-out happens *only* when a cat is relaxed – the length it hangs down being a barometer of relaxation. That would make interpretation simple if relaxation was not caused by many things. We may relax because the environment has nothing to make us tense, the extreme example being a sensory-deprivation tank. Or we may relax after physical exertion or a high-fever that leaves us utterly exhausted. Do I confuse relaxation and exhaustion? I doubt it. In either case, the body shuts down all processes extraneous to existing. In both cases, the feeling is good unless you feel you must be up and about because you do not accept the benefit of sitting or lying still. A veterinarian with a shallow understanding of cats may tell you tongue-out *only* shows a cat is sick (exactly what I thought when I first saw it!). Indeed, it *may*. For that reason, older cats tend to do it more than younger ones. But the "only" is all wrong. When you are sick, or beleaguered by various bodily ailments, there comes a time, or a level of discomfort, where you lie back as you were drunk. You feel good because you feel less. A more aware vet would say it might show your cat needs a check-up because a cat can feel well, or be perfectly content, even when it is sick. (In this respect, the cat is a much better patient than a dog who, in Robert Louis Stevenson's words, *"connects . . the uneasiness of sickness and the consciousness of guilt."*)

So, in short, kneading is a psychological and tongue-out a partially physiological index of a cat's condition; and neither is by itself a completely good or bad sign.

neoteny & nostalgia

What does a cat think of when it tongue-outs or kneads? Does it think of its mother? Of its childhood when it could imbibe what it kneaded?

Probably not. Most of us have no such specific memories and there is no evolutionary advantage to keeping them. But the cat is feeling *something.* Anxious or satisfied, such a cat is in a receptive mood, a vaguely dependent frame of mind called *"amae"* in Japanese. We might call it a *longing to be loved* that is itself a form of love, an unconscious way of making up to or opening up to someone. This is particularly true for tongue-out, as kneading, like any motor-activity, is largely self-centered. You know this because the cat with its tongue out and eyes closed (eyes, another chapter) usually turns toward you as silently as a sunflower faces the sun.

Both behaviors are usually combined with purring (pg.113), a fact which emphasizes the fact that even a sick cat may be well where it counts, in the heart. It is a baby happily cooing to itself and to its mother, a puppy offering its belly to a hand as it wags its tail and pees. And since we are talking about grown cats, we might call it a desirable form of regression akin to what we call *nostalgia.*

Cats may not always walk alone, but they are never far from lonely. Like us, they miss more than they will ever know.

a blue raccoon

We once had a raccoon that sucked her thumb until it turned a rusty orange, all the while sobbing in that delicate cricket trill that inspires French poets more than English ones, either because the word "cricket" is less mellifluous – the k-k-t consonants better fit the sound-sense of the term "playing ~ ," with its hard-edged rectitude – than the delicate *grillon,* or because the English have tin ears.

H.R.M. Gill (I do not spell out her name lest family uses it for a password) had been abandoned by her mother, or dropped by a predator. She was tiny, still, blind and covered with ants when we found her. Nursed by eye-dropper, doll bottle and baby bottle (graduated tit-size, one service even Mother Nature cannot offer!), this spoiled racoon slept and showered with us – delightful when she wasn't biting our toes or prying her snout into our mouths (imagine waking up with someone breathing down your throat!) – accompanied us to school, rode our shoulders as we swang like Tarzan from branch to rope to rope to branch on a giant banyan, guarded our watchdog Lucky the Dalmatian in his old age from a neighbor's ferocious young dingo-like Speedy, who once made the mistake of catching her before she made it up the tree (she rolled underneath and tried to give him a sex-change operation), enjoyed playing in the restroom by pooping and fishing in the toilet bowl, unrolling the paper and flushing things like my mother's only pearl necklace down into the septic tank, and once enjoyed the honor of biting the three-time world ocean power-boat racing champion (and my father's business partner at the time), Jim Wynne, on his calf, drawing ample blood and a loud bellow after Jim gamely grabbed back the olive she had stolen from his martini and put it back into his drink, forgetting the three rules of raccoon etiquette: 1) What is yours is mine; 2) What is mine is mine; and, 3) Never, I mean *never* laugh at me!

Following this last incident, H.R.M. Gill – always a handful, as you can see from the photo with sister Susan left & Prudence, me or a friend right) spent a couple weeks in her cage. I argued that the bite was justifiable given the multiple breach of raccoon etiquette, but the adults had to consider the outside chance of rabies. She was also confined when in heat; and this was when she sobbed the most. It hurt to listen because it was so beautiful. Raspy grief may grab the ears, but only sweet sorrow burrows deep into the heart and remains. I still hear her today. She had many reasons to be lonely. Motherless and incapable of fitting into the world of man or raccoon, she was a real misfit. Her life was not all bad – she was fat and well cared for – but she had cause enough to sob.

lonely cats

There is a poem by Bella Akhmadulina.

Ty dumaesh, shto ya iz gordosti	*Do you think it out of pride*
Khozhu, s toboyu ne druzhu?	*I walk alone and not with you?*
Ya ne iz gordosti - iz goresti	*'Tis not from pride, but sorrow*
Tak pryamo golovu derzhu.	*I keep my chin up as I do.*

More literally (giving up the rhyme) it ends *"I, not of pride, but of grief / hold my head so straight."* One wonders if that might not apply to some cats. That cat who walks by with a "humph, don't even try!" or "hands off!" body language may, deep down, be sad for lack of a relationship allowing it to *amaeru,* or open-up. Even your proudest most independent-minded cat – Ôsama king of cats (pg. 139-40) – is not wholly content. If you follow him closely, you will catch him kneading. Some cats knead more than others, but all of them do it. The corniest pun is true: *Cats knead the world!*

and dogs?

So, if we look at nursing-related mannerisms rather than general motor functions, it is the cat rather than the human that seems to be exceptionally juvenile. We shall play with play, the most common index of juvenility, elsewhere.

Suffice it to say that it is ludicrous to attribute *our* play to *our* playfulness and a cat's to some pressing biological matter unless, that is you believe we, unlike other animals, did not evolve. And, if neoteny is where evolution is heading, the cat is already there with us.

Ah, but what about the dog? It may not purr, knead or stick out its tongue like it is nursing, but it surely is as youthful as a cat isn't it? On the whole, yes. Anyone can see that play-wise more puppy remains in a dog than kitten in a cat. If the cat retains more *infantile* mannerisms, the dog retains more *childish* ones. The frantic wagging, begging and excitement at goings and comings are all traits of a juvenile ingratiating itself to its mother and other dogs. But only the ears back when pleased mentioned by Darwin seem truly infantile, if, that is, you imagine puppies squeezing in side-by-side for nipple space.

Since the juvenile is more outgoing than the infantile, the dog is the more obviously youthful animal – and some breeds of dog have been bred to degrees of dependence not found in cats – but, speaking for the cat, infancy *is* the earlier stage of ontogeny and that means one can not out-neoteny a cat without acting like a fetus.

cat tails

Classical Kneading Cats. Lucretius observed what is now called r.e.m. sleep, i.e. rapid eye-movement, and related the body movements and sounds made while dreaming with the daily concerns of the animals. I do not believe he mentions cats kneading awake, but seeing such fine detail concerning any psycho-physiological process, wonder if any other ancient writer did.

Grey Flannel Suit. Occidental Males were once as playful in their dress as Occidental women are today. Even soldiers enjoyed colorful, and often personally modified dress. The Great Sartorial Renunciation, as Pflugel called it, was also the first step away from *homo-ludens* and toward the drably uniformed worker in the authoritarian workspace of modern times that once excluded women but still enslaves men.

Breast-kneading Cats. Doubtless, the same happens in Usania, too, but fundamentalist Christians, body-negative feminists and the utterly immature regulatory commission's enormous fine for revealing the breast prevents it from airing as a funny video. Will we ever grow up?

***Tongue-out* as *Sick*.** While it is true that the tongue does tend to hang low more often when a cat is in ill health, perhaps because a cat husbands its energy by relaxing, it is so much more! Conceptually speaking it opposes the lungs which expand in death and require energy to exhale (though oddly enough, inhaling *seems* the voluntary one as we more often conscious of doing it, perhaps because of making an effort to do it deeply). Especially in mammals where the tongue is used to lap water or wrap around food, it extends when muscles stop holding it in. To me, the most puzzling tongue is that depicted by Mesoamerican art. I believe I have read it identified with what might be called bravado in life. Panthers are often so depicted. Considering the ferocious way brawny Pacific Island men stick it out and down as they do display/threat dances, there may be something to it. Expert opinions are welcome for glosses to future editions.

***Stevenson*.** Robert Louis Stevenson wrote an essay called "The Character of Dogs." I have it in his *Memories and Portraits*, Colington edition vol. 20 of the works of ~ . London, with no date. He held that dogs were bred to be "man's plate-licker," toadies, to live "with man as courtiers round a monarch" and he expanded upon the significance of that for various sorts of dogs. Here is the sentence following what I quoted, the last of his paragraph on the vices of dogs:

> To the pains of the body he often adds the tortures of the conscience; and at these times his haggard protestations form, in regard to the human deathbed, a dreadful parody or parallel.

There is much truth here, though individual cases will differ. On the whole, I would rather be in a house with a gravely ill cat than a dying dog.

***How a Raccoon Sucks its Thumb*.** The nail of the thumb was not in H.R.M. Gill's mouth. She sucked the butt of the thumb and up the side. When you think about it, that is the part of the hand we use to wipe tears with!

do cats (really) love?
Compared *to* What!

I love in the cat, the independent and almost grateful temper which prevents it from attaching itself to anyone.
                      Chateaubriand (from *Puss In Books*)

To love her [a cat] steadfastly without being loved in return – these things are not often possible to the Anglo-Saxon nature.
                                Agnes Repplier (Ibid.)

As soon as they're out of your sight, you are out of their mind.
                      Walter De La Mare (from Ibid.)

When a cat shuts its eyes, you disappear.
                            Leonard Michaels: *A Cat*

In a cat's social life, you are marginal unless it wants attention.
                            Leonard Michaels (Ibid.)

It can scarcely be denied that cats tolerate us, whereas dogs adore us.
    Jeffrey M. Masson: *Dogs Never Lie About Love*

the stereotype

Is the trait described above meant to be a fault or an ideal? All of these authors love cats and do not mean to defame them by writing what amounts to a claim that cats are pathologically independent. One finds something analogous in Japan, where the West is (or, *was*, in the 1970's and 80's) often stereotyped as an insanely Hobbesian dog-eat-dog society by writers who claimed to personally find it an attractive alternative to the safer but stifling culture they lived in. If you ask me – *With friends like this*, ...

the reality

> *Sometimes he sits at your feet with an expression so gentle and caressing that the depth of his gaze startles you. Who can believe that there is no soul behind those luminous eyes!*
>
> Theophile Gautier (from P.I.B.)

> *Often he would sit looking at me, and then, moved by delicate affection, come and pull my coat and sleeve until he could touch my face with his nose, and then go away contented.*
>
> Charles Dudley Warner (from Ibid.)

Note the grammatical difference in the quotations of "the stereotype" and "the reality." The *unloving* cat is "a" generic animal, "the" fiction. The *loving* cat is a "he" or "her" (second quote on last page), *i.e.*, an individual, and the words of Gautier and Warner in every detail testify precisely to experiences I have had countless times.

The loving look of a cat is beautiful to behold. It is love as pure as a cool mountain spring. The depth of the gaze is not just startling but occasionally scary, if you, like me, are not certain you want to be loved *that much.* Perhaps you have seen the way a cat that loves you wants to lie right on your pillow so as to occupy a space that time would put inside your head. Yet, it never stares as if it would bore its way in. It is soft and open. Only in morbid moments, do you find yourself fearing the cat's love might either swallow you up or burrow within to displace your mind with its matter.

The loving look of a dog is different. It is so intense, you can almost see it straining against the leash of the dog's ego. If the dog is not trained to restrain it, the affectionate force of the id will break that leash and lick you all over. You, popular musician. Your dog, the adoring mob. Call it groupie love, *a crush* or *mania.* And no dog grows out of this puppy or teenage love. A dog may slow down but I doubt any ever become as placid and gentle a lover as a cat.

love is earned

They say, women are proud, wherein made the trial?
They moved some lewd suit, and had the denial . . .

Joane Sharp (1617)

Cats, as most books on cats never fail to mention, do not give their heart to just anyone. While one should not confuse matters of love and sex, the above-quoted lines from Joane Sharp's *"Defence of Women"* come to mind when I think of those would maintain that cats are cruel for being slow to fall in love. When we are lonely and want an instant shot of love, a neighbor's cat may not be as a good bet as their dog, but if you want to enjoy the fruits of hard earned love, the cat is your perfect lover.

Two big qualifications.

First, all dogs are not cheap. Try mooching up to a one-wo/man dog and you may have your nose bitten off. When cats and dogs are compared – or, rather, *contrasted* – we usually find a relatively aloof Persian or Siamese set against a hopeless softy like a cocker Spaniel or collie. That is hardly fair, but our expectations are matched, so who complains? I have not known many breeds of cats but I would not be surprised to find some to be puppy-like seekers of easy love. Nor would I be surprised to find that wolves that, like a cats, generally avoid your eyes, have the same loving gaze as a cat. Who knows but that the most loving of eyes are the ones generally shy of contact.

Second, cats may just require more subtle wooing. Once you know how to do it, you can make many if not most of them yours almost as fast as you can a dog.

So said, there still is love and then there is love. Real love takes time. You can make acquaintance with a cat in minutes and become good friends (when the cat decides to make you part of its route or drops by to play) in days. But you need months, or, with some cats years, to *earn* the soul-melting gaze that comes from the bottom of an adult cat's heart. What young Christopher Marlowe claimed with respect to humans clearly does not hold for cats, who almost never fall in love at first sight. If you call this playing hard to get, it makes cats sound bad, but I would call the demand that we *win* their hearts, prudent if not laudable behavior that bonds us.

There are, of course, exceptions, some apartment cats are so grateful for news from the outside world brought by stinky old shoes that they will literally fall for first-time visitors bearing such rich presents on their feet, but this is an anomaly resulting from sensual deprivation and does not always last.

witnessing love

If you do not have a deep relationship with a cat, but would see its look of love, find a cat with kittens. For a mother cat, like mother people, can be observed gazing with wide-open eyes upon her creations, pouring out love as freely as the sun gives light, or, should I say *moon,* for what we see is also a reflection of the goodness in nature. If one believes love must be returned, it is wasted; for, usually, and this, again, is true for people, we may best observe it in the mother when the little ones are fast asleep.

Of course, this is not the eye-to-eye direct love-look. But it is impressive, nonetheless. To watch any animal giving its all to raise its children is heart-warming. The cat is *particularly* inspirational in this respect, because it goes "into love" with the same intensity that it goes into heat. Veterinarians can attest to the fact that mother cats will adopt almost *anything.* (Even *birds!* See the excerpt from Thomas Brown's *Interesting Anecdotes of the Animal Kingdom* (1834) in *The Vintage Book of Cats*) And, despite their species' finicky reputation, they do it more than dogs.

Mother cats begin to fill with love weeks before they give birth. As soon as their tits start enlarging, even the most ornery Queen (an English term for the counterpart of the Tom) loses her chill. It is as if she swallowed a love potion. Her eyes look with affection on all. Obviously, her genes are behind this. A gravid queen must turn on her charm if she is to find a human protector, a home, before she gives birth. (Dogs, more likely to already have a secure place, need not change so radically; so, they don't.) But, that does not make the metamorphosis any less marvelous.

If such a cat comes to your window, it is possible to get into a loving look relationship in a matter of days or weeks at the longest. You are not being taken for a ride. The cat (as a being rather than a taxicab for genes) is not thinking about reproductive strategies. A cat may rub up against you for a tidbit or a pet, without caring if you exist. But no cat can fake a look. If you would check the veracity of my claim, be kind to her. The experience, however, will not come cheap. Soon, you will be stuck with her whole family and perhaps be forced to betray her love to exercise some family planning the hard way.

loving is lovable

> *Riko kneading Yoko's hand / Not quite as confused as when first pregnant and sounding like a crow [wretched meows] / Encounter Riko in the bamboo [grove] and she doesn't move away at all [born wild, she feared me outside] / Thrilled to be petted she gives in completely. (my notes 4/19/87).*

> *Like a lover doing as would be done, mother cat is most open to caresses – infantile herself. (Ibid. 1992)*

When a cat wants to be licked, it licks. The mother cat who eagerly sucks kittens' asses wants them to suck her tits. About to give birth, Riko kneads as she would be kneaded. She loves us: she would be loved. And vice-versa. Her overwhelming love and desire to be loved even conquers fears she acquired in a traumatic kittenhood when the feral cats could not be allowed near the apartment in the daytime because harboring "pets" could get one – a poor man, a renter, like me – kicked out.

I exaggerate the symmetry. But the details don't matter. What counts is the fact that the outgoing and incoming vectors of love grow together. If there is some chemical imbalance – or balance, if we prefer to consider it normal to be in love – that makes animals loving, it also would seem to make them lovable. At least, I have observed that to be the case with cats.

Pregnancy is said to greatly increases a woman's olfactory powers. This is supposed to help her stay away from foods dangerous to her fetus or nursing baby by making her hypersensitive and thus likely to choose mild-fare. After she moves beyond the initial nausea as her body adjusts to housing a foreign body, it also makes her eat more. That makes good biological sense, but, why not consider something more interesting? I hypothesize that psychological tests will show the belly and the heart expand *pari passu* – women love more when they are pregnant. Euphoria, as the Greeks and the Chinese knew, is round.

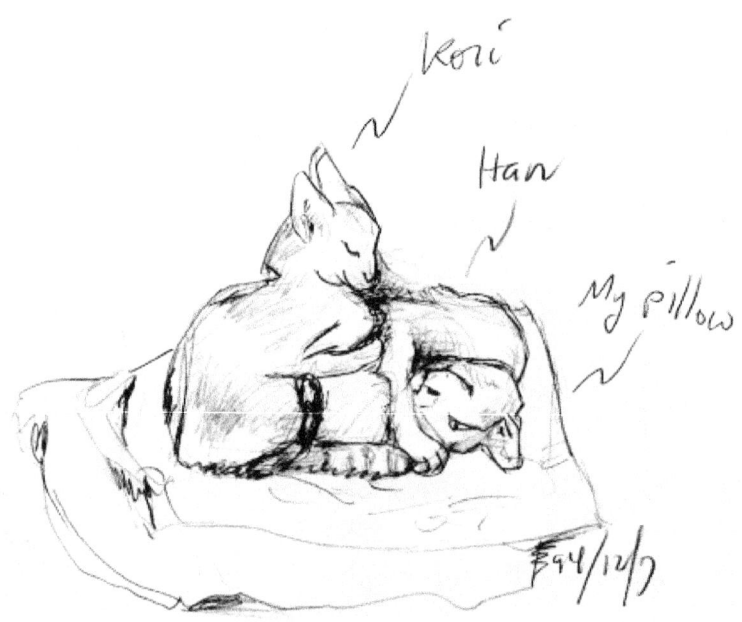

The above shows Kori and Han-chan before Kori went to the vet to be neutered and came back insane, and before Han-chan picked up the cat-AIDS-like disease that afflicted him in his final years. Kori worshipped him and he loved her attention. I think the angle of his eye may be a bit off. I was concentrating on the overall arrangement of limbs and their position on my pillow where Han-chan went for love of me and Kori followed for love of him, her favorite and at this time only uncle.

interspecies' love

> No wild animal – and the cat is a wild animal – can accord even the most trusted human being a higher degree of friendship than he would grant to his own species under natural conditions.
>
> Konrad Lorenz (*Man Meets Dog*)

Sleeping kittens do not see, much less return their mother's gaze of love. And, I am not certain that *any* cat other than a sleeping kitten gets to bask in that gaze. Kori was so fond of (I almost write addicted to!) her uncle Han-chan (who, you recall, helped mother her) that she would rush to greet him every time she came in. Though old Han-chan's mouth stank to high heaven, she alone licked around it. And, when I put Han-chan to sleep, she stayed up alternately licking and sleeping on his corpse all night long. But, I never saw the two looking into each others eyes that way.

Poor Mad Kori shows her love for ailing, smelly uncle Han-chan. 1/98

Even dead, uncle Han-chan remained larger than life for poor mad Kori who spent the entire night with him, after the vet came after work to put him to sleep (pg.105). Here, five hours after death, she rests her hind foot under his jaw and burrows down between her own legs and, it would seem has yet to realize he will not be waking up. 3/98

Kori + dead Han
1:Am (5 hrs after d)

When Lorenz writes "the fact that an adult tom-cat will accept a man as a companion in natural surroundings leads me to believe that neither the domestic cat nor his wild forebear is nearly such a social recluse as is commonly supposed" (Ibid.), he is absolutely right. But if the cat only *exchanges* the look of love with a human being, as I hypothesize, his above-quoted categorical assertion may be wrong.

I would guess that the relationship between our pets and us create special conditions which can build upon natural potential to create a different if not "higher degree of friendship." What cat can give another cat the food, protection and massages we can offer, not just for a year, like a mother cat to its kittens, but year after year? And could not this constant care give rise to a love that exceeds the love a cat feels for a member of its own species?

If some men can love an imaginary Being more than they can love their fellow man, surely a cat could love us with a love beyond that given to other cats! (If you read Lorenz carefully you will see he specifically writes "no wild animal." So he might respond "a human is not wild." I am not so sure. Perhaps the biggest question to ask – or to debate – would be are we more like cats or dogs?)

"Then Pussy Launched her Ultimatum"

The image of tiny Puss clinging to the back of fleeing Grumpy bear in Seaton's splendid classic *Lives of the Hunted*, with the understated title "Then Pussy Launched Her Ultima-tum," or, rather her dauntless action has impressed many generations of readers; and everyone who has had a mother cat knows it is a true story, or should be. You will have to imagine the picture, for my old copy of the book with the illustration I planned to reproduce was among the many losses poverty (quick moves and lack of time and space to order things) brings. Let me just say the cat was drawn so small compared to the bear that she might have been mistaken for a flea.

Yes, I know. Mothers who fight to death for their children are a dime a dozen in the animal kingdom and we who feel these mothers are heroic will always have our noses rubbed in the power of *instinct*. While I am a Darwinist and have no intention of denying the genetic component of behavior, an unconscious urge neither negates individual courage nor explains what is going on in the cat in question. Throwing out words like *instinct* is no substitute for observation and thought? *We have a mystery here.* We have an animal overflowing with love, yet a lethal weapon with a hair trigger.

In the next chapter, *How Han-chan Almost Killed a Man*, we will delve into that mystery.

the reverse side of love

> "All dog caretakers. . . have marveled at the exuberant greeting their dog gives them after a brief absence. . . . We tend to explain it by assuming a kind of stupidity: the dog thought I was gone forever. . . . Yet a lover is entranced to see the beloved after even a brief absence – and dogs are all about love." Jeffrey M. Masson (Ibid)

Dogs are the very embodiment of a joyous reunion. Cats, on the other-hand, are known for *not* greeting their "caretakers." As Susanne Millen put it, *"they feel you have behaved very badly and may not be civil when you return."* (*Cat Quotations*).

This does hold not true for *acceptable* absences. When I regularly left in the morning and came back at night, my cats, would either run out to greet me as I approached or be waiting at the border of their territory. It is the nature of the greeting than differs. If dogs want to jump up and into us and, according to one theory, force us to regurgitate, the cat would do the reverse: Kuro'ko-chan and Kori troubled me by contesting day after day to be the first to commit suicide under my foot! They were so good at throwing themselves down on their back just before I stepped down, that I could not come up the walkway without recalling the ancient religious practice called a juggernaut. A puppy dog is quick to bare its belly and the assumption is that it stands a better chance of avoiding being killed by psychologically disarming a potential killer by showing it gives up and puts itself at the other's mercy ahead of time, but the cat's behavior is puzzling. You will not find the same directed toward other cats unless it is to cling and bite them.

For short irregular absences, the dog-cat difference is simple. Dogs always make a big deal of it. Cats rarely do. Returning from an hour in town, my cats only made a big deal of me if they thought I was carrying fresh fish. From the human perspective, this is normal. Human parents, children and spouses act pretty much the same way. So only someone who mistakes the dog's hysterical life-long crush for normal behavior, could consider cats cold for disregarding inconsequential comings and goings.

Long absences are a far more complicated matter. Leonard Michaels puts it beautifully. You return from a trip and "your cat acts haughtily, as if it doesn't care you're home, as if it hardly knows you." (Ibid.) The "as if" is what it's all about. The cold back *is* your greeting. That is only natural. The cat who loves you trusts you. Not understanding your excuses, it feels betrayed. Barbara Holland's cat stayed by her day and night when she was sick; but returning after ten days in the hospital:

> . . . he refused to greet me or even meet my eyes. . . . Now, he walked a few feet away and sat down with his back to me. He was very angry, but I had finally come home, and he began to wash. He spent the remainder of the day washing; it was a long disagreeable job – he was an perfect Augean stable of cat . . . but when he was finished he glittered as before. He still didn't speak to me, though. It was days before he forgave me and things were the same between us. *Secrets of the Cat* (1994)

Rather than the silent treatment, I have been "greeted" with a chorus of angry, accusatory meows – a strident attention-grabbing *hey!* followed by a descending – not asking but telling – tone that told me off in no uncertain terms. *"Where the hell have you been!" "If you think that present will put things right, forget it!"* Or, more simply, *"Go to hell!"* And all I can say in response is *Mea culpa! Mea culpa!* I do not actually use those words, but I do make apologetic meows of the same high type I make when I step on a cat's tail by mistake. It is true, as Susanne Millen continues, that "after you have apologized, normal relations can be resumed," (Ibid) but, as Barbara Holland noted, the cat may take a while to accept your apology.

A cat has every right to act that way. A dog may be an angel. But a cat, when it comes to matters of love, is only human.

love & responsibility

Vicki Hearne had two very important points to make in her philosophical essay, *Adam's Task*. First, training an animal to behave is dependent on its attentiveness. Mind-as-IQ means little. What counts is whether or not they mind *you*. And, second, the usual animals chosen to example intelligence, chimps and gorillas are not as bright as dogs and horses when it comes to *social* intelligence, defined as the ability to live and work with us. After all, she argues, we must keep the former behind bars.

Where does the cat stand in this? Hearne did not make that clear. Her chapter on cats, as we have seen, is pure poetry.

My opinion is that cats are socially as intelligent, as responsible as dogs. They may not defend you from an intruder; but I believe this is because they are only programmed to defend kittens and territory, unlike dogs who fight for the pack. Cats also think *you* are responsible for just about anything – even the weather (no joke! They blamed me for it) – and do not feel you need help. But my cats, at least, usually behaved incredibly well. Having grown-up with a dog who was a faithful companion, I assumed its contrary, the cat, was out-of-control and was amazed to discover differently. From an earlier manuscript:

> *1) They go to sleep when I do and patiently wait for the alarm to go off when I set it late, even keeping quiet when I reset it for thirty minutes more snoozing.*
>
> *2) They read my lips, leaping through the window at the count of three as I open it for just an instant (no heater, in the winter), veering sharply left or right to cross my bay-window desk on the side indicated by my hand signal.*
>
> *3) They generally come when you call if you have a good reason to call them and humor you by playing when you want them to.*

I was not exaggerating. Even locked in by mistake, without a litter-box for the day, they usually manage to hold it in! Cats are marvelously attentive to our genuine wishes. Once they know your lap-top is sacrosanct, they will not walk on it (though some may pretend to do so to catch your attention).

Only obedience for obedience's sake – something demanded by pushy little children and tyrants, such as, judging from his own words, the God of the Old Testament – disgusts them. In other words, they are sane adults.

This is not the case with dogs. For all that obedience-on-demand, you cannot trust most of them to behave. You must take care to keep things physically out of their reach. It is easy to understand why children almost always prefer dogs and most writers choose cats.

love & tricks

It is not that I would have cats out-dog dogs. I am just tired of reading generalizations about untrainable cats. Many do not deign to do tricks. Many humans do not care to, either. Other cats, like Han-chan, not only are easy to live with; but can be trained to do many tricks. And, more remarkably, if we mistake the stereotypical cat for all cats, Han-chan liked to perform. He would eat anything given to him as a reward for a handshake, *even though he was full and had no interest in the tidbits a minute earlier.* Is that not proof that he is eating to reward *me* for playing with him? (The next time you find uneaten biscuits on the floor, make your dog do a trick for them. If that increases the dog's appetite, this phenomenon may be common to all performing pets, not just cats.)

Still, Han-chan was not like a dog who will do a trick for you ten out of ten times. For he did not so much obey my commands as comply with my requests. He had to be in the right mood (which he usually was), or else I had to humor him first. In either event, my enthusiasm as transmitted by voice and hand was the *sine qua non* for success. He almost never failed to answer audibly when I called out for a meow to impress someone on the telephone for he could tell I really wanted him to react and was not simply testing him. On the other hand, he would only rarely consent to obey a request to roll-over and seemed to do it just often enough to show me he knew what it meant. Difficult tricks sometimes had to be psyched up to. To get a double paw high, *"Gimme ten!"* (sometimes *"Ryo te!"*, which means "both hands" in Japanese) – I hate the usual term *"Beg!"* – I usually had to begin with a regular handshake, proceed to the left-hand shake ("*okawari*!" or "change!" preceded by the honorific prefix "o," was the word I actually used) – actually, words were not needed for he learned which of his hands should respond to which of mine! – and the high right-hand shake, or *"Gimme five!"*

He liked the simple handshake enough to offer it voluntarily at times. It was no mere reflex. If I opened my fingers rather than taking his paw, he would stretch his out and if I, taking his hand, squeezed it, he would match me squeeze by squeeze. I cannot say for certain Han-chan's action was conscious for it might be a sort of extension of yawn-catching to other behavior. I had to stop asking or rewarding him for one trick – shaking his head as one might shake water out of ones ears – because he began to do it all by himself as a way of requesting food. He knew the trick really interested me, because I couldn't help laughing at it. He was right, but I feared the rapid shaking might addle his brain. For signaling exchanges, we ended up confined ourselves to his flicking his tail tip when I clicked my fingers.

Hanchan's most impressive trick was so subtle it would ordinarily not be recognized as one. He would stay still for me to draw him and only move once I told him it was OK. He knew how much I wanted him to stay put, how disappointed I was when he moved when I was only half-done, and, he loved my *attention*. The more I drew, the more euphoric he became. Han-chan may have had his eyes closed, but he seemed to literally bask in the light of my eyes. Only his tongue, the thermometer of an old cat's heart, moved. By the time I finished my picture, it would hang down to his chin! Its extreme length *also* reflected Han-chan's poor health by this time, and despite the first line of this paragraph, is no trick, but it does reflect the length of his pose and his euphoria. If cats may be born to pose, Kori (shown above him on page 21) struck one good pose after another, like a professional model. A good camera with a motor-drive might have turned her into a feline super-star. But only Han-chan tended to stay still as long as I needed him to. That made him my best model and holding such a pose for a long time is and is not a trick.

Kori happy to be with zonked-out Han-chan in this Picasso-ish sketch.

Pregnant With Love. The inflow of loving feelings that accompany pregnancy is probably not specific to cats. I would not be surprised to find more single women pregnant with one man's child falling in love with and marrying another than might be expected. I would like to see surveys about personal attractiveness or political feelings and so forth that might reveal whether the heart of pregnant women softens as I imagine it would.

Going Into a Love Heat. Reading Temple Grandin's *Animals in Translation*, I see my observation of love-drunk cats has a chemical basis. Oxytocin, which "shoots up right before a mother animal gives birth and helps her be a good mother." The same chemical rises in a pet dog, and I would guess in a cat that feels it is loved (though it does not explain the extraordinarily tight relationship to feeling good and meticulous grooming in a cat). I thought licking/eating-out kitten's butts made the male Han-chan ecstatic because the odor had something he craved, but maybe it is the actual ingestion of the Oxytocin (and not just the opiate – if it *is* an opiate, pardon! – passed from mother to kitten in the milk that did the trick.

♪ ***Drawing Note, FYI*** Perhaps you have noted the late night-hours. That is because most of the notebook with the best pictures was filled over a winter and I would sleep in because the valley was very cold in the morning. I generally was asleep by midnight or one and up at dawn for the rest of the year.

the trials and tribulation of a social animal
how Han-chan *almost* Killed *a* Man

> If cats are aloof and independent I can't for the life of me figure out what has been climbing, leaping and crawling Into my lap through all of my childhood and adult years. Roger Caras (*Celebration of Cats,* 1986)

> 'Walks by himself' is usually taken as an allusion to the solitary existence cats are supposed to lead. However, I hope to point out that there is more to it than just that. Paul Leyhausen (in *The Domestic Cat*)

'surprising' or old?

A 1994 *New York Times* book review of Elizabeth Marshall Thomas's *The Tribe of the Tiger* by Christopher Lehmann-Haupt tells us that *"What is most surprising about her portrait is that, contrary to Rudyard Kipling, cats do not really walk by themselves, waving their wild tails in the wet wild woods, but in fact are highly social."* Obviously, the reviewer had not done his homework. Little serious written on the over the last half-century does *not* make just that assertion! In the cat chapter of his largely convincing classic *Man Meets Dog* (1953) even the dean of modern ethologists, Konrad Lorenz, both demonstrates (by detailing body language) *how*, and argues *why* (as sociability is not born overnight) he came to the conclusion *"that neither the domestic cat nor his wild forebear is nearly such a recluse as is commonly supposed."*

Why, then, do so many people still believe the fiction?

denatured cats

It is, of course, because fiction grows from a kernel of truth. Many cats we encounter reinforce our prejudice. Partly, it is because the more subtle way cats love humans, as described in the last chapter, is liable to give us the wrong impression. But, the main reason is much, much sadder. It is because there are many wacko cats out there.

I only came to realize that after I had experienced life with three generations of cats under a single roof. The tough old grandmother (Mama Cat) was the boss, but did not always insist upon her way. The mothers and grandmother cooperated on child-rearing. The cats had their spats, but no more than we see in human families. On hot and muggy days, most cats preferred to rest, or sleep, separately against the large river stones in the shade. Otherwise, they loved each other's company. One day, it dawned on me. The asocial creatures I had indeed come across in the past, were the feline equivalent of human feral children!

That is to say, *most* cats we meet are psychologically disturbed as a result of being separated from their mother and siblings at a tender age. Petted by their owners, most are in better shape then the touch-deprived monkeys in Carpenter's classic study, but the general principle is the same. We are talking about millions of mental cases serving as the paragon for a species!

Some ethologists justify the cat-as-a-solitary-misfit, by claiming individual cats in the wild would need a vast territory. Carnivores, they say, are expensive. Tigers seem to back them up. But, *whoa there!* What about lions? They are a hell of a lot bigger than house-cats, but they still manage to live together. Might not our pets be descended from cats even more social than these lions? If that is true, even kittens that are separated from their family relatively late are unable to fulfill themselves as truly social cats.

And, as I show in the chapter about *tanuki,* the racoon-faced fox of Japan, it takes three generations to completely socialize an animal. Until colonies of feral cats of various breeds, living in areas with plentiful food (so they won't be forced to hunt separately) for about ten years – allowing extra time for three generations of male adults – are carefully observed, we cannot even be sure of the one part of the "solitary cat" stereotype most likely to be true: that "the cat is a solitary hunter."

a most social cat

Han-chan is what you'd call a mama's boy. He grew up and stayed at home. A week before his younger sister Kori was born, eighteen-month-old Han-chan resumed nursing their mother – my observation is that many males try to nurse their mothers and often get away with it up to age three! – and, after she was born, spent as much, if not more time in the cardboard box with her and the other kittens as her mother did! He greatly enjoyed letting her nurse him – or, should I say, becoming her pacifier – and helped lick her ass (not just cleaning, but shit-eating, like a mother).

When Kori had her own litter a little more than a year later – she actually finished growing up while pregnant! – Han-chan did more to care for their toilet than she did. Partly, that was because she was the cat equivalent of a teenage mother with an attention disorder, and partly because Han-chan just loved kittens and they, naturally, loved him back.

On the last page, we saw Han-chan sharing the kittens with his niece, their mother. Here we see him taking care of them by himself. Note the way they even go for his nipples! Kori may have been out hunting or simply wanted some time to catch up on sleep as she was always a thin cat and needed to husband her energy. Han-chan's narrowed eyes show his euphoric state. I wish I had carefully noted the date of Han-chan's operation. I *believe* this was prior to it.

Unlike the time when Kori was born, Han-chan was not actually in the box when they were born. He must have been outside for I have a note of his first approach: *"Han-chan moves close to just born litter like a mantis."* Or, a stick-bug, for I recall he was ludicrously stiff!

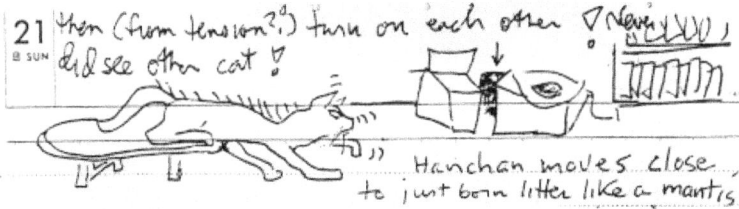

The picture shows him hair-raised stepping from the table in slow-motion. Was he apprehensive of Kori, or fighting to control his own excitement? As elaborated elsewhere (pg 273), Han-chan would learn to touch tiny finger-spun tops so gently with his paw, that they would keep on spinning, where other cats either whacked or ignored them. But, that was years later. Han-chan was not yet a model of self-control. Consciously or not, I think he feared what he might do to the kittens and, for a few days, exiled himself to the far side of the room.

Then, suddenly, he was mothering the kittens. He could not sit back and watch when Kori slacked off. But, he still had a lot of kitten in him, and sometimes got carried away. Like when he saw two kittens in a tissue box and was unable to restrain his urge to join them. Suddenly, the kittens were literally sent flying as Han-chan tried to cram himself into the box, which could barely fit his head. After a lesson in futility, sliding about the tatami, head in box, he tore it into shreds! Meanwhile, I laughed myself to tears.

But, on the whole, he was more responsible a "mother" than his half-sister Kori!

defending kittens

I lost the perfect expert's quote about how male cats are not supposed to defend kittens. But, after what you have just read about Han-chan's love for them, you can probably guess what's coming next.

One day, the kittens were playing under the dense shrubbery in the tiny front-yard. Their mother, Kori, was nowhere in sight. I was conversing with Han-chan, who was lying on the cement surface of the second floor's outdoor corridor, when an old man came up the hilly path with a typical Japanese dog (sand-colored, a cross of a stocky sled-dog and a sharp-snouted coyote). The dog was minding its own business – sniffing and peeing on both sides of the path – and did not even *look* in the cats' direction. But the instant he came into Han-chan's line of sight, it happened.

Han-chan flew off the side of the corridor, hit the ground, ricocheted up and landed square on the dog's back. The dog bolted. His leash was around the old man's hand. If it had not slipped off before the man was pulled over far enough to fall, tumble down the stairs, hit his head (or had a stroke or heart-attack) and die, the following day's tabloid headlines would have been *"FOREIGNER'S ILLEGALLY KEPT CAT KILLS SENIOR CITIZEN!"*

Later, the next-door neighbor – mother of the girl I gave the mouse to (pg.280) – related excitedly that she had to walk her even tougher dog (his muscles felt like steel) on a different route than usual because he too had been attacked by, and feared Han-chan. Han-chan, the most cowardly cat I ever had, was, I quote: *"terrorizing the neighborhood!"*

a shitty hypothesis

Genetics say it makes sense to defend one's nephews and nieces. But, still, how can we explain the transformation of a hypersensitive cowardly male into a fearless mother cat?

Watching the incredible shit-eating grin on Han-chan's face when he finished prompting the kittens' bowel movements, the answer suddenly came. We have seen a lot of research on the beneficial effects of mother milk – the opiate effect that helps kittens/infants sleep, the anti-diarrheal effect, and so forth – well, what about the effects of kitten shit, which concentrates ingredients found in that milk?

If the mother cat's love increases before she gives birth, her fearless attacks are seen after she gives birth. Could Han-chan have discovered, or unwittingly become a demonstration of the bravery-enhancing qualities of kitten-shit that would suggest a mother's hormones include something other than what makes them so loving that also makes them so brave? Or does whatever prompts love simultaneously make us brave. Or, does being in love (with mates or children) itself create some other chemical reaction that makes us all lion-hearted? We do, after all, do things we would never dare to do when we have a crush on someone.

the Queendom

Toms may stink up a lot of territory, but they do not monopolize it. They are like nations living dozens of miles apart, asserting a 200 mile economic zone over their shared international waters. There are many scuffles, but everyone knows they are just playing around. When a female comes into heat, the males gather round, sing up a storm and quarrel like cowboys at a cathouse on payday. For all their fighting – and the misery old toms cause young toms (pg 161-2) – they are far more tolerant of competitors than lions.

It is the females who must hold together a cat's pride, i.e. guard their gene pool by maintaining a resource base for their descendents and relatives. In a chapter on "spacing problems" in *The Domestic Cat*, Liberg and Sandell write:

> "there is no published evidence of active defense of core areas by group living females, but the complete lack of female transfer between groups . . . . , while male cats obviously move between groups, does point to some kind of repulsion of strange females."

Some kind indeed! I was sitting on the veranda, when Mama Cat flew past me into the garden and through a hole in the thin hedge. At first, I only registered a grey blur. She had not uttered a sound, and the suddenness of her passage, like a bullet or rock from out of nowhere whizzing by, gave me goose-bumps. I noticed the thin calico from the farm-house just across the road on the far side of the field, about a hundred yards away, just twenty or thirty yards off, in the recently harvested spring onion field just as she saw Mama and turned tail. Mama closed on her so fast you would think she was standing still and hit her so hard that they both went flying. Mama caught her again on the bounce and surely would have killed her if she didn't somehow manage to flee. (Let me add that the kittens were safely inside at the time and almost half-grown. As far as I could see, they were in no immediate danger. I suspect she was still nursing them, but, unfortunately, I was not yet recording such vital details.)

That was the only time I have ever seen such an "active defense" of cat against cat; but it was enough to tell me why the only other strange female cats that ever called on me were Mama, herself, and years later in a different city when I had no cats, Chikurina, both the first of their lines. A female cat may not have an economic zone as wide as the male's, but her sovereignty over her Queendom is absolute. A female vs. female defense makes perfect sense, for if males are not great hunters but females are, their competition would threaten to her offspring's survival.

The standard view of cat territoriality has it that "there is a strongly defended territory which is larger for the male than the female" (Julie Clutton-Brock: *The British Museum Book of Cats*). The fact that queens generally allow male visitors to enter their territory without visas and do not patrol the boundaries might give one this impression; but if "strongly" means the defender is dead serious and *no quarter is given* to intruders, then the experts are wrong. By that definition, only females qualify, and males don't own *any* territory. They only play king of the mountain over as much of it as they can keep by huff or by bluff.

Kori & the tanuki

The third and last active defense I experienced, after Mama Cat's torpedo and Han-chan's ricocheting leap was by Kori, the generally careless young mother, and the victim was neither cat nor dog.

The kittens were small. The window was open. Three or four tanuki, raccoon-faced foxes (pgs 283-92) visited. The other cats recognized them and, knowing they meant no harm, remained relaxed. Kori was in a box in the far corner of the room, about seven feet behind me, sleeping or nursing her litter. *Was*. The next thing I knew she was flying by my shoulder and out that window to slam into and knock over one of the fleeing *tanuki*.

While *tanuki* are more considerate of a cat's nerves than dogs, they seem to enjoy manipulating cats with their superior savoir faire. Even outnumbered, these clever foxes can usually psyche-out cats. They make odd, clucking and drumming sounds. Letting a cat face them down, the second the cat averts its eyes to eat the contested food, they rush the cat, while loudly scuffling over the leaves, causing the cat to flee without physical contact. But this time, there was no time for tactics. Kori, alone, routed the entire pack.

Three things favor a charging cat. First, the attack is so fast the attacked animal has no time to consciously identify its attacker. All it can do is register a projectile closing quickly. That automatically triggers a fleeing response, for no animal wants to wait-and-see, for such a bet sometimes can cost a life. Second, the silence is unnerving. Most threats are loud, dressed in impressive noise or bright color. They are supposed to make you think, thereby preventing a fight. Tanuki actually enjoy such inter-species games which they usually win. Here, thought is bypassed entirely. Third, as the cat will be moving far faster than the trespasser when they close, if they do actually collide, the bluff is not over as the tremendous impact will seem to the struck party to have come from an animal the size of car, rather than a cat.

punishing my pride

While females usually rule, once the first mother, Chikurina and Aunt Riko were gone, and everyone kept was desexed, Han-chan became the spiritual mother and leader of the little desexed pride. He took it upon himself to call for food while the others generally kept quiet. As noted elsewhere, when food was limited, he waited for last – the opposite of lion males! – and rarely exercised his ruling right except to obtain more raw tuna and the highest place to nap. All of the other cats made up to him whenever they met. And I made no bones about ruling over Han-chan and his pride. Living in a one-room apartment no bigger than a dinghy where it was forbidden to keep cats, anything that caught the landlord's eyes, nose or ears would ruin it for all of us. As I have related, cats are attentive to what matters. But, I must confess that my cats' super-egos did not develop spontaneously. I helped by using a water-squirter and a pea-shooter to put *the fear of god* into them.

These disciplinary devices are the secret to raising well-behaved yet loving cats (and dogs) and here is why:

◎ First, the value of any negative re-enforcement diminishes by the square of the time elapsed since the undesired behavior. To run across the room to whack a malefactor means a lot of pain for you and your cat for little effect. *Instant* punishment means minimal punishment. ◎ Second, cats are liable to sulk, and good at paying back the punishment by puking or peeing in strange places. It is best to distance oneself from the punishment, to make it as impersonal as possible. At first, squirt or bean (I use soy beans and am careful not to hit the face) the cat when it is not looking your way. You can gain the effect without the resentment, and even console the cat later. ◎Third, the device will prevent problems in the future. By the time the cat realizes that Divine Punishment comes from you, it will usually be enough to merely pick up the weapon to keep order at a distance. Han-chan, quickly discovered that the pea-shooter was impotent without the soy-beans, but that turned into a blessing in disguise, for I realized I could crinkle the bean bag out of his sight for a pea-shooter that worked around corners! ◎ Fourth, the pea-shooter in particular, can make repelling troublesome Toms easy. At first, Han-chan, seeing the weapon that helped detail his super-ego, ran, too. But before long, he and the others all learned the pea-shooter was *their protector* and not to be feared, unless they did something wrong. Han-chan would meow to high heaven to get my attention, and wait to rush the tom the instant *after* the bean hit him and put him off-balance! Water is just too messy and the range insufficient.

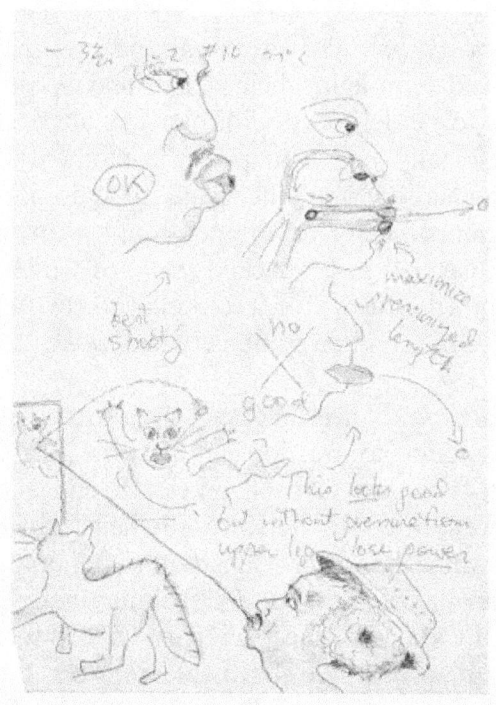

I have no pictures of me using a pea-shooter, but you can see I also learned to do it with my tongue. If you would try, take care not to breath in the bean, which is placed far back in the rolled tongue.

Fifth, it is so much fun! Don't pity the cats, for water and beans are nothing compared to the rough discipline cats dole out to each other. And, don't fear retaliation. Once cats learn what is expected of them, they do not sulk, glower at you, stare you down or misbehave in predictably unpredictable ways, as they do when you punish them for something about which they have no clear understanding, which is the case for all punishment that is not instantaneous. They may not look as guilty as a dog, but they know what is and is not fair, and readily accept deserved punishment. The only problem is that they sometimes turn it into a game; but, what the hell, I'm up for it! Yes, even disciplining, done right, is fun for all.

vicarious vs. jealous

If your cats are a family, like mine were, they react in one of three ways when you pay close attention to another cat in the house.

Vicarious reaction. The other cats narrow their eyes in pleasure and through their ears and posture show themselves to be delighted with me. The angelic Kuro'ko-chan occasionally began to purr the moment I began to stroke Han-chan! On the other hand, they do not at all like to see me punishing, or playing too rough with another cat, unless that cat had just whacked *them,* in which case they readily admit the justice of it. No one rushes to defend its sibling, but I have gotten some very bad *looks*.

Jealous reaction. Not as pleasant as a vicarious one, but nevertheless good to see, for it proves the cats are *paying attention* to you and to each other. It can also be very funny. Shortly after gentle Kuro'ko-chan learned to shake my hand, which had been Han-chan's monopoly, I shook Han-chan's hand right after shaking hers, and was astounded to see her place her paw on his forehead and push him off to one side. I was pleased to see her do the same thing the next time I lined them up for handshakes before dinner. Evidently, even an angel has a weak point. She can get jealous.

Ignoring. Finally, they can just ignore it. But, that is a purely theoretical reaction. Related cats, at least, are so attentive to each other, and all cats are so attentive to the relationship between other cats and the owner that, I would guess, the cats only pretend not to care.

I forgot to mention, my cats – some more than others – helped call my attention to cats waiting outside the window to be let in, by going over to the window and meowing until I did my duty. Even cats do not live in a dog-eat-dog world. Given half a chance, they cooperate.

beyond diaspora

In a chapter in Serpell ed. *The Domestic Cat* (1988), Eileen Karsh and Dennis Turner say "emphatically 'no'" to the practice of adopting cats before they are weaned to bond them with their owners. It is enough to have them handled by humans during their "socialization period." They, and many others, also recommend we keep two cats from a single cat family if we keep any, so they can amuse each other when we are out and better amuse us when we are in.

Amen. But it is still not good enough. We need to support larger families of cats, so several generations can enjoy a more natural social life. I think two *dozen* cats would be best. Obviously, that is far too many cats for most of us to even consider caring for in our own houses or apartments. Ideally, dozens or scores of neighbors would cooperate so that all cats owned on the block, or town, could be related without increasing the total feline population to the detriment of the local ecology.

The only problem is that we have not even *begun* to do the same thing for *our* children. The rest of the world should have joined China and promoted the one-child family long ago, but the dearth of children so necessary for the welfare of our species and the survival of biological diversity is unnatural for a society. If our culture was both reasonable and compassionate, we would be designing our blocks or buildings to compensate for the low density of children through collective dining rooms, and playrooms. Parents would be encouraged to take turns caring for each other's children. But, no. Our heartless nuclear-family diaspora is taken for granted and, from the looks of things, we would sooner run the planet into the ground than behave responsibly.

Alas, we are like our cats, and not solitary animals. I am afraid our fortunes ride together and, at this time, our future does not look good.

cat tails

A Dog-eat-dog World. Apologies to dog people. I also know dogs will come running when a fellow dog cries in pain and, less commonly, call attention to another trying to get inside. But, idiom aside, I have not heard anyone claim that dogs were asocial, so I champion the social cat. You might say that I follow Kropotkin who was well aware of competition in Darwin's theory of evolution but chose to concentrate on cooperation, which also interested Darwin, because it was being overlooked.

Mama Cat vs. Chikurina. Mama cat was the first homeless cat I took in. She appeared below my kitchen window cooking = burning fish in the Japanese style. I did not see but *heard* her, or, rather, heard an odd hissing noise and wondered if my bicycle tire was leaking. When I cracked the window, I heard a louder hiss and saw it came from a woefully thin mongrel cat. I had never been approached in so odd a manner but thought I *better* give her something lest she jinx me or something. After a few months, she moved in with her kittens. I had no litter box as I kept the doors cracked (low crime in Japan) and they did it outside. She remained the Alpha cat even when her toms outgrew her and did not hesitate to whack anyone who got out of hand. I had yet to take notes, much less draw pictures of cats, but I keep a clear memory of her swishing by me like a missle to strike that strange female out in the field. This is all we will hear of her in this book about cats born of a green-eyed brown tabby who seemed almost a tigris in her pronounced pattern and the confident gaze. She suddenly appeared as if by magic out of the bamboo forest (*chikurin*) and appealed to me through the open window with the most musical meow I had ever heard. Unfortunately, Chikurina disappeared two years later, leaving me and Yoko (who had moved in and, like the cats, was not supposed to be there) with her barely grown kittens. If she had remained, she would surely have become a major part of this book.

a pictorial chapter, for seeing is believing.
The Sleeping Cats or, rather, *Cats*

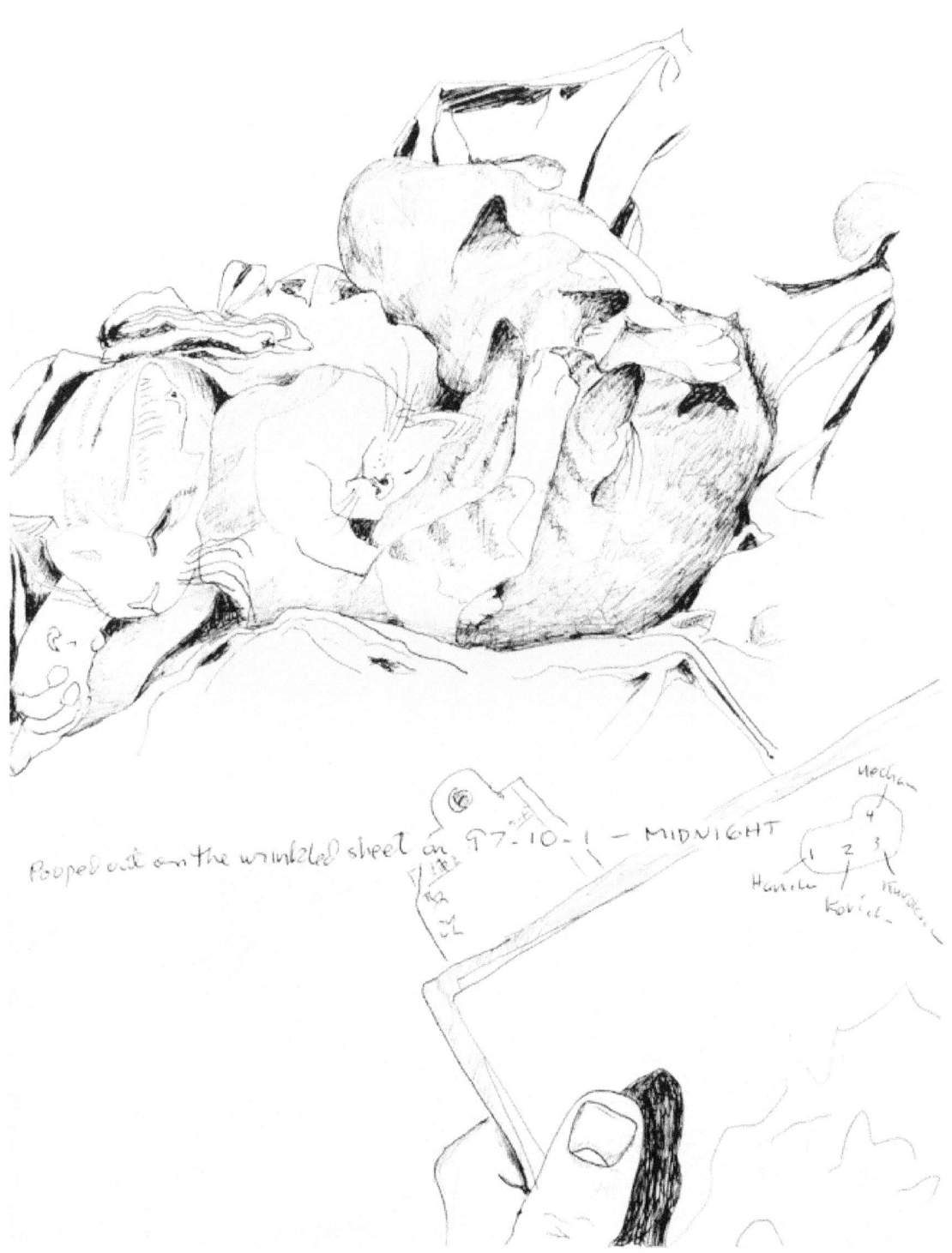

This looks far better lightly colored. Kori's winter coat belies her svelte figure. The *hakusai*, a Chinese cabbage best-known for use as *kimchee*, a fermented Korean condiment, but also good in soup with ginger and chicken, is a winter vegetable that even grows in the snow. The central part of it is missing for I grew tired of drawing because of my poor eyesight. The direction of the shading lines indicates colors. The haiku may help explain why it is so warm inside on the third day of the New Year. I will let you guess what "First Princessing" means.

nikai ongaku de gomakasu hime hajime

The second floor
covers it up with music:
First Princessing

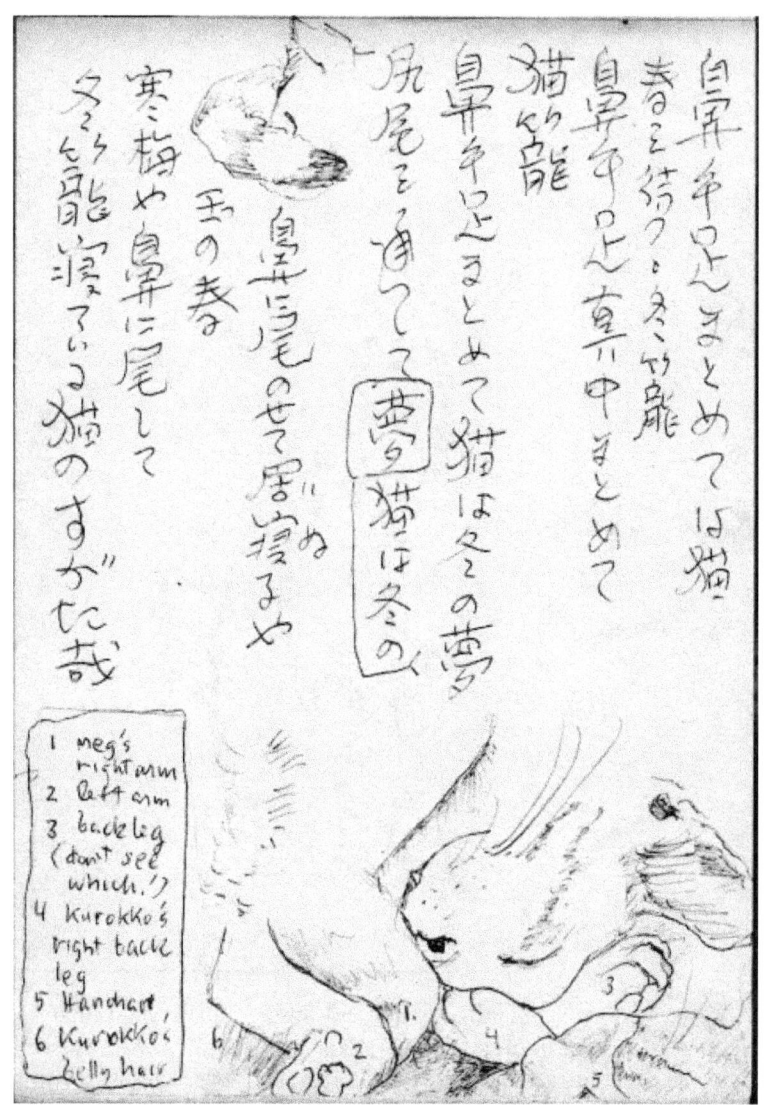

The pictures shows part of three cats. This was drawn on a day I was drawn to the sleeping paw, nose and tail. Some of the haiku:

> wintering in:
> is not a sleeping cat
> the form of it?

nose and paws
gathered together, cats
wait for spring

gathering in
its nose and four paws
a cat winters

> tail laid across
> its nose the cat sleeps
> into the new year

How related cats socialize when 50-80 degrees. Han-chan is licking Meg the hunter as Kori looks on happily. She moved twice as much as anyone else and is *also* shown facing me with a mosquito sucking her brow. They are all lying between my legs.

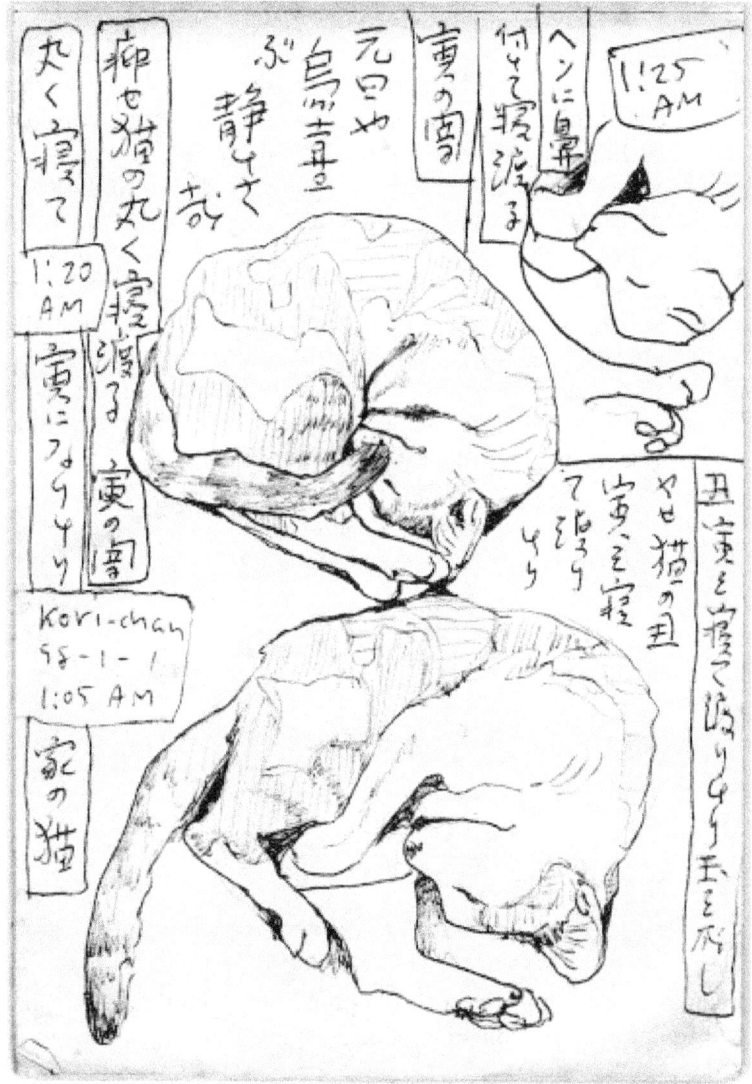

Ovaries used to be associated with hysteria, but Kori-chan came back crazy after they were taken out. She had always had the most shapely legs (not fore-arms) of any cat I knew and seemed to show them off even as she slept, assuming more impish postures – not the sprawl that Han-chan created or the ball of Meg. Unfortunately, the body proportions are way off here. The arrival of the Year of the Tiger haiku are bit better.

Nose to navel
fast asleep she crosses
the Tiger Dark

Curled up asleep
tonight our house cats
become the tiger

the skinny cat
curls round to sleep across
the Tiger Dark

Sleeping cats have many points to make and we will find them in other chapters, too. In this chapter, following a brief aside on living in the cold and the aesthetic and behavioral discoveries made observing a single cat sleeping, we shall consider collective sleeping as the best proof of the sociable nature of the cat. That is something found only in the winter. If you, like me, lived with many cats without heating, and furthermore, left a window open far enough for a cat to come in and out all night in sub-freezing weather, you know what I mean. I suspect that few people know what I mean. But, before proceeding, let me add that I did hang up a blanket cut so it functioned like a dog-door, so the temperature only fell a bit below freezing before dawn allowed me to man the window. Here is a picture of that window device (left). Note how the cat misuses it:

I would love to jump right to the point, but the only picture that will fit below is sick old Han-chan sleeping alone:

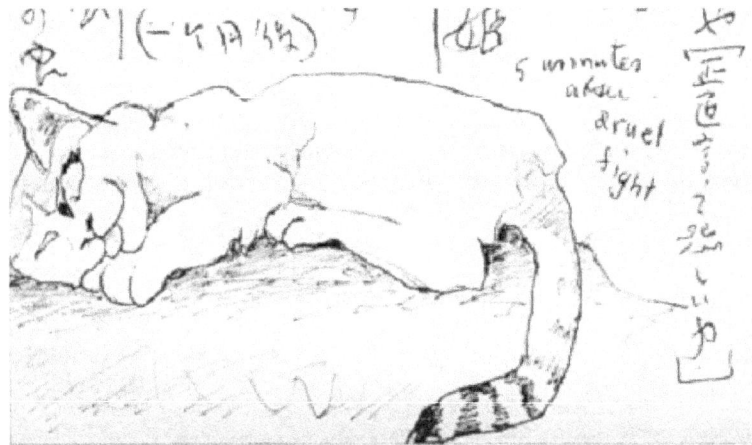

The next picture is what cats do in the winter. First, a cat that sprawls out large in the summer will make a tight ball to sleep. That was when I discovered that Han-chan, whose pattern I thought was purely haphazard, actually – or, seemingly – grew in much the same way as the continents when they broke away from the original singularity, Pangaea. In other words, when Han-chan balled up he took himself back billions of years.

The *ume* (conventionally plum or flowering apricot). It blooms in the coldest part of the year. If you read Japanese, please *don't* – the haiku are awful. Old Han-chan sleeps while blossoms on a cut branch light up the room and a call attention to ear hair. I am eager to get on to the socialized sleeping that you will find most interesting, but let us see a few more of the one-cat sleeping first. This next picture did not come out right. As written, the ear got too big and I failed to capture what impressed me as a perfect yin-yang sign.

I include this so-and-so drawing here to give you the translation for my notes which read as follows in Japanese:

> *Originally, cats in the winter competed for the center. They formed an endless cycle where one after another throws himself into, no, squeezes or wedges into the very middle of a pile of cats. But when there is an anka – a small water-bottle-shaped heating pad I got to warm up near the window so my computer would not literally freeze – that original form can no longer be seen. They turn into modern cats and struggle to monopolize the pink-colored small island called an anka.*

Above: the conceptual discovery noted. Below: a close-up that exaggerates Kori-chan's paws latching on to the *anka* for dear life. Maybe a "raft" would be a better concept than "island!"

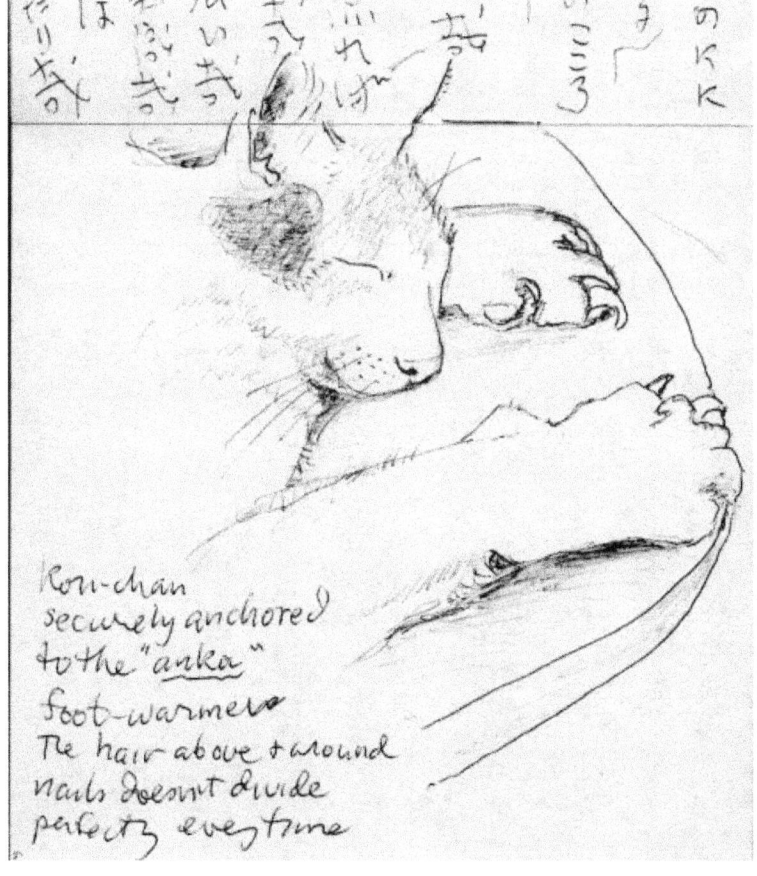

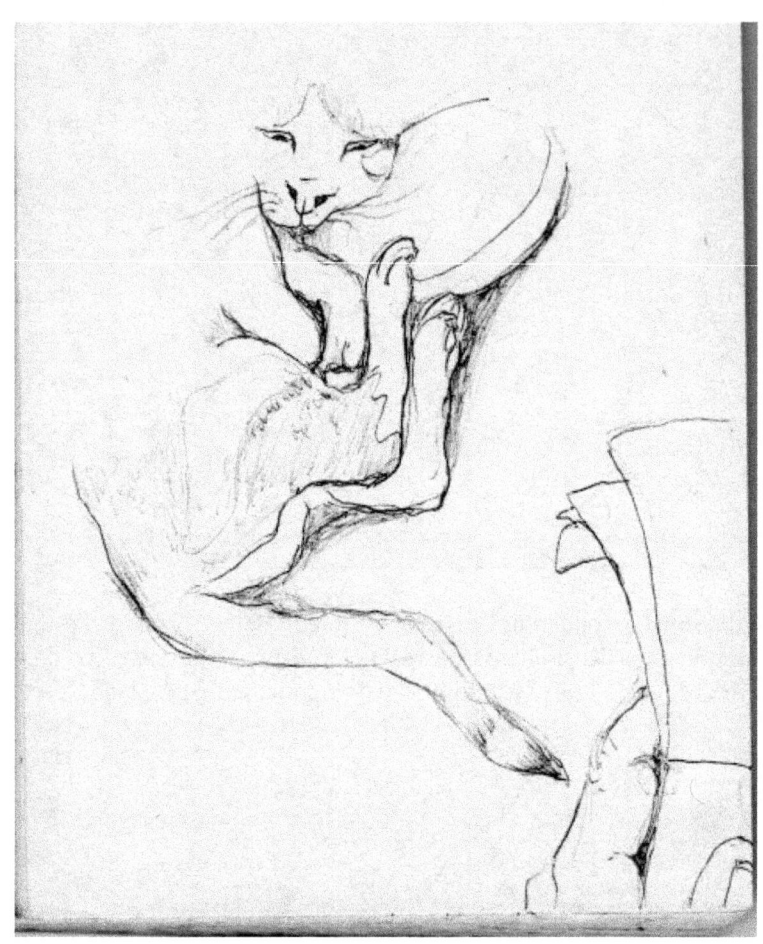

Below, we can see some sharing. Must not have been too cold! The *anka* is under the sheet between them. Bottom-left, Han-chan

The light colored part from the anka container is cut and pasted in my notebook, which was a pad of dark, i.e. natural newspaper. The catch-phrase above says "♪ *Warmer than our house's Tama,*" which suggests most Japanese know cats are warmer than people and may have found that useful as central heating is almost non-existent there. Oddly, another place warns people not to let pets sleep on them. Tell *that* to my cats!

The Reverse Yawn, or Stretching in the Winter!

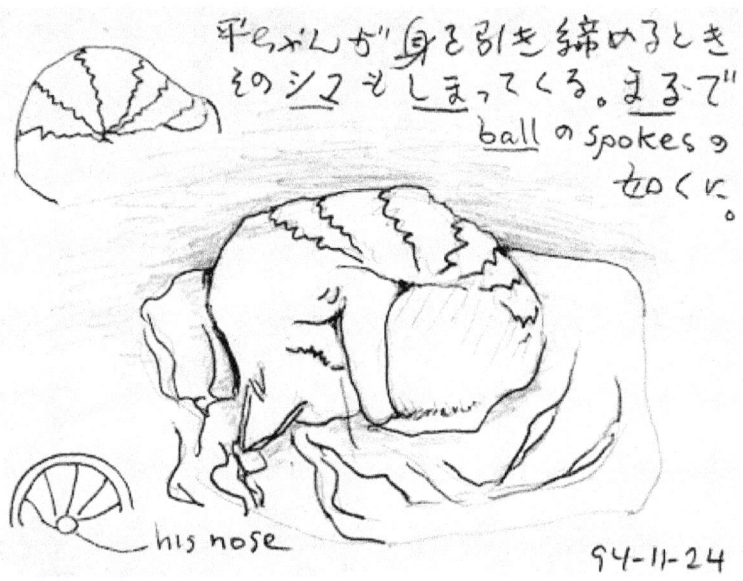

We are back to pattern, but rather than rejoining continents, we have stripes coming together in the center to become spokes on a wheel. I reinforced the idea with a fine pun on *stripe* in Japanese but misspelled Han-chan (半ちゃん not 平ちゃん)!

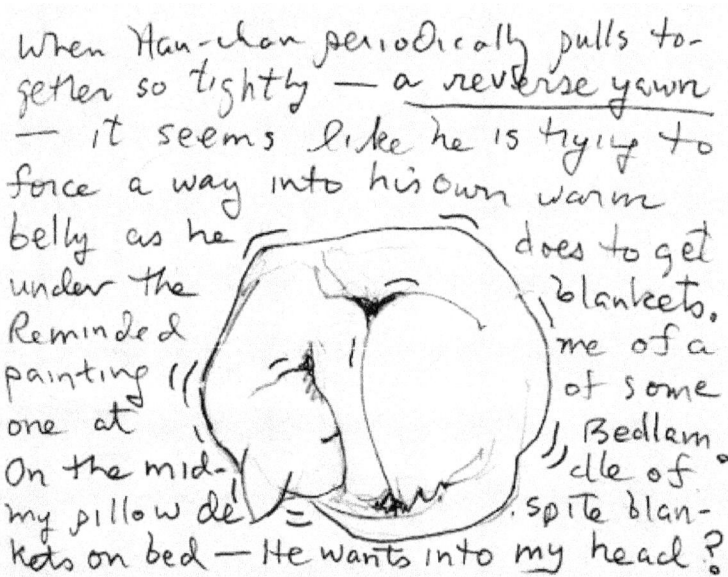

Forget the superficial! A reverse yawn. Is this my discovery and coinage? All cats love to yawn. When it is cold a conventional out-style yawn loses body-heat so cats have come up with in-style. My notes on Han-chan wanting to be inside my head are poetic but said yawn was not only demonstrated upon my pillow.

More Variations on the Squeeze Yawn

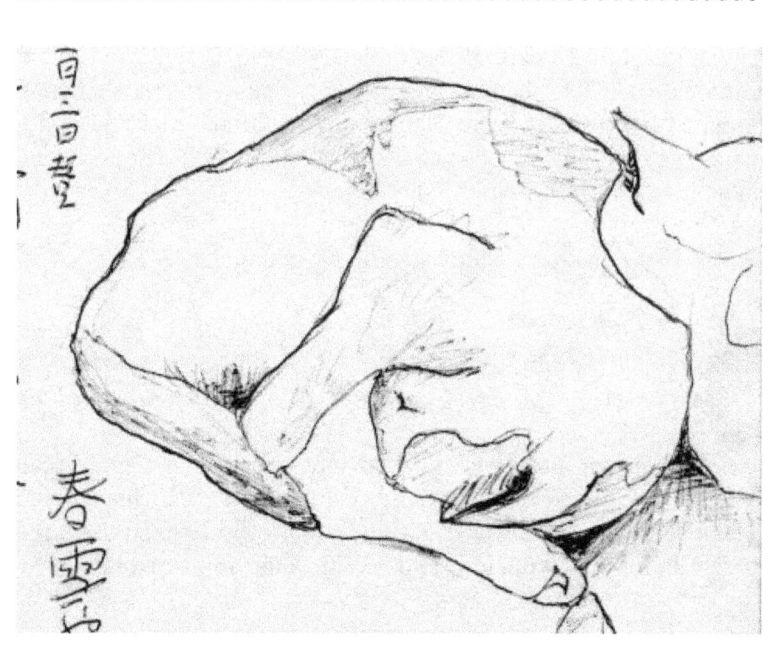

Paper kimono used to be typical winter clothing, especially for old men. As the homeless know, paper is extraordinarily good at keeping out the cold. In other words, newspaper can keep in enough heat that a cat-ball is not necessary in an unheated room. Besides, old Han-chan is lying on my legs – I am sketching propped up in bed. Were Han-chan not old and sick, he might have been tempted to check out the "Long-tails" (azure-winged magpie) mentioned in the first haiku:

onaga ya tsumaru hi no saundo efekutto

Long-tails! What
a sound effect for the sun
forced to set!

The cramped sun
you can hear it go down
squealing magpies!

Below that is a haiku by Shiki: "Right underfoot / I spot green grass: / a withered field" or to English the flow: "A winter field / i spot some green grass / right underfoot" and I substitute a red umbrella for the "withered field." With some adjustments:

By my feet, I still find green grass: a red umbrella.

Han-chan sleeps in a loose one-cat ball. Meg (unless I drew Riko too fat) is balled up but wide awake and watching me sketch with her ears – how else to describe the attentiveness of an alert cat with closed eyes? Over her head, there is a name, Issa 一茶. My slightly long haiku (*idenshi kara yoi'ko no neko ka fuyugomori*) does not English well, but let me try:

So, do their genes
make cats behave so well?
Wintering in.

Issa had poems about cats behaving like angels in the season no animal wants to be out in the cold. I wrote his name where I did to show my poem was a follow-up to his. Better I wrote *it*, too, but I neglected to do so. My handwriting shows it was cold.

Kuro'ko-chan, the brown tabby's coat was too time-consuming to draw and Kori-chan's below (right) too complex.

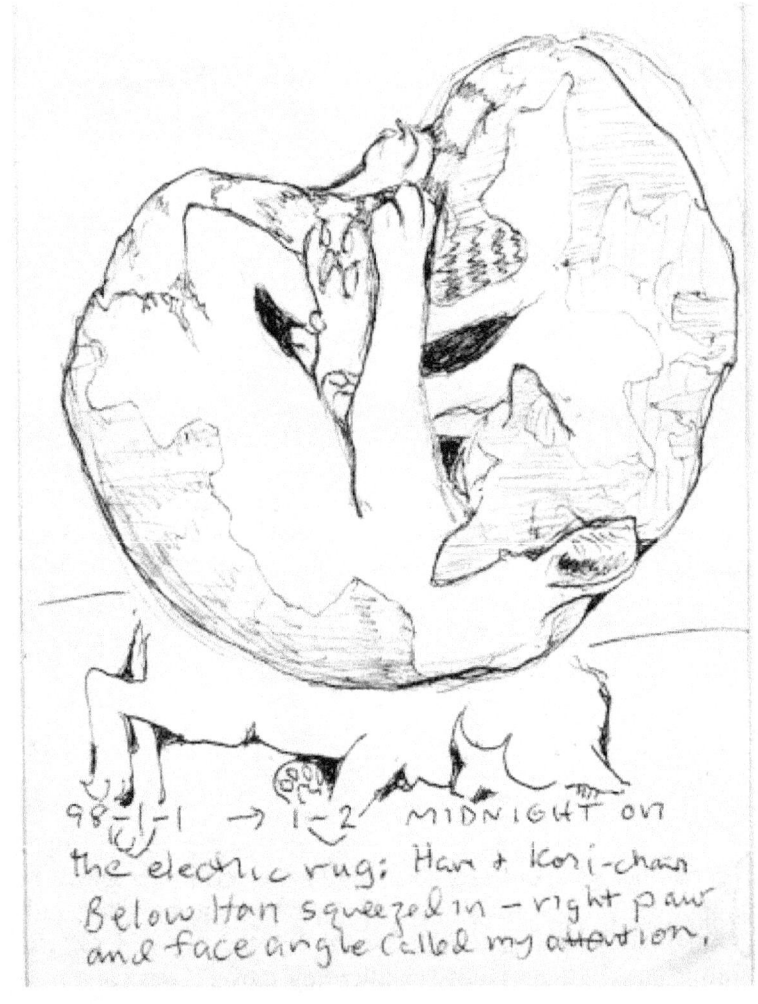

On the last page I see I got a little electric rug. That, too, was for the computer. And, I forgot to mention it, but I had to bend a desk-light bulb down close to the little Mac and incubate it 15-minutes every morning before it would consent to turn on! The above was my last New Year in Japan. Yoko, the cat's favorite snowball-bowler (pgs.95-6) and I had separated and I was alone with the cats who were happy with the heating Mac forced on me. The next drawing takes us back a few days to X-mas, which was usually an exhausting day as it started with a full-day of cleaning at the office (in Japanese companies even the brass does it) – I did windows mostly because of my reach advantage and because I insisted in singing while I worked and that got me outside. After that you drink and eat and catch your flu for the holiday. Cats do not need much air to sleep with, but they want it warm:

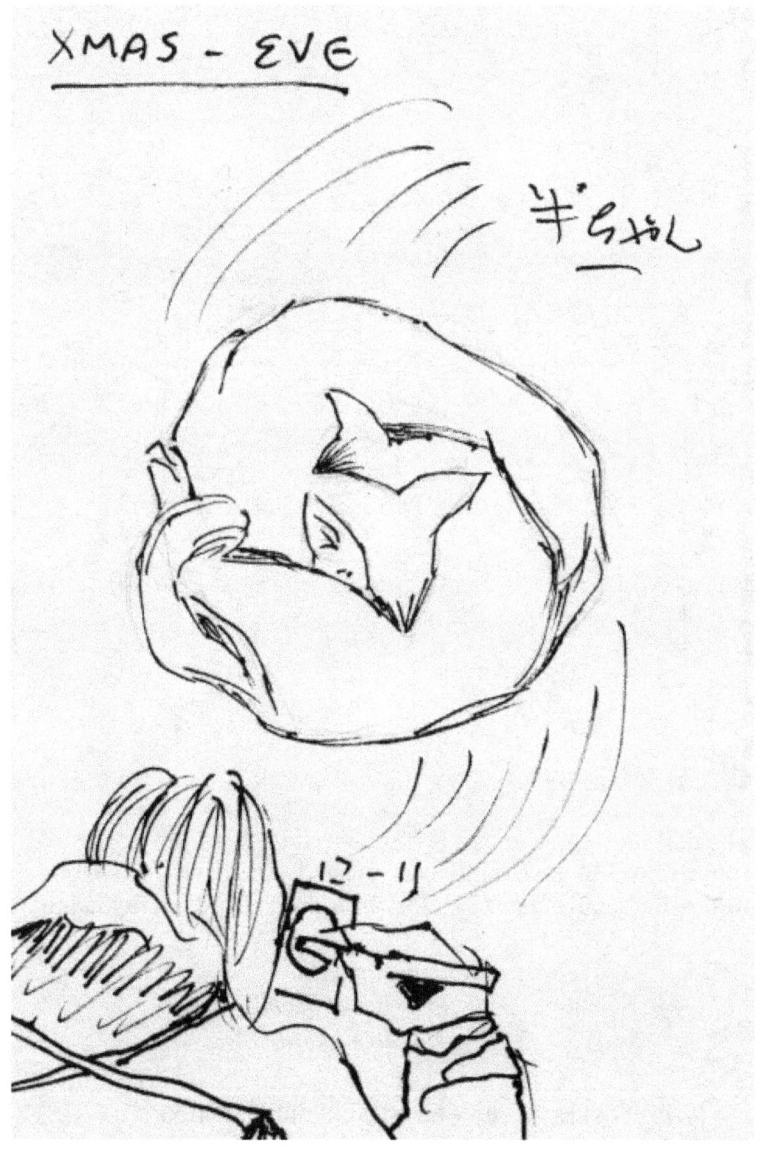

Needless to say, the picture on the last page of two cats making a sleep-ball also makes a yin-yang. I wish I knew why Kori-chan had become Rori! The X on my back is a tasuki, a device you can make with a long sash or cord to hold bulky clothing in. Yes, we have now finished with one-cat balls and started two-cat balls.

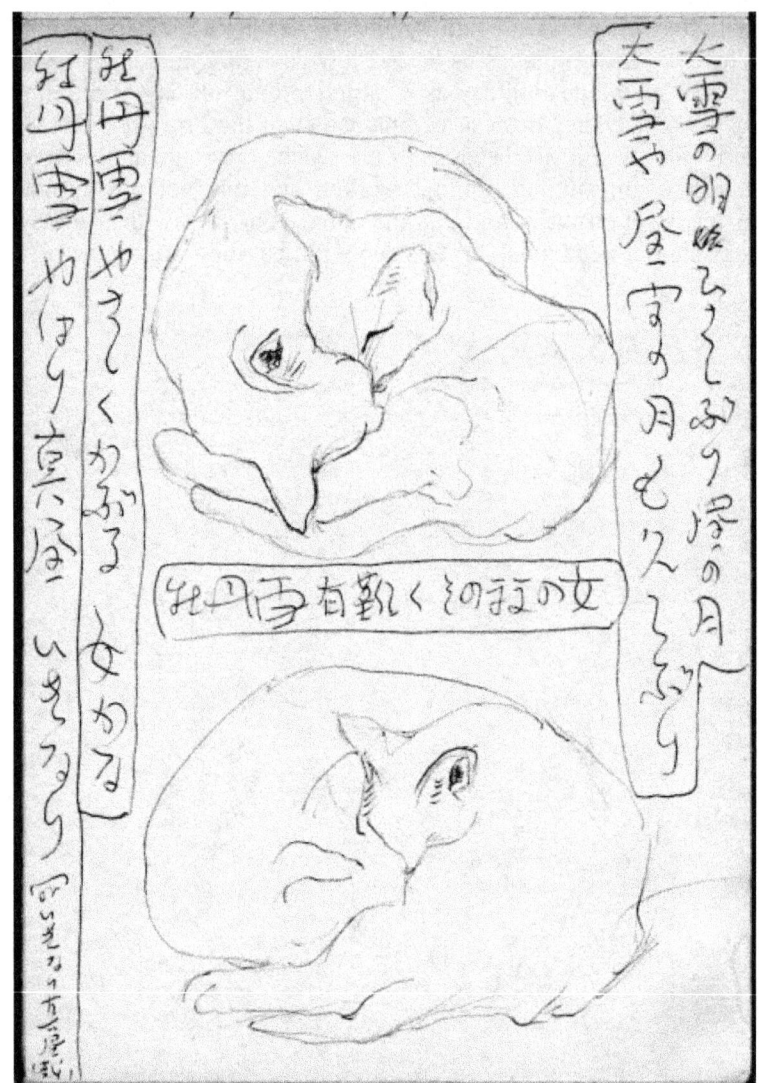

The dark in the ear above is disconcerting, but I never claimed I could draw. In fact, until cats pushed me to try, I was much worse. Let me Romanize and try to translate three of my haiku:

Heavy snowfall –
How long has it been?
The daytime moon.

ôyuki ya   hiruma no tsuki mo hisashiburi

Snow like cotton
gently crowns the head
of a woman

botan-yuki yasashiku kaburu onna kana

Snow like cotton
i'm grateful she left it
as is, on her

botan-yuki arigataku sono mama no onna

In a better reproduction, this looks good. Focusing on details of Kurô' kô's face, I lost the greater picture and her sweetness –

Now we are up to three. Han-chan, on the left, is happily attentive to my drawing and delighted to have the other cats' heads near his belly, for he was, as we see elsewhere, exceedingly enthusiastic at mothering. The room would be cold but not freezing, for the cats have their heads up. It might still be Autumn as the following is specifically so:

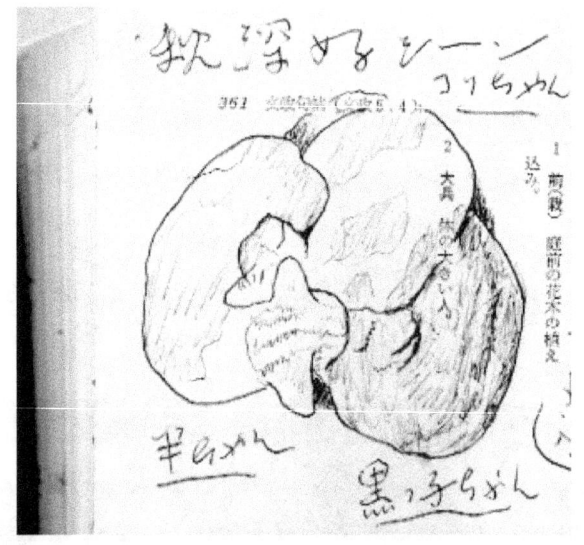

I lack a good picture of a four-cat sleep-ball. Why a rectangle. Because the cats cover two of the pillow-like anka (heaters). I lack drawings of large sleep-balls because the rotation of cats from the perimeter to the center – climbing over and squeezing in – every five or ten minutes means there is movement before I can finish drawing. That is where a photo (below) comes in handy. Han-chan is the kitten on top. Zoro, the mother of the small white cats in the center and heroine of the Battle with the Blue Boss, is on the right, facing her alley-cat-like brother whose ugly stub tail cannot be seen, tail touching her other full-tailed brother.

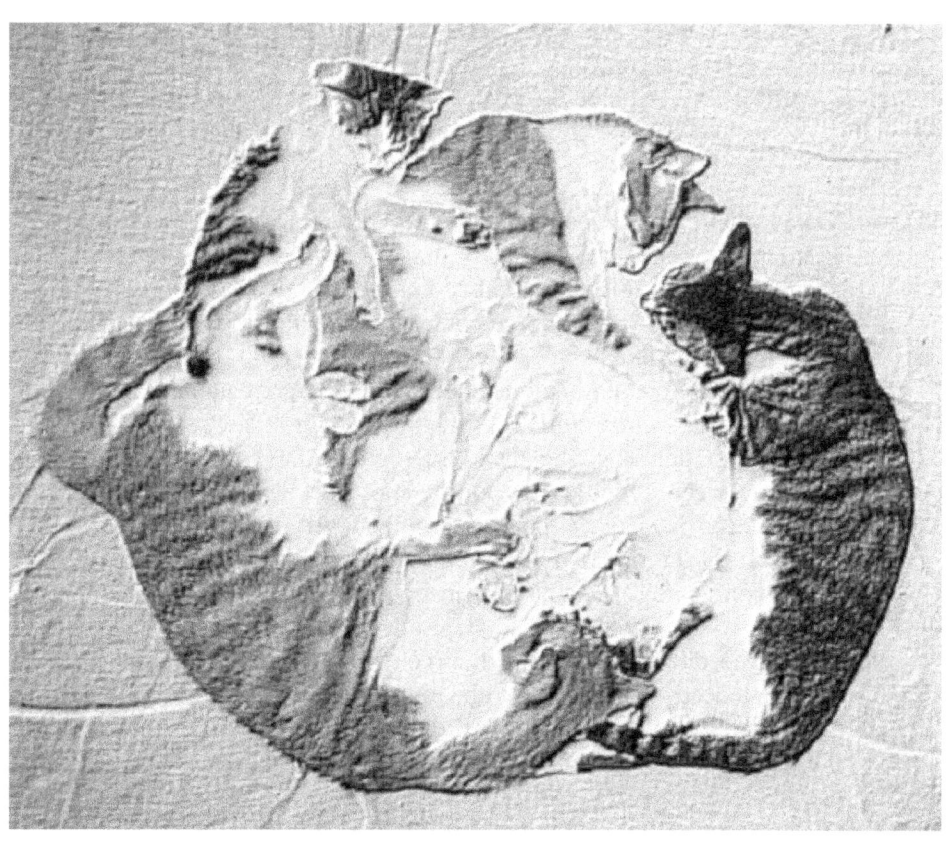

cat tails

1. *Cat Sleep.* My intent was to stick with pictures in this chapter, but I read the following in Jeffrey M. Masson's *The Nine Emotional Lives of Cats* and felt I had to comment:

> Maybe cats have lucid dreams – that is, dreams in which the dreamer knows he is dreaming. They sleep remarkably lightly. They can hear the faintest sound of a mouse's footsteps and be instantly awake and alert.

I know that cats like people must learn to recognize dreams as dreams when they awaken as they must learn to recognize mirror images and TV images as fake, but beg to differ about the blanket statement (made in the context of asserting the oddity of not purring in dreams – not a good argument for purposeful purring, as a cat could imagine another party in a dream and purr to communicate contentment, as dogs wag their tails in dreams). It is the case that cats who spend the night, or much of the night out, may sleep soundly for hours. The black cat with me at present goes out like the proverbial light when he is on my bed alone during the day. Much of what is taken for sleep at other hours, unless the cat is able to adjust completely to human hours (the case with Han-chan, who slept all night in my right armpit with his head on my shoulder after Yôko left and must have slept deeply indeed to put up with my snoring!), is closed-eye alertness, as discussed elsewhere. It may be that some cats have insomnia, but I would guess they are like people, a mix of heavy and light sleepers.

living with a hypersensitive cat
the Very Thought *of* It!

After writing the title of this chapter, I went into the kitchen to make coffee. Returning, I noticed Han-chan wore a large clear right-triangle. So something *had* fallen off the edge of my desk ten minutes earlier!

I knew what happened. Han-chan thought the triangle falling over his head was *my* doing. Since he trusted me completely – I could even do the schoolboy trick where, palms together, you aim straight at the eyes pretending to give a two-hand karate chop, splitting them apart to bypass the head at the last instant, with Han-chan not even *blinking* – he was content to leave things where I put them. No, he was *more* than content. He was *delighted* with the attention. Where most cats will frantically remove a clothespin hanging from their hair, I have decorated Han-chan with *dozens* of them *and he loved it.* He trusted me to remove them; and knew that meant more *skinship*, if I may borrow a Japanese word for touching that is good for the psyche.

Don't get me wrong. Han-chan was not one of those dull cats that react to nothing, sleep all day and have only one meow, like a thin black one that wandered into the publisher I worked for, Kôsakusha. Who knows if it was an excess of social contact (our office was next to a university) lead-poisoning from growing up by a highway, early abandonment, or autism (who says it is unique to humans?) that left him barely alive except when someone played a tape of Jim Nollman jamming with a pod of Orca. Judging from the way the usually unmoving appendages on his head perked up and his eyes got a wild and utterly alert look, orca song tapes should be marketed as catnip for the ears!

No, Han-chan was not like that. He was generally alert yet not jittery, or reactive, like cat with frayed nerves, lap dogs only their owners like, and all turkeys. If I were out and a triangle fell on him he would have quickly pulled his head out of it. So, when I say he was *hypersensitive* – we finally arrive to the subject of the chapter – I mean something deeper than mere neurosis or instinctive nervousness.

imaginary snow

It is a cold winter morning. The other cats go out the window with trepidation and, perhaps, a butt-warming spank from the author, but as soon as they answer the call of nature that got them from *futon* to window in the first place, they are happily tearing off across the snow as if high on something sometimes called the same.

Han-chan, too, got as far as the window. Han-chan, too, got a pat on the butt (actually, on the thigh muscle which is *their* gluteus maximus). He came *close* to jumping. At one point, he was poised half-way out the window and I gave him *a push,* more than enough to make up his mind normally. But not this time. He was as solid as a rock. As a mule. As the founding father of Aikido, who, legend has it was still unmovable and unliftable by a number of young musclemen when he was in his eighties. Then, Han-chan backed in, turned, and vigorously shook his back legs, one at a time in my face. That shake is exactly what he does when he steps on something wet – dew, rain or snow equally disgust him. But this time, it was different. *Han-chan had not gone outside.* His feet were dry. Han-chan shook off *imaginary* snow from his feet.

*   *   *

The other cats rush off ecstatically over the freshly fallen snow while Hanchan

This is the kind of thing that can only happen to a cat with a phenomenally strong imagination. Or, should I say *a cat who thinks too much?*

Han-chan's dislike for deep snow was beyond question. My interpretation of his action as being the result of an overly vivid imagination is not. It might be countered that Han-chan did not *imagine* stepping in the snow, but merely *saw* it and responded with a somatic *"Yuck!"* Even so, the specificity of the body language was undeniable. It is not a general indication of discomfort, but how Han-chan *concluded* encounters with wetness. It was not just *"Yuck!"* but *"Brrrrrr!"* and *"Wet!"* as well. The pantomime may not have been consciously performed; even I have my doubts as to whether Han-chan really meant to tell me something with it, but snow did not fall often enough in Tokyo to make a Pavlovian response probable. It seems more likely that what, more than anything else, triggered the foot-shaking was his hyper-active imagination.

flea circus I – game trophies

As a matter of fact, Han-chan found many things *yucky*. One particularly hot summer, fleas were his main obsession, but before focusing on him, the broad picture –

Living within a giant bamboo grove with a thick carpet of leaves in a damp corner apartment cut deeply into the foot of a hill upon old *tatami* (straw-mat), *all* my cats were flea-ridden and my mountains of books and notes, guaranteed that even the occasional fumigation could not get all of them. I once removed fleas with tweezers. I could get hundreds in minutes and stuck them on masking tape for easy counting. So long as your eyes hold up, it is a pleasurable sport that might be favorably compared to tiny hand-held computer games. I am not alone in finding it fun. Novelist Komatsu Shigeo compared it to *hunting* and even had *off-seasons* to give the population a chance to recover. In an interview in the Japanese monthly *Sinra* (special feature: *Tale of a hundred cats and their owners*), he says his record is 462 fleas on 88/6/26. The photo of one of his specimens shows only 179 (neatly scotch-taped down three to a row in four columns) taken between 8:50 PM and 1:00

AM July 10/11 1987. I am not so patient or fastidious to spend *that* much time hunting and displaying fleas, but I found one short note in my 1989 diary (years before I found that used copy of *Sinra*):

> *7/30   Tweezered 115 fleas at one go from Ao-chan alone in approx. 30 minutes*

That is 230 fleas per hour as compared to 45 per hour for Komatsu-san. But, to be fair, he probably caught most of his fleas in the first half-hour and had his statistics ruined by the law of diminishing returns. Moreover, his cat is a Han-chan look-alike, while Ao-chan, soon to mysteriously disappear, was pure white. Komatsu was having to cope with mixed terrain, while I had all my fleas out in the open. If I counted for calico Meg, or brown tabby Kuro'ko, my statistics would surely have dropped to less than a flea per minute. After ten years of such heroics, by 1990 or so, I learned how to use a flea-comb to good effect. The combs never come with decent instructions, so readers who dislike tweezers, flea-collars and powders, listen up:

> *Always keep combing until there is enough hair together with the fleas that they don't try to flee when you pull the stuff off the comb. Immediately drop it into a waiting jar of soapy water, cap it, give it a few shakes so the hair and fleas are water-logged, remove the cap, comb the cat and repeat the process. After you finish, the foul soup may be dumped into the toilet and flushed. With this method you can do in more fleas in five minutes than a tweezers can in an hour.*

Flea hunts are fun; but we have so little time and so many fleas. If I had a wife and a child, those fleas could be used to gain me time alone with the former. *"OK, kiddoo, see how many fleas you can get off the cat! A dime for each, and make sure they are stuck to the masking tape, for I will not pay for any that escape!"* And, if I added that I would subtract a dime from his or her earnings for every flea I could find on the cat after the hunt was over, we would be guaranteed silence and utter privacy for at least an hour. One can well imagine becoming so dependent on such fleas as to require them to be captured alive, placed in a jar and returned to the cat after the results were tallied up.

flea circus II – self-preservation

> The flea, a persistent pest, disturbs the rest of sleep, and unhappily despises the tranquility of that most agreeable contemplation wherein one enjoys supernal delights. By a luckless progeny of the body . . .is man molested, so that he may reflect that his own body is the heritage of worms. (Alexander Neckam 13th century, transl. George Boas)

The real comedy began when Han-chan discovered that fleas were liable to pounce out from the holes in the tatami or spaces between books when he was drinking from the water-bowl in the corner of the room. Since none of the other cats appeared to notice it, at first, I thought he was just being hyper, perhaps because he was bitten by one flea just as his tongue reached out tentatively for that first lap of water one time. But his apparent paranoia persisted, so, returning from work on a warm day, I tested the area for fleas before letting the cats in. My bare sweaty foot served for bait, for it is not true that the difference in human and cat body temperature – they are hotter – renders us *immune* to cat fleas; they are happy to make do on our warmth and blood in the absence of cats or the event of overpopulation. A dirty T-shirt laid on the *tatami* by my foot added to the bait and helped me see better and, sure enough, many more fleas appeared by that water-bowl than anywhere else.

I do not know if fleas are just drawn to moisture or, *use* water bowls to ambush cats because the cat smell is concentrated in that area. But that was academic. The fleas *were* there and Han-chan, not unreasonably, boycotted the water-bowl for his favorite alternative and sign for it, the kitchen sink (pp104-5).

This was the hottest summer in recorded history in Japan, where the humidity is even worse than the Eastern seaboard of the USA. I must admit the fleas got out of hand. A term used in Issa's haiku to describe his own hut a hundred and fifty years before came to mind, *nomi-jigoku,* "flea hell." Indeed, the only good thing coming of this was an explosion of flea *ku* which provided balance for my hundreds of mosquito *ku*. I tried to tell myself the poems were ample compensation for the sleep deprivation. But I was thin and only had so much blood to give, and what with having to share it with the ferocious thicket mosquitoes, so large you could count the stripes on their legs, I had to take *some* measures for self-preservation.

At first, I let the cats enter the apartment before me when returning from work in order that they, not I, vacuum up the waiting horde. I must admit to feeling a little guilty, but weren't *they* the ones who brought them in the first place? And wouldn't *I* remove the fleas from the cats by flea comb later? This procedure was worked out shortly after I noticed how, after coming home to the hot apartment, I was instantly beset with ravenous fleas. At least, they didn't come out to greet me as Issa claims his did (he was gone for days rather than just a day); but they did shimmy up my socks and work their way into the holes of the fabric to get to my legs heated up from climbing the long hill home.

After a few days of this, I decided to simplify the process and spare the cats by placing a bucket of detergent-filled water handy *before* going to work and, on return, entering first, and sitting still for a few minutes to encourage all the fleas with ants in their pants to go for my socks, which I would then strip off while pulling them inside out and submerge into the waiting water.

flea circus III – the dirty look

The other cats were happy to go in first and put up with the short wait though they could not understand what it was for. Only Han-chan did not buy the deal. Not at all. Whether or not I went first, he refused to go in until the room cooled off, which took only five or ten minutes, for the room was small, the windows large, I had a good fan and the surrounding woods were cool. But even then, he knew I was not getting *all* of the fleas and added the entire *tatami* floor to his boycott. For days – or was it weeks? – in a row, he bounded in seeming terror from veranda to kitchen via chair and table-top, and if a single flea or imagined flea reached him, he went right out the window leaving me with a very dirty look.

The only thing that eventually brought Han-chan's paws back down to the *tatami* was the periodic routing of said fleas by a new invention, an anti-flea spray with a long needle to inject it – whatever it was – deep into and through the tatami (also between books piled vertically and horizontally where the wall met the floor). As you can imagine from what I have said so far, I almost had to tie him up to get him to give the *tatami* another chance.

That *dirty look* – actually, an imposing glare generally saved for looking back over the shoulder – is what most interested me at the time. I could have sworn Han-chan held me *personally responsible* for the fleas in the room, and was *demanding* that I *do something* about it. Imagine that – *Je acuse!* from your cat.

Guilt on my part? Perhaps. But consider the fact that on these occasions, Han-chan always managed to bound across the room in such a manner as to spill my coffee, graze my ear, step on the stereo or otherwise *sin*, and then respond to my angry yell with the body language of a "Hrmph!" rather than fleeing out of sight or putting on a more suitable contrite look (never as hangdog guilty as a dog but clear enough to someone who has lived with cats, it involves a low posture and total avoidance of eye contact). And, this, despite the fact that Han-chan was usually the most considerate cat I have had the pleasure of knowing.

flea circus IV – sleeping with han-chan

How considerate? Well, for a start, Han-chan is the only cat I have known who *always* cleaned his feet before getting into bed with me. Any cat can be taught not to dirty the bed by having his or her dirty paws shoved into his own nose or mouth. But they tend to forget or get haphazard about it on wet, chilly days. Not Han-chan. He caught on so quickly I cannot even remember teaching him. Maybe he watched me. I never get into bed without first rubbing my feet together like a cricket. I assumed *everybody* did so, until a human bedmate laughed herself silly about it. If you, like me, seldom clean the floor, and go about barefoot, such rubbing is necessary; my plucky cohabitant – she stayed for five years – ended up copying us.

After she left me to the cats and my imagined loves, Han-chan always slept the entire night with his head on my shoulder or the edge of the pillow. Because of a neck injury in high-school, I sleep on my back all night, which makes me an ideal person to sleep with, or at least offsets my snores. Well, Han-chan *also* stayed put. Why I do not know, but it is no small accomplishment for a nocturnal animal. Since I had no heating and the window was left cracked for the other cats all night, every winter, it literally froze inside. Again, Han-chan is the only cat I've known patient or farsighted enough to refrain from tunneling down into the warmest part of the bed only to have to claw their way out over my sleeping body a half an hour or so later. Who can say whether this was because he wished to avoid hurting me, was afraid of my reaction, or, knowing I disliked him tunneling down, simply wished to please me. I think the most likely explanation is that Han-chan, unlike the others, *knew* – that is *could imagine* – that if he waited he would soon be warm; or, conversely, remembered what would happen *later* if he chose instant gratification.

the situation. I say this because Han-chan is usually very considerate. He is the only cat I have ever known to be absolutely certain to clean his feet before getting into bed with me. He is also the only cat I've known patient enough to refrain from tunneling down to the warmest part of the bed in the cold of the winter (only to have to claw their way out a half hour later). Han-chan knows — that is, can imagine — that he will be warm if he waits; or conversely knows — that is, can imagine — what will happen later if he chooses to be snug in an instant. When Han-chan bounds accross the room in such a manner as to spill my coffee or hit my pillow within a hair's breadth of my ear, and when he responds to my angry yell with an expression of "Hmph!" or a wild glare, I'd say Han-chan is not only saying "I hate fleas" but "do something, it's your responsibility!" to me.

So when Han-chan did something he *knew* disturbed me, and added a glare to boot, I do not think I was imagining things when I interpreted it not as simply *"Yuck, fleas!"* but *"It's your fault, asshole!"* It seemed that he who was so considerate to me expected something in return. And that included keeping the place safe for a sensitive cat.

flea circus V – getting the future

I was that rare child who actually ran from "shots" – once, I hid outside the doctor's office and Mom had to threaten to call the fire department to bring me out of hiding. To tell the truth, my balls still retract at the mere *thought* of a shot, so I can readily identify with Han-chan's hypersensitivity to fleas and doctors (after getting a shot once, he hid from all male visitors – the vet was male – for years!). But, at the same time, I won long-distance races with bloody feet, endured months of tough manual labor (chaining boats to tractor-trailers) in a hundred degree-plus heat where no other *anglo* lasted more than two weeks and spent many winters in Tokyo without any heater despite lack of insulation on my Miami-born body. I do not write this to boast but to make a simple point. It is possible to be both hypersensitive to sharp pain and exceptionally tough when it comes to enduring duress.

Han-chan, for all his sensitivity, was the only one of my semi-feral cats to have learned to put up with the flea comb and to appreciate it when I tweezered fleas off his forehead. Speaking of which, here is a paraverse of a Japanese simile:

*broad enough
for a family of fleas
my cat's brow*

The simile is "as narrow as the brow of a cat" – All the other cats struggle, and look at me as if to say *"Why are you torturing me like this?"* Naturally, I showed off tweezered fleas to all the cats after I remove them. In Japanese I would say *"Look at this!"* Sometimes, there is a flicker of recognition on the part of the other cats, but when I finished, they would flee and the next time, give me the same old tortured response. Only hypersensitive Han-chan always bore with the discomfort – because the teeth are so narrow, it is quite a tug – and remained by my side after I finished. This might be a male trait. Many toms bear up to so much discomfort one could almost call them masochists. Perhaps, Han-chan is only unique for being of a different sex than my other three friends. He is, after all, the only male cat to have stayed with me longer than three years. Or, it might be that Han-chan was the only cat with intelligence enough to connect the grooming with the removal of the fleas.

& mosquitoes!

The bamboo grove boasted an extraordinary parade of mosquitoes. The big *yabuka* (thicket-mosquitoes) fell with an audible plop on the tatami even when not full of blood. One could pretty well drain a mouse. Then, there was a daddy-long-legs variety that luckily didn't bite, a normal everyday medium-size, itchy-bite fiend and, most horrid of all, a small breed that *filled* so fast and painlessly you only learned of your contribution after you gave it because they over-drink and, like heavy birds on water, literally bounce across your skin or the sheet on their blood-balloon bellies to gather up enough energy to take off!

Han-chan was the only one of my cats to appreciate my cramped mosquito net – an umbrella-like fly-guard (*hae-cho*) intended to protect a tray of food on the table, to which I added a foot-wide strip of sheet to the bottom edge to skirt the gaps made by my body and the covers.

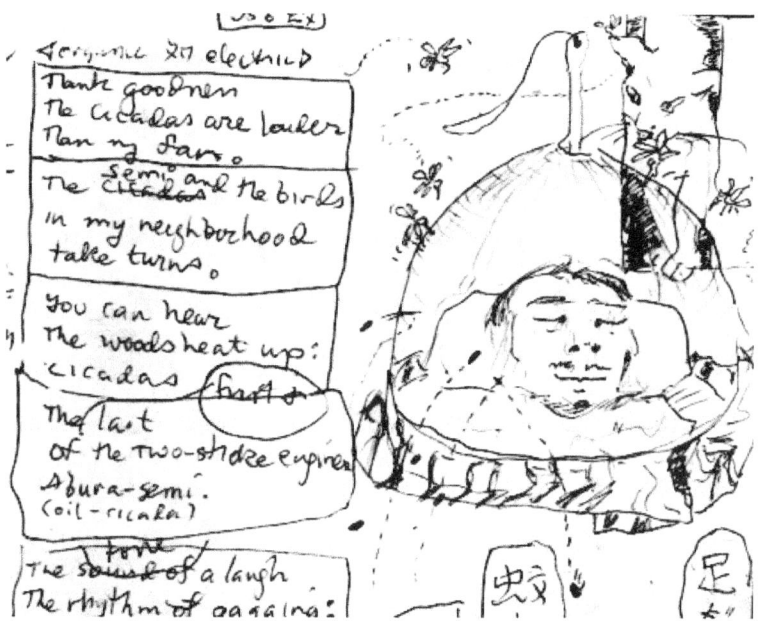

With barely enough room for Han-chan and my head and shoulders, the slightest movement brought his delicate ear-tips into contact with the net and reaching distance of the mosquito. Yet, Han-chan always *asked* to be let in, and remained there until dawn. In the hottest part of the year, there was no comfort in keeping close to me – cats slept apart from each other, too – but he *learned* that the net shielded him from mosquitoes and fleas (they could squirm through the eyes of the net if they tried but fleas ambitious enough to surface at night always *lept* for us, so they bounced off), and slept cooler for knowing he was safe.

Depending on how you think about it, Han-chan was very sensitive and, hence, cowardly, or exceptionally far-sighted and self-controlled. Or, perhaps, the first gave birth to the second. In my own case, I have little doubt that what strength I may boast is largely born of weakness.

The feline gourmet, or anticipatory disgust

Han-chan's hypersensitivity, not surprisingly, includes food. He is no more picky than your usual cat, that, to be fair, is no more picky than your usual human would be if forced to eat a monotonous diet.

Think about it: Do we give our pets the variety animals enjoy in the wild? Do we give them the variety we enjoy ourselves? When cats express misgivings about their food, it is usually for good reason. They have either been getting too much fat or protein and need a change, or, they have had to suffer the exact same protein and fat mixture day after day after day – the similarity of pet foods is no less horrible for being mandated by nutritionists – and are bored with food of whatever flavor it claims to be. How would *you* like to eat what amounts to k-rations every day?

But Han-chan is exceptional in *the manner* in which he expresses his likes and dislikes. Only Han-chan could tell by the sound of the wrapper when I opened a pack of *sashimi* (raw tuna) from fifty yards away and through closed doors, while cats in the adjoining room had yet to catch on to what's up. I did not mind sharing some of it with him *in exchange for silence*. He *needed* red meat fish for, like me, he could not handle fat (I cannot absorb it, and he, after becoming infirm, drooled like a cow when he ate anything fatty). Fish oil may be great for some hypothetical animal, but it does no good unless one can absorb it. But Han-chan could not be bought. He was no sneak. He invariably belted out his loudest *"Chow time!"* meow, and the others came on the run.

Usually, the perfect gentleman, he would wait for the other cats to finish eating before beginning himself. When there was not enough, he might even call for more, though circumstances – such as my feeding him before the others come in – conspired to let him eat his fill first. Yet, sometimes, he did something as funny as it was inconsiderate. The moment I began to open a kind of cat food he did not care for, Han-chan would turn about and paw at the newspaper (always topped with slick advertisement pages so the food would not soak up newsprint) as if to say, *"This is shit! Take it away!"* I suppose it was thoughtful of him to tell me this while the food was still in the can, but it was selfish when you remember that three other cats who did not necessarily share his taste were eagerly waiting to eat! Then, again, he may have thought he was talking for all of them.

mr fastidious

> This looks especially bizarre on a hard floor on which they may sometimes scratch without effect for minutes on end. *The Domestic Cat*

Covering up leftovers or disliked food is common enough: Yet, Han-chan was the only one of my cats to *consistently* and carefully cover up not only the remaining food, but even the soiled paper it rested on. This generally meant folding the newspaper over upon itself; but when the paper wouldn't cooperate, or the meal was served on a plate, Han-chan availed himself of *any* material within reach and Han-chan had a very long reach. He managed to pull the sheet off the *futon* bedding on several occasions and, once, pulled over my desk chair on top of it! More commonly, he enlisted a dirty sock in the cover-up. This was no doubt very effective as the sock surely outstank the tuna and even challenged sardine.

Han-chan knew I did not appreciate this compulsive cleanliness, but he could not help himself. After years of problems – even manuscript blown off the desk was not sacred, we worked out a compromise. *He* no longer went in for heroics, and *I* made every effort to *quickly* cover up or throw away the offending paper. Specifically, this meant Han-chan made a few perfunctory scratches on the edge of the newspaper and pointedly looked my way. Then, I did my duty. If I did not, Han-chan did it *his* way, and I had no right to complain.

There are two basic theories about how cats have come to cover up food. The hygiene theory stresses the benefits of not leaving food to rot and draw parasites, not to mention enemies. This fits closely with the cat's well-known preference for clean surroundings, unlike most dogs who prefer the stink of familiarity. In other words, they cover up their food for the same reason they cover up their scat. The other theory, the cache theory, is self-evident.

Males are said to be more thorough coverers than females. I have five hypotheses why this might be so. 1) Males, who are continually jockeying for position within a bully-or-be-bullied clawing order, fear revealing their condition (evident from the smell of the scat) to outsiders, whereas females in their all-or-nothing world of absolute territoriality (pp 37, 51-4) are unconcerned. 2) Males, being poorer hunters, catch less and must cache more if they would eat regularly. 3) Males are less likely to bring food home and share it, so they stash it away instead. 4) Males, because they wander more are more likely to harbor parasites likely to endanger relatives. 5) Males dislike the smell of waste more than females who lick their kittens' asses and swallow their feces. Or, 6), it may have something to do with dominance, where the boss of the household is in charge of covering up food (in which case, families of cats with a dominant female may contradict the above.)

Since Han-chan covered up food he did not wish to eat as well as food he was too full to eat, it would seem that whatever the biological explanation may be, cats are thinking *"Yuck!"* And, as in the case when he shook his feet at the snow, Han-chan, at least, reacted *before* the actual experience, at the very thought of it.

Over the last years of Han-chan's life, I would sometimes show him the can and wait for his opinion before opening it. Since Han-chan came to know a vigorous scratching would never fail to get him *other* food, it is possible that he was sometimes doing it not because he really disliked the first food offered, but because he wanted something *better*. I wish he could have known how grateful I was for being entertained by a cat who would bury his food before it was open!

qualification: cats and snow

Han-chan did not dislike *snow*, just the cold and wet aspects of it. On pavement, one snow-ball at a time, he *loved* it. In fact, *all* my cat friends were big on winter sports. A page from my diary of 1990 (see drawing on top) shows what I mean.

> *Snowball bowling, of which there are 2 types – with hard balls like ice hockey where cat chases it as it goes by, & soft ones thrown to collide with the cat or else just over head and break when hit with paw into a localized blizzard, & Yoko [my cohabitant] & Koriko [Kori] did it for over 1/2 hour, no gloves for her & no gloves or shoes for Koriko who refused to come in and called us back out.*

The Japanese in the upper right side of the picture credits Yoko with the invention of snowball bowling, which we did on the snow-free concrete porch of the apartment building. Were cats our size, those soft snowballs would be the size of cantaloupes! The cats were so turned on by the game, they didn't even mind being struck now and then. Because the balls explode on impact – think of it as reverse bowling! – the cats must feel that they have won every time they demolish a snowball, even if pieces of it hit more than their paws. The picture below it shows a game that *I* invented before Yoko started to bowl snowballs because she was too sweet to throw them at the cats as I did. The tree depicted was actually a bush, so that the top had the twigs needed to catch and hold snowballs:

> *Cats climbing bush to catch incoming snowballs or bat them down from branches – even if person [after a person] stopped throwing – Futsukakoshi [the neighbor, a middle-aged woman] says "I thought they [cats] just sat around the danbo [hearth or heater]!"*

Took K-chan outside to see if she would still play with snow. balls. She no longer takes them head on like a bowling pin but enjoys watching them hit edge of concrete next to her as shown above.

cat tails

Ao-chan, the White Cat. All who met Ao-chan, meaning Little Boy Blue, believe he must have been kidnapped. He was the rare snowy white cat with two bright blue eyes yet perfect hearing. Another white kitten, born to Mama Cat at my previous residence, was not exceptional, yet adored by a neighbor who said he, "too good for" me, belonged at a shrine! Meanwhile, she called a much brighter brown kitten "dirty" and *detested* her!

Real Flea Hunting! With games of skill, the more tenuous the contact, the more pleasure. Plucking with tweezers beats using your fingers but, unless the sadistic joy of popping fleas – which, if they kept you up at night can be as satisfactory as achieving the long sought triumph over a recalcitrant pimple – is your aim, you are still too *close*. For sensitive souls, at least, the greatest satisfaction comes from trying to hit moving targets at a distance. Christina, the healthy young Queen of Sweden whose penchant for early morning study cost poor Descartes his life (he caught cold and died), had a miniature crossbow devised especially for shooting fleas. Where exactly those fleas were hunted is not said, but it is pleasant to imagine a ruler who had eyes for small things as well as large.

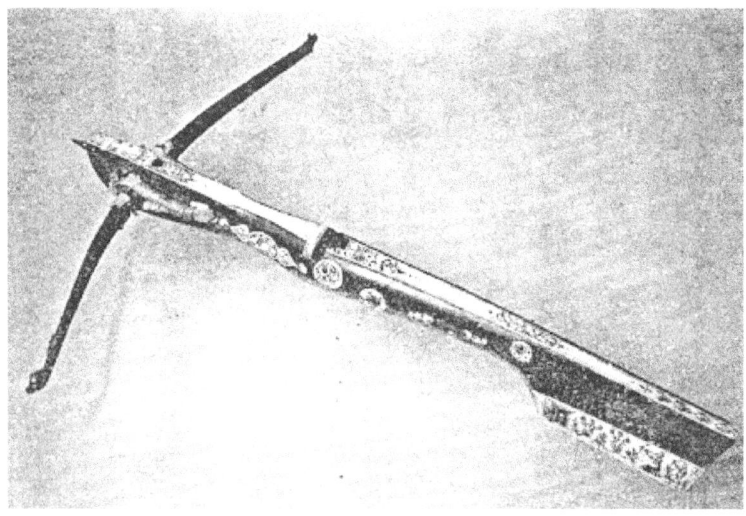

If Your Cat is Terrified of Fleas. Temple Gradin (*Animals in Translation*) points out a fine paradox I never noticed: "It's the most fearful animals who are also the most curious." She figures it because the stolid big-boned animals have less need to be worried about their surroundings than the more delicate animal. And, pointing at Arabian horses she adds more tentatively that "fear seems to correlate with intelligence, too." As a thin-boned ectomorph by (pre-mature) birth myself, and, speaking for cowardly yet always curious Han-chan, I like to think all of this is true, but I do know some stolid yet curious cows.

Han-chan Not My Only Sleep-mate. While Han-chan was a plus in bed, my other cats tended to get in the way. The drawing from a greeting card on the next page shows how they pinned me down as surely as a specimen, night after night.

from silent meow to talkative tail
Conversing *with* Cats

French novelist Colette was a firm cat-lover. When she was in the U.S. she saw a cat sitting in the street. She went over to talk to it, and the two of them mewed at each other for a friendly minute. Colette turned to her companion and exclaimed, *"Enfin! Quelqu'un qui parle francais."* (At last! Someone who speaks French!) – from H. Exley: *Cat Quotations* 1997

meaningful meows

If you would understand cats, learning a little Japanese or Korean would be a good start. *Why?* Both put their entire emotive force, or *tone*, into the tip of the tail of the conjugation or adjective-as-verb at the end of the sentence, rather than dispersing it here and there in the manner of our more complex stressed sentences. English tone, while more important for the overall syntax, is, on the whole, not obvious enough to teach us the language of tonal change. With Japanese and Korean, the length of the last vowel, or vowels – they almost always end in one – is about the same length as a cat's meow and equally variable in tone In English, expressive, or shall we say, musical, phonemes are pretty much limited to song: (*"Glo-o-o-oria in Exce-elsis"*).

The *direction of the tonal change* counts most. A rising tag (end of a vocalization) sounds plaintive and attracts others, while a falling one may show discontent or even anger and warn or threaten others ("may," for complex nuances arise in combination). Controling for distance, the *volume of the tone* indicates the degree of import of the message, whatever it may be; and *the direction of change in the volume* accents the meaning inherent to the melody.

The *accent* for a rising tag is usually on the end, and that of a falling tag on the beginning.   Since a rising tone tag has no desire to scare at the start, it tends to start quietly and works up to the final appeal, which, echoing, keeps pulling on the other's heartstrings after the meow ends. Since a falling tag tends to occur when the cat wants a quick response from the other party, the scare that sudden loudness provides is desirable, so the accent comes at the start of the tag. And the quality, or *grain of the tone*, as with humans, helps identify the speaker, communicate his or her physical and psychological condition, rested vs. tired and calm vs. excited, respectively, etc. and, thereby modify the content of the message.

Examples of "Sentences"

A$_{A_{U_{U\ U\ U\ U\ U\ U\ \ U\ \ U\ \ U\ \ U\ \ \ \ U\ \ \ \ \ U}}}$

A sudden, loud and high (i.e. shrill) start that holds briefly, followed by a quick slide down, grain roughening as the "meow" fades away is a protest about being hurt unfairly. The surprise and pain is registered first, as an emphatic "Oow!" or "Hey!" dropping to a clear "Cut it out!" and tapering off in a tagging "Will you?" or a warning, "You had better!"

U$_{R_U}$ $^{R^U!}$ U $_{R_U}$ $^{R^U!}$ U $_{R_U}$ $^{R^U!}$

A slow gargling grain like a cricket chirping but slower, between a crisp but not loud start and a short rising tag repeated at least three times says "Listen up! I've got something interesting to show you, you better come fast, please!" The tag is optional and may be dropped when the other cats are attentive enough to come running at the gargle sound alone. If even the plaintive "please!" tag fails, the final gargle may end on a brief accented falling note creating a pushy plea: "Come see this, damn it!"

M$_I$au^U!!   M$_I$au^U!!   M$_I$au^U!!

This is a lost adult cat calling out for someone he might know who is lonely but not carrying anything. For now, let that do. Despite Collette's claim, I doubt French is more cognate than English with respect to Felinese. Even with a nose cold, my cats never sounded particularly nasal. But the graininess does recall a certain chanson singer . . .

the cat who cried fish

The real combinations are more complex than those given above. Cats may emphasize statements by *continuation* and/or *repetition*. Each repetition can grow louder until you give in to the demand, meow them down, whack or squirt them; or it can slowly fade away – Are you *sure* you can't do it?" "Not a even a wee chance of it?" "Sure, sure?" until the meow is silent. And, even then, as we shall soon see, some cats continue by lip synching!

Not all meowing has a clear message. Some meowing is only for the sake of meowing. Caterwauling, which is to say a crowd of male cats meowing up a storm, may be part threat and fear one against another, but also seems a form of musical harmony, or rather *jamming,* more pleasant for both the participants and the audience (were it not for the outlandish hours chosen for the performance) than our opera, perhaps because it is improvised rather than aped.

While the basic elements of tone are universal enough for all sane cats and humans to ascertain whether a call is or isn't a threat, is or isn't happy, the details of the message often depend on context to be interpreted. Part of that is the character of the speaker. For example, a mother cat that has it all together will add more gravel and volume to her call when she brings back a prime item, such as a roasted fish or a live mouse than for the more conventional skink, bug or other so-and-so tidbit. This way, she naturally teaches the kittens to discriminate between degrees of urgency and to jump to when they hear an emphatic gurgle. But a young mother who has not found much worthwhile and is, perhaps, a scatterbrain (some cats are), may completely lack such subtlety.

<u>*kittens come quick!*</u>

a mother cat
anything she brings back
is advertised.

haha-neko ya nani motekite mo ko o yoburu
(mother cat: anything carry-come even, child/ren calls)

This haiku of Issa's could have been written for Kori, who once had me laughing until I cried for making more of a fuss for *a single lima bean* (probably flavored by shaved bonito in the soup stock) than her more reliable mother Chikurina would have made for the head of the neighbor's dog. I learned not to get to excited over Kori's catches until I saw them, and, needless to say, so did the other cats.

the universal and the particular

When you pick up the universal nuances of Felinese, you will find it a cinch to communicate with cats. You need not stop at listening. You may *demand* attention from cats, catching their ear with an abrupt and shrill start, descending quickly to a thick grainy threat or scold, finished off with a plaintive high-rising tag to show your intentions are friendly. It even works to call back strange cats impolite enough to give you the cold shoulder.

But, with your own cat, you must do this only when you really want to catch your his or her attention. If you do it frivolously, *i.e.,* just to test or show-off your cat's responses, he or she will learn almost immediately that your cat talk, however fluent, is like the image in the mirror or television, fake and unworthy of any response. The more you talk, the more you will be ignored. Like Kori.

In this respect, it was interesting to note how Han-chan reacted to certain tones made on my home-made one-string fiddle . At first, he would start and assume a ready-to-flee posture every time I'd do a falling glissando. I'd laugh and assure him that no harm was intended by blinking my eyes. He'd blink back, and assured all was well, settle down. Next, he would still start, but not need my reassurance to realize things were all right. Then, finally, he stopped starting and only his ears still reacted apprehensively, if only for a moment. Finally, even those revealing ears paid my fiddle's falling glissandos no particular heed.

There is a thin line between tuning in and out. It is said that cats make poor laboratory subjects because they are quickly bored. Not really. They simply have no tolerance for bull-shit; they do not react to what they have determined to be *meaningless.* Cats do not mind repetition if it is for real (or, they can *convince themselves* it is real, as we shall we in another chapter, cats do play make-believe). I do not know whether the decision it is conscious or not at first. But, once the ears (or tail or whiskers) stop twitching, the stimulus might as well be the sound of a regularly scheduled night-train. Awake or asleep, we do not grow *bored* with hearing such a train, we grow oblivious to it. Cats, likewise, do not get bored. They become *oblivious* to things, and people who take obedience for obedience's sake for granted mistakenly think this proves they are aloof.

styles of felinese

> The language of a cat is as individual as fingerprints, and the wonder of it is that it's understood by us and other cats without anything resembling a commonly agreed-on vocabulary." (*Secrets of the Cat*)

For once, I beg to partially disagree with Barbara Holland. She makes a good case for the individuality of cat-talk, citing everything from a little black cat who "never opens her mouth to say anything, but speaks in her throat, to herself" to an elderly siamese "who speaks in deep chest tones, as if from a bellows, in an infinite variety of yet to be invented vowels." While none of my cats were that spectacular, they, too, showed great differences in vocalization.

But *speaking* and *hearing* are not the same thing. If we can hear (or lip-read) and understand, than we *do,* by definition, have a common vocabulary. It is simply more tonal – as opposed to phonemic – than English, the language we are used to. The tonal syntax we have pictured and discussed – is readily understood by any cat which was part of a feline family when young, and even the unlucky loner can handle the basics (rising as friendly and falling as threatening). Hence, I can communicate with most cats using what I learned from some despite the variety noted by Holland.

The individuality of a cat's voice fuses with each cat's overall communicative style – which, is to say, how a cat gets along with other cats and people – and is most meaningfully introduced together with a total characterization of the cat.

han-chan speaks

Han-chan always spoke when spoken to. His Felinese had the broadest tonal range of all my cats. One of his calls made me think of a word I normally do not use, *ennui*. It was, I think, the most touching short melody I have heard (only some crickets come close). Ah, to have been a composer and capture it on paper! Coming to appreciate his range, I selfishly *insisted* he use it. Whenever he turned into a monotonous bore, which thank goodness, was not often, I chastised him and meowed to him in some of the more interesting ways he himself had taught me, and rewarded him when he came around. I am all for talking, with people or other animals and the more the better. What uses less energy, what is more sustainable, than talk? But it *must* be *interesting*. Human or feline, I do not abide broken records.

Sometimes, however, Han-chan's vocality was trying. When he did could not wait for me to divvy up the bloody raw tuna he craved, or open a can of catfood for *another* cat's dinner – sheer kindness or a paternalistic desire to make it seem to the other cats like he was responsible for the treat? – his loud and *insistent* calls could be irksome, especially, if I just got an important phone call or was otherwise indisposed. On a couple such occasions, I was amused to see his neice, the sweet-tempered brown tabby Kuro'ko-chan turn and clinically whack him with a sheathed-claw paw in mid-forehead! I do not know if it was for my sake or her own delicate ears, or for both of us, but I was very grateful as it never failed to shut him up.

Oddly, he never raised his voice for water. Maybe no cat does but I only noticed it with Han-chan because he usually spoke up. Instead, he discovered how to lick the faucet of the kitchen sink, setting off a trickle of water. This brought me running to scold him – not so much for spreading germs but because he was likely to knock something over – and lift him off by the scruff of the neck, before noticing there was no water in his bowl and meowing out my *mea culpa, mea culpa*. Then, I filled it. Lesson learned, Han-chan kept leaping up upon the sink. Before long, he understood that when I was home he did not need to actually lick the faucet. It sufficed to make a loud enough dish-sound, a ring of glass or chink of porcelain, to make me come running whenever he wanted that water bowl filled. I would have preferred that he meow by the bowl, but he enjoyed working for food and drink. Doing tricks gave him more appetite for foods he might not otherwise have wanted more of and he would stop eating food on the saucer or newspaper to tear open a bag of said not-so-favorite food for the pleasure of removing a piece at a time and eating it from clenched paw. Moreover – we are now back on the sink – if I did not respond, Han-chan still had his water. The only problem was that water was not always what Han-chan wanted. Once he realized how well kitchen noises caught my ear, even when I was hard at work and oblivious to most sound, he used them for calling my attention to many things. He would do this by tearing off in the direction of whatever the problem was when I came in to give him a piece of my mind. Occasionally, however, he did it simply to get my attention, feeling it better to be scolded than ignored. Years later, I would learn that some cats would actually *bite* their owners in such a situation.

From 1996-8, Han-chan suffered a long illness of a "Cat AIDs" variety. Treatment was way beyond my income and family circumstances demanded I move back to the USA. He had been too sick to vocalize for so long that I could not remember his last meow. I convinced a very gentle veterinarian to put Han-chan to sleep in my apartment. As the opiates kicked in, pain gone, he began to purr. The vet said it was a reflex. Comfort is comfort, conscious or not. I was relieved to know Han-chan experienced well-being at any level. As his eyes slowly dimmed, I repeatedly called out to him *his* favorite words, which were not in Felinese, but Japanese. "*Neyô, Han-chan, Neyô!*" ("*Let's go to bed!*"). Hearing these words, he would drop everything and run to join me every night, so he could be settled down with my right arm for his pillow when I turned off the light with my left hand. The vet, apparently assuming my out-of-place Japanese was an odd foreigner's way to wish his cat to die fast, kindly reassured me: "He'll go to sleep soon." (My eyes fill with tears even now, whenever I recall this). Han-chan did. He died purring. ♪

a cat like tinker belle

Kori inherited the most musical meow of any cat I knew rom her mother Chikurina. The timber lay between the two most beautiful sounds in nature, the trilling of a cricket and chiming of a bell cicada. Like a *shakuhachi* (Japanese flute), the acoustic thickness varied from a clear monotone to opaque polytone. Her name is short for "kôrogi," cricket.

Had I the means, there are thousands of projects I would seed. Among the hundreds of an aesthetic nature, there are two for cats. One is breeding small ones, for I sometimes see perfectly normal little gems but know of no such breed. Another would be the creation of a breed or breeds of *musical* cats, valued for the tone of their voice rather than form or markings. One could start by offering a reward for the most musical meow at cat shows, or on U-tube and go from there. Unfortunately, I had to have Kori desexed without passing on her miracle.

Worse yet, she returned from the vets a total basket-case. Like Tinkerbelle, whose tiny mind could not fit two emotions at once, but lacking Tinkerbelle's ability to reflect, Kori became a holy terror. (It might be that the anesthesia left her starved her brain of oxygen, but I suspect, it was the shock of the trip and the animal hospital. Ever since this, I have *insisted* upon sleeping medicine to partially knock out a feral cat before moving it anywhere.)

Give her a warm look and she has an instant love-attack. Looking lovey-dovey straight into my eyes, she climbs right up upon my chest and starts kneading. Her claws are only partially sheathed (all too common for adult kneading), but you reject her advances at your peril, for she clings if you try to remove her! When she wants something, Lord have Mercy! She does not ask. She *acts*. She will 'accidently' run right over your bare flesh leaving scratches and punctures behind, leaving you to figure out what she wants! Only one of her behaviors required no interpretation. Jumping from the bookcase upon my crotch clearly served to wake me up. Until, I managed to kick her sky-high by reflex a few days in a row, I had to sleep with a basket over my lower-belly! I'll spare you the drawing.

Even when she was sane, Kori got into spats with Meg and the two often glared at each other. Now she hissed aloud just to see her, and took a claw-out swipe at her if she came within range. At first, Meg answered each hiss with a whack of her own. But, eventually, Meg came to realize that Kori's hiss no longer meant what it used to. On the other hand, all a cat she liked (*i.e.* Han-chan) had to do was give her a warm look or lick her and if she did not respond directly she would *instantaneously* pass on the good emotion by licking another cat.

With all animals, to various degrees, emotions demand to be vented. "Purring would seem to be, in her case, an automatic safety valve device for dealing with happiness overflow" writes Monica Edwards (l.s. but a marvelous English writer) about her cat. That would be correct for *all* cats and not restricted to happy emotions nor to purring. But what made Kori's case uniquely instructive was that she did it as suddenly and consistently as the flicking of a switch. You could see her jolt to it. That was abnormal, for if there is anything a cat is not, it is an automaton. It was not easy living with a crazy cat, but what we shall call *Kori's Psychosis* – or, should we call it Tinker Belle Syndrome? – is, in retrospect, interesting to say the least. Her heart was smaller than Tinker Belle's. It could not only not hold more than one emotion at a time, but could not store more than a nerve's worth without discharging it!

meg the manipulator

Me-chan, or Meg, the roly-poly calico, who from the looks of her should be impervious to the cold, just cannot manage to go out in the morning. I leave the window ajar with a cat-door flap cut in an old blanket serving for a curtain; physically speaking nothing is stopping her. So what does she do? She picks a fight with Kuro'ko-chan or Kori-chan (before Kori went insane), taking care to nip them hard enough to make they squeal, which makes me jump up after her and swat her behind as she scoots for the cat-door.

This, like Han-chan's method of filling the water bowl, is a perfectly logical – indeed, fail-safe – method of communication. Meg was not much of a meower. She saved her voice for calling others together when she returned from her hunts with something worth showing off. But she knew I demanded quiet in the morning and was not about to put up with quarreling. Confident that I *will* come after her, she heads straight for that cat-flap, whereas, normally, she would dive under the table after misbehaving. Sometimes, it is enough for her to know I am in hot pursuit, while I, knowing that, may take only one step *as if* I would pursue and she goes along by not glancing back. Usually, however, she manages to catch my hand, or rolled-up newspaper, and, backside freshly warmed by the spank or whack, dives triumphantly out into the cold woods to answer the call of nature. Mind you, she never did this in the summer. She was simply using me to help her through the winter.

Me-chan's occasional mean behavior began early. Born a weeks after her mother's daughter gave birth, she was the smallest kitten in the house. Moreover, male kittens tend to push their weight around and make their little sisters squeal. One day, Me-chan did something I'd never seen happen. She attacked the larger kittens who picked on her when they were fast asleep! She did this more than once.

Even when they woke, as of course they immediately did, she would continue to beat the hell out of them, aided by both psychological surprise and their slowness to recover full awareness, probably as a result of the narcotic effect of mother's milk. Before long, Me-chan was getting the respect she deserved all day long. In her unprovoked winter morning attacks, she did not at all mind it if the other party was napping. To think that a clever tactic, totally justifiable at first should later be put to such a selfish end!

I fear that Meg (her calico coloring and plump body seem to require the additional "g") has unwittingly re-enacted the history and the tragedy of the entire "weak" human species.

kuro'ko-chan the sweet

With an insanely insensitive cat like Kori, lack of communication makes *you* suffer. With a sensitive cat like

Kuro'ko-chan, you will not suffer, *she* will. Kuro'ko-chan never asserts herself. She could be dying to pee or drink water and you would never know it. Her name was taken from the black-robed Noh puppet manipulators who walk or roll around the stage that you are not supposed to see. Although she got it shortly after birth because her feet had shiny black pads and *"kuro'ko"* literally means *Blacky*, it describes her character perfectly.

I am afraid I may have been partly responsible for her reticent nature. Once, when she was little and one of her claws punctured my skin and drew blood, I instinctively whacked her. It was one of those rare times when the wound aches down to the finger bone, and I pushed the bloody digit against her nose and hit her again very lightly and made some painful sounding cries so she'd know how much this hurt both of us.

She went off looking *very* forlorn. None of that "I'd bite his head off if I was a tiger!" glaring eyes stuff. Most cats would be over it in an hour. But that night, she was the saddest sight you ever saw. She didn't regain her appetite until the next day, but remained strangely subdued like a child that has cried his heart out. I felt *horrible* about what I'd done. I had never known a cat to be *that* delicate. The memory still hurts. Kuro'ko-chan grew up to be the best natured cat I've known, kind to every cat she met. But she would never again would rough-house with me and never learned to give me the present only a psychologically healthy cat can give, a love-nibble bite.

Communication with an angel must be handled very delicately. I am far from rough-natured, but I could not help thinking this cat should have been owned by a woman with a gentle voice and softer hands than mine.

Kuro'ko did not care to be picked up or petted. "Normal" caresses were just too much for her to handle. She preferred to be stroked *very* little and *very* gently. Or, better yet, just to be looked at! Of course, with a very soft gaze and not up close but from a distance. Amazingly, that alone was enough to set her off purring and treading the air in ecstasy.

& her silent meow

With Han-chan, I exchanged real meows. With Kuro'ko-chan it was enough to mime them. No, it was *better*. She preferred it that way. I first wrote about this in an illustrated letter sent to a friend a couple days after making the discovery. The letter, reproduced on the next page, is copied on the back of a copy of a dummy page for a Louis Vitton handbag pr magazine edited by my employer, an impoverished avant-garde Japanese publishing house. In direct translation, the catch-copy reads "SOPHISTICATED EXPRESSION. LOUIS VITTON'S FACE." (I love LV. *Why?* The phenomenal popularity of his utterly tasteless design allows me to immediately spot bores I would avoid). What is really "sophisticated" is – if I may forget my customary modesty – the conversation enjoyed by Kuro'ko-chan and *moi*, the translation (I was writing in horrendous Japanese) of which reads as follows:

> *I have accomplished a FIRST in the annals of human-feline communication*, the exchange of voiceless meows. *This child [sic] normally replies in an extremely soft high voice that is often too low to be heard at all; so the other day, I thought , Well! If that's how it's going to be, I [Here I used the obsolete first-person pronoun used by Natsume Soseki's cat in his novel "I Am a Cat" (My spelling-check suggests the famous novelist found on the 1000 yen bill is a misspelling for – CAN YOU GUESS? . . . "seasick" – I think we have the makings for a new game here!) for "I"] I, too, am going to try an un-voiced, visual neow [The monolabial "niao" is close to the Chinese for "I love you" and, in my opinion, is closer to reality than "meow/miao" for most cats. The only cat I know who tended to sound bi-labial was Ohsama, the Persian described on page 139]. So saying, I tried to actually put this into practice [Had I written in English, I would have said "Here goes nothing!"], and was completely successful with this first venture into silent conversation".*

Kuro'ko-chan and I both loved our silent conversations and did them every day. The drawing shows our joy, *but may be wrong about an important detail*, something more readily perceived by a native of Japan than of the Occident that is the subject for the *next* chapter.

After returning to the US in 1998, I was disappointed to find "my," or, rather, Kuro'ko-chan and my, *silent meow* was not only old hat to many but actually *the title of a book(!!!),* in English, written from the perspective of a cat. Here is a quote from the same:

> I cannot begin to tell you how effective the Silent Miaow can be for breaking down resistance, always provided you don't over do it but save it for the right moment. The technique for this is ridiculously simple. You look up at the subject, open your mouth as you would for a fully articulated miaow . . . . except in this case you permit no sound to issue. . . . . It appears to sum up for them such a burden of unhappiness and need that we are not able even to give voice to it. It is an un-cry of despair and longing that pierces more directly to the human heart than the most self-pitying miaow of which we are capable . . . (Translated from the feline and edited by Paul W. Gallico)

The photo of the silent miaow by Suzanne Szasz shows only the bottom teeth of the cat, while her photos of "The Active Miaow" on the next page show the upper teeth, too. Not all voiced meows show the upper teeth, but I recall that almost all silent meows show only the bottom teeth. The body language may be especially endearing for not baring the fangs and for the bottom lip, which hangs loose in delicate suspense – the opposite of the tight upper lip, sweet and unguarded, like the sentence-ending *"-wa"* of the women of the Pleasure Quarter in early modern Japan.

Japanese and the cat's tail

The literary giant and staunch proponent of Japanese aesthetics, Tanizaki Junichiro admitted to a certain amount of jealousy toward cats in his essay *"Kyaku-girai,"* meaning "the guest-hater" or "*I hate guests!*" It is the cat's tail that this curmudgeon coveted. If he only had a tail to communicate with, Tanizaki wrote, he would not have to actively participate in stupid conversations with visitors but could simply twitch his tail to indicate he was listening when he was not.

> "The tail also provides a tangible clue as to whether a cat is listening to its owner. Call a cat that is listening and it usually responds with a slight tap or quiver of the tail." (FLORIDA CAT OWNER'S HANDBOOK)

The handbook shows Tanizaki knew what the tail was for, but the reason he desired one so badly loses something in translation, for you must know one of the unspoken rules for conversing in Japanese is that indicate you are following the other party by vigorous nodding and exclamations, even if no more than grunts, *every few seconds*. Not to do so dries up the conversation. I have long found this amusing, considering all that has been written on the Japanese ability to read one another's minds. If English speakers rather than Japanese had to make such responses, Japanese intellectuals would be falling over themselves to explain how it shows an inability of Occidentals to intuit each others minds owing to rampant individualism, polycultural confusion or something of that ilk.

Unfortunately, you cannot just grunt at random or in regularly timed intervals. The grunt, usually *"Hai!"* (translated "yes," but far less meaningful by virtue of its ubiquity) or *"Un!"* ("uh-huh" or "yea") nowadays – must be inserted at just the right time. In fact, it is called an *"aizuchi"* and is defined in my Kenkyusha dictionary as "alternate hammering ((by two blacksmiths))" and, together with the verb *utsu*, or "strike" means to "give responses that make a conversation go smoothly."

It is acceptable to close your eyes like cat in a Japanese conversation, but you cannot close your ears or your mistimed grunts will give you away as surely as a musician who, for whatever reason, loses track of what the others are doing and enters a discordant note. So, even if he had a tail, Tanizaki would still have had to pay close attention to what his guests said, lest he twitch his tail at the wrong time or in the wrong way. So, he was wrong about the utility of having a cat tail. It would not have released him from the responsibility of speaking Japanese.

Does Purring Say Anything?

There are several books titled *How to Talk to Your Cat*. The author of the second (chronologically speaking) of them, Lynn Allison, notes that "author Roger Caras" claimed purring "has little to do with happiness" and begins "when kittens are in the nursing stage," and that cats purr "when they are in some distress," such as labor, and quotes, "Cats purr when they are sick or even injured," indeed,

> they purr when they are dying . . . Contentment just doesn't seem to do it. Profundity seems to be the key. When cats are profoundly anything – contented, in pain or any form of extreme behavior – they seem to purr. (Caras: *A Cat Is Watching* 1990)

When I feel either exhausted by digestion, brain-poisoned by septic bowels, or otherwise miserable, I find what I would call "deep groaning" happens to help. I would guess that groaning, if it can get some vibration going, improves blood circulation in a manner particularly suited to increasing the intake of or processing of oxygen, which brings good feelings or at least dilutes the poison in the blood. This has led me to believe that we are not talking about an either/or question here. Whether the cat relaxes and purrs from trust or from exhaustion, including that coming from infirmity, the feeling is pleasant. My dying cat did not experience distress, but thanks to purring, or as indicated by it, he *was* content. Recall if you will, the quiet pleasure of total exhaustion from engaging in endurance sports which I believe shares something with being in labor. There is a fine line between agony and euphoria.

Purring may be seen as an extension of deep breathing, which both comes of and increases contentment. As such purring proves the cat a what might be called a natural adept. So much for metaphysics. The reason why I brought purring into this chapter is that I read Jeffrey Moussaieff Masson's take on it:

> Cats do not purr for themselves, . . . but for us and for each other and even for other animals they like. I have not heard of a cat purring in the presence of a favorite toy. . . (Ibid).
>
> If I am right, . . . purring is a form of communication, and what is communicated is contentment." (*The Nine Emotional Lives of Cats*)

Masson also noted in support of his hypothesis that while cats sleeping with him purred themselves to sleep, they never purred while sleeping, though one might expect they had pleasant dreams, and purr when fed "only, . . . when we are present." This idea of purring for others seems odd coming from Masson who elsewhere in the book depicts cats as solitary animals that "do not apologize" unlike "species like humans and dogs that are sociable and depend on others for security, safety or pleasure" who "need signals to show they are sorry" and "have to be able to apologize;" but hypotheses, unlike tested theories, are not required to be consistent. Masson wonders whether a cat purrs when observing another cat's pleasure because the cat imagines the pleasure felt by the other, the pleasure of the other itself pleasured the cat or if it was automatic as "purring is, like a yawn, contagious." I feel it is the last two reasons, but would like to point out that purring is like yawning in more ways. We find yawns pleasant, yet we do not yawn in our dreams (ot, at least, I never have). I think that is why cats do not purr in their dreams: both are a motor reflex and naturally not encouraged by the sleeping body.

Cats may purr eating alone if they caught their own food and judging from the way my cats have eaten things they do not much care for after being gently stroked, they do not find meals neither presented nor taken very pleasant. It is not so much that they have no audience as they are not experiencing either of their ideal mode of eating. And, I might point out that they, or some cats, may purr while kneading furry rugs alone on a chilly day out on a veranda with the glass doors closed (see the *Kneading the World* chapter). Masson wrote that, unlike r.e.m. dreams, "cat daydreams . . . appear to trigger purring," and mentions his cat that, sitting silently on the edge of his hot tub "suddenly, for no discernible reason" began to purr as evidence, supposing imagined she had to have "imagined some pleasurable situation" and that while he was present

> so the purr could in theory be directed at me, but since her eyes are closed, and she is not paying any direct attention to me, I believe she is in the throes of imagining something wonderful. (Ibid)

A pleasant thought but, to me, it makes more sense to imagine a vague contentment with the cat very aware of Masson's presence. Just because the cats eyes are closed does not mean it is not paying attention. Japanese at meetings annoy Occidentals by closing their eyes to listen intently. I would bet the cat's ears were alert and absorbing and reflecting Masson's contentment in the bath. Indeed, the way people open up in a warm bath is remarkably similar to the purring experience of a cat. That takes us to our last perspective on purring. It is about *letting go*. Clea Simon, who would make felinity female, something that bespeaks more of our culture's ideas of masculinity and femininity and the gender ideology of Usanian society than cats *per se*, writes that cats teach us "emotional bravery."

> "no matter how frightened we are of our own vulnerability, they seem to tell us that sometimes we must let down our guards and curl up on a friendly lap." (*The Feline Mystique:* On the Mysterious Connection Between Women and Cats).

Men in Usania have traditionally been the uptight sex, but this is, indeed, one front women have come to put on, call it the armor of a "liberation" that was in part an embodiment of Puritan male ideals. I associate purring-as-letting-go-and-trusting-others with a state of positive dependency Japanese call *amae,* though no Japanese ethologist that I know of has noted that. That state is exemplified by the human baby and, if you recall, we did a first take on purring in the chapter on neoteny.

the silent meow revisited

The silent meow alone has a half dozen interpretations. Barbara Holland and I have experienced and separately emphasized its role in what might be called *loving communion* (pgs 109-112). Paul Gallico,– or, rather his cat – on the other hand, sees it as a useful *tool for begging*, but characterizes it in Suzuki Daisetsu-like *"un-"* terms of *Zen* (No contradiction here, isn't begging part of being a bonze?). Like words and body language, context can give the silent meow many meanings. One, I witnessed not only from Kuro'ko-chan, but from Han-chan and the others, was the last peep of a cat *about to give up asking for something*. Liv Ulmann's description – especially her *"~ing"* adverb and adjective – is perfect:

> She claws at the window, meows and looks beseechingly at me where I sit reading . . . When I come to the window, she no longer meows with sound. Only the mouth opens in a silent imploring prayer. (l.s.)

Only the shy Kuro'ko-chan broke the pattern. She sometimes *began* our conversations with a "silent imploring prayer," because she knew that I did not like to be disturbed while writing and, bless her heart, felt compunction for calling my attention. So, for some cats, at any rate, the silent meow is also a way of signing *"Pssst! I beg your pardon, but . . ."* Finally, cats suffer jaw/throat problems which take away their voice – Han-chan's cat AIDs forced him to use the silent meow more than he had previously – and must communicate with a deaf cohort (common especially among the blue-eyed) more often than dogs or humans, so the availability of a lip-synch back-up system may be an evolutionarily explainable redundancy.

cat tails

***Caveat re. Japanese, Korean* and animal language.** For all the advantage of a meaningful melodic tail and drawn-out vowels for making one attentive to felinese, Japanese and Korean are far from purrrfect. Like Latin tongues, there is no vowel sound for purr/grrr, and almost all native speakers cannot mimic it even if they try. For cats, an extended "u" (as in *dew/do/due*) captures most growls (but not dog-like low ones) but not purring , usually described as "sounding the throat *gorogoro*."

Tonality. Linguists think of English, unlike Japanese and Korean, as "a tonal language." That, practically speaking, means our tone is more important for the syntax, *i.e.,* the meaning of the entire sentence. As it happens, while a Georgetown student in the early 1970's, I dated one of the six daughters of the founder of the Lado method of marking English sentences with lines running over and under and dog-legging words and phrases to show the tonal accent to foreign students and even helped photo pages for one of the prototypes with it! Maybe we can have an example illustration in the next edition.

No such system is needed for students of Japanese. Though the tonal tails in Japanese and Korean should be called to the student's attention, they are small enough to be approached and mastered naturally, as is that of Felinese.

On the Inherent Significance of Sound. Arguments about whether sounds have inherent meaning or only serve us in an arbitrary capacity as signs go back at least as far as Plato. I believe there is much more significance intrinsic to particular sounds and sound-sequences than the all-too-sure Saussureans would have it, for it is not a matter of either/or but degree, and even includes some universals. I was delighted to find an oblique mention of this truth in Temple Grandin's *Animals In Translation:*

> In the brain, logic and reason are never separate from emotion. Even nonsense syllables have an emotional charge, either positive or negative. Nothing is neutral. That's what you have to remember.

She wrote this in the context of a discussion of pain and suffering (which she carefully demonstrates are not identical). To apply it to my argument, the first sentence needs to be revised to "In the mind, *sound* is never separate from emotion."

Responsive Conversation. The reality of a language requiring a responsive listener and one that does not is hard for someone not fluent in the former language to feel. The best testimony of its significance I have come across was in a book of cultural anthropology stories – to literary ethnology, what animal stories are to nature essays – by someone named Quigley or Nigel or something ridiculously English or Scott, who could not get more than one-line out of a people said to be sympathetic and boasting great stories to tell. His failure went on *for months* until someone finally told that he had to make frequent clear responses of interest if he hoped for them to continue talking. A Japanese anthropologist with a tenth of his vocabulary in the native tongue and a tin ear would have recorded long stories from day one, for he would have responded every few seconds whether he really understood what they were saying or not!

Apology and Universal Language as Instanced by Cats. I believe I have something about apologizing to cats elsewhere, but we have a good lesson here:

> I do not love a cat – his disposition is mean and suspicious. A friendship of years is cancelled in a moment by an accidental tread on his tail or foot. He instantly spits, raises his rump, twirls his tail of malignity, and shuns you; turning back, as he goes off, a staring vindictive face, full of horrid oaths and unforgiveness; seeming to say, "Perdition catch you! I hate you forever.' But the dog is my delight . . . (Peter Pindar vol. III)

The dog, Pindar (John Wolcot, 1713-1819) writes, will decide after a moment that it must have been his own fault and will make up to you. Had Peter Pindar only known to immediately let out wretched-sounding squeals, the higher pitched the better, and with the ends of each squeal rising up and beyond our hearing range, the cat would be over his resentment in seconds. Whether that is because the cat thinks you are sorry, that both of you have been hurt by the same invisible presence or that it feels sorry for you and forgets its pain, I do not know. The point is it works and proves the universal significance of basic sounds.

Paul Gallico, my dictionary and the Silent Miaow. I had never heard of the man until I encountered the book in a used bookstore and the book was, on the whole, far from impressive, so I was surprised to find Gallico, Paul William (1897-1976) in my *English-Japanese Shokugakukan Randomhouse Dictionary*. I guess journalism and short-stories could get one immortalized in mid-20c Usania! Personally, I would have preferred the dictionary to include Peter Pindar, the prolific poet whom I mentioned above, but my guess would be that he, being long dead, had less pull from the grave. Or, he was not dead long enough, for the BC Pindar was there . . . But, to return to Gallico, if it turns out that he was indeed the first person to point out the silent miaow, then he does deserve the entry. However, in that case, it should be altered to make that official and start, "the discoverer of the silent miaow," or "meow." As it is silent, I don't suppose the spelling really matters.

Cats that Must Be Taught to Felinese. After returning to the USA in 1998, I met a cat that was linguistically speaking almost completely deaf and dumb. He showed up at my mom's condominium a kitten so beautiful (long blue-grey hair) and obviously needing help that she fell for him. Lost or abandoned, he was spaded too young and unwittingly named Natasha. A cat who played with siblings but not with humans can have great difficulty understanding how easily his claws hurt us, but such cats do know very well the difference between a strong bite, a medium bite meant to hurt a bit but not draw blood, a gentle bite at the end of a play-fight or other event where one appeases the still upset party by allowing oneself to be bitten and the tender love-nibble. This cat was obviously separated from its siblings at birth or near to it as it had only one bite and it drew blood. It eventually learned to give me a gentle bite when I desired to stop playing with him and he felt upset by not winning enough (like a 3-5 year-old boy who who will calm down after being given a shoulder or belly to sock). *As a rule, a cat that has not mastered the body-language of the social bite also lacks linguistic skills.* I had to work hard with Sasha to teach him to listen and respond to basic tonal meow syntax. He learned to hear and eventually speak, to a degree. I am willing to bet that my knowledge and ability to reproduce basic felinese made this work better than any random signs would have. I also taught him to jump over my leg and later foot and, on his own, he became a pointer. That is, he hated drafts (of air, water or sound) and would lie at a distance from the problematic window-siding and point so exactly at it that humans came to depend on his advice and go for the putty.

***Whisker* Body Language.** No whiskers were mentioned because my sketches of them got lost in one of the many moves one too poor to own a home must suffer and, not seeing them, forgot; but felt I ought to elaborate after reading the following in the above-mentioned mini-book by Lynn Allison,

> Whiskers that extend straight out seem to reflect inner contentment. Watch out for whiskers that are either pulled back tight along the face or bristling around the cheek area. This is a very clear indication that Kitty isn't a happy camper. Whiskers convey a cat's mood and intentions. (*How to Talk to Your Cat* Mini Mag 2000. The address is Boca Raton - advice right from the mouth of a rat?)

Straight out is neutral position. Pulled back generally indicates aversion to being touched. You need to watch out for either hurting the cat's feelings or, if you push too hard with the wrong cat, a bite. Reaching whiskers (they do not only move at the base creating a "bristle" effect, but more incredibly curve slightly forward to make a parabola when fully forward) indicate curiousity and playful intentions, so you need to "watch out" if your cat cannot keep a nip within the force level safe for your skin. But, you cannot accurately read the whiskers of a strange cat because the individual variation is tremendous. My sketches of whiskers were made because I noticed my best hunter (especially of moles) Me-chan, or Meg, whom we shall read about soon enough, usually had her whiskers slightly forward rather than straight out and when I brought her something to sniff – anyone who loves their cat (or dog) should bring sniff-gifts to them when they come home – and literally grip them!

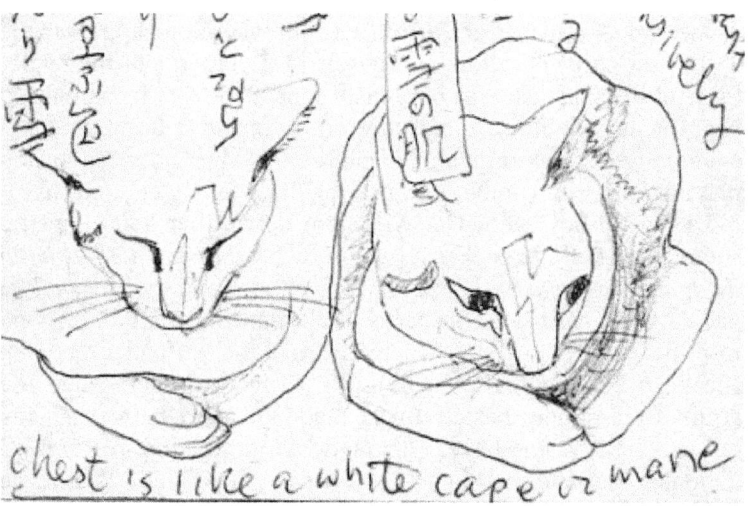

You can see Meg's somewhat-forward whiskers here. Somewhere lost in my notebooks is a cartoon where they extend forward to form a cage within which a mouse is trapped! The shy Kuro'ko-chan, on the other hand never reached her whiskers forward and tended to pull them back when approached. Allison mentions that whiskers "can be a barometer of your cat's health," which may be true; but I would call them a measure of a cat's personality, which, if we establish a "normal" could be called, instead, a measure of mental health! I think some very interesting studies could be made of whisker angle and cat behavior and we might even find patterns of variety in sub-species (variations) in domestic cats.

Felinese, the Most Popular of All Animal Tongues? A quick check of published work on cat language at Google Books suggests the cat does not have the tongue of animal book authors.

How to Talk to Your Cat - Jean Craighead George, Paul Meisel - - Juvenile Nonfiction - 2003

How to talk to your cat - Patricia Moyes, Nancy Lou Gahan - 1993 - 118 pp ("Talk sessions should be frequent and prolonged; they will bring comfort to both parties.")

Cat Talk: The Secrets of Communicating with Your Cat - Sonya Fitzpatrick - 2003 - 288 pp

If cats could talk: the meaning of meow - Michael P. Fertig - 2004 72 pp

The body language and emotion of cats - Myrna M. Milani - 1987 - 294 pp . "To demystify often enigmatic and disturbing feline habits, Milani begins by examining the anatomy, physiology, and body language of cats." Kirkus rev.)

Communicating with your cat - J. Anne Helgren: 1999 - 176 pages I talk to cats Annie Lawson - 1995 - 64 pp

The Cat I.Q. Test - Melissa Miller - 1996 - 198 pp ("A recent University of Pennsylvania study concluded that 37 percent of American cat owners talk to their cats regularly about the events of the day or . . .")

Who said cats can't talk? H. Boots - 1995 - 121 pp

The Cat Who Could Read Backwards - Lilian Jackson Braun - Fiction - 1986 - 191 pp (Cats have a contempt of speech. Why should they talk when they can communicate without words? They manage very well among themselves)

Cat talk: what your cat is trying to tell you. Carole Wilbourn - 1979

Cat Talk: The Secrets of Communicating with Your Cat Sonya Fitzpatrick - 2003 – 288pp

Cat talk! Suzanne Smither ("America's most loved and most trusted animal psychic")- Cats - 1999 - 97 pp

What is your cat saying? Michael W. Fox - Juvenile Nonfiction - 1982 - 80pp

The Cat Whisperer: The Secret of How to Talk to Your Cat - Claire Bessant - 2002 - 184 pp ("This book, written by a leading cat expert, will guide you toward forging a more meaningful bond between you and your feline pet.")

If Your Cat Could Talk - Bruce Fogle - 2007 - 160pp ("Based on expert research and a specially commissioned veterinary survey")

How to Speak Cat: The Essential Primer of Cat Language - Alexandra Sellers - 1998 - 192 pp ("Cat owners are notorious for doing just about anything to please their pets. Now, with this remarkably original language primer, they'll be able to do their ...")

The language of your cat - Frank Manolson - 1977 - 157pp

Cat Speak: How to Communicate With Cats by Learning Their Secret Language - Bashkim Dibra, Elizabeth Randolph - 2003 - 256pp ("From acclaimed animal behaviorist and trainer Bash Dibra comes a remarkable communication guide that can help owners keep their cats happy, healthy, . . .")

How to Speak Cat! - Sarah Whitehead - Juvenile nf - 2008 - 96 pp

How to speak cat and dog language courses - I. S. Strange - 1982 - 26pp

Understanding your cat - Frank Manolson - 1984 - 157pp (The feline face, often so inscrutable, is capable of great expression. Indeed, almost every thread of the cat's being has a language...)

SOME USAGES OF FELINESE

Cat country: a satirical novel of China in the 1930's by Lao She - Shê Lao - History - 1970 /1987 - 295pp ("freedom" in Felinese means "taking advantage of others, [being] non-cooperative, creating disturbance" "Felinese, Houyhnhnmese, and Newspeak all share one common feature.")

For the love of cats - Amy D. Shojai, Irene Gizzi - Juvenile Nonfiction - 1995 - 216pp ("Reading the subtleties of felinese requires a quick eye, for cats rarely prolong their silent dialogue.")

The Cat Companion: The History, Culture, and Everyday Life of the Cat - Amy Shojai - 1992 – 128pp. ("Felinese is not easy to master; cats communicate with body posture, tail and ear positions and movements, ...")

The Essential Kitten - Betsy Sikora Siino - 1999 – 96pp ("Experts speculate that silent "felinese" developed in wild cats as a way to communicate without alerting enemies or prey to their presence.")

OTHERS

Cat Wrangling Made Easy: Maintaining Peace and Sanity in Your Multicat Home - Dusty Rainbolt - 2007 - 269 pp ("Ch.2 Felinese as a Second Language")

Humans and other animals: beyond the boundaries of anthropology - Barbara Noske 1989 - 244 pp ("Roger Tabor tried to become accepted in the world of London feral cats by talking cat language (glancing, yawning, keeping the right distance)")

Roger Tabor's experiment seems the most interesting to me.   You?

I am embarrassed to admit I have not read any of the above, though I have read other work by one

the shy animal, or far from ecotopia
Smiling with Closed Eyes

I have leafed through dozens of books on cats, less to learn about the cat than to discover which of my thoughts are rare – and, therefor, worth expanding – and which are not. There were some big surprises. I had not expected *anyone* to scoop me on the "silent meow" which turned out to be a book's title and actually include words about the phenomenon, while I anticipated *everyone* would describe the cat's closed-eye smile or, as this alert state is *the* most obvious characteristic of cats, if by *obvious* we mean something that differentiates them from dogs and Occidentals.

a strange occidental bias

It is a safe bet my assumptions came from spending my entire middle age (25-45) with cats and in Japan, where it is the rare cat cartoon that does *not* depict or book that does *not* include a photograph of a cat sitting or lying with its head raised attentively *with closed eyes.* The caption never bothers to explain what the cat is doing. Why? Because *all* Japanese naturally *know.* Why? Because they do the same thing themselves.

Han-chan, on the left, is clearly listening attentively with closed eyes.

Kori is delighted to be snuggled up against Han-chan whose poor health may be ascertained by the disarray of the hair on his lower back and his open eyes showing his is out of it. One of Kori's ears is cocked for Han-chan & the other for me, but her eyes are closed for both of us. The poem has me hearing a suzu-mushi (little bell bug) while the plum blooms. I did not yet know the bug was the onset of my horrid tinnitus!

Books written in English, on the other hand, rarely show a cat with closed eyes unless it is actually sleeping. And, even when a cat is *not* sleeping, they often claim it is! Even a photo of a cat with one ear cocked forward actively listening for the shutter and whiskers erect in scanning position – not to mention subtle facial clues I can read but not recognize – i.e., *the very picture of awareness,* may still be turned into a "sleeping" cat by the caption, as was the case even in an otherwise observant book, *The Silent Miao*.

why cats close their eyes

> "Full closure of the eyes occurs in two contexts: sleep and appeasement. When two cats are fighting and one is forced into submission, it often performs what is called "cut-off," when it turns away from its tormentor and closes its eyes, trying to blot out the frightening image of its rival." (*Catlore*)

Unless the cats I lived with in Japan were peculiarly oriental, Desmond Morris was wrong to limit "full closure" like that. He actually broaches the broader phenomenon in passing, for he says "*half*-closed eyes" (my italics) are "an expression of total relaxation and one that signals complete trust and confidence in its owners." Let me assure him that cats at home shut their eyes *completely*. Did he balk at introducing the fully-awake cat with its eyes happily shut because he told us that "an alert cat has fully opened eyes," because he could not imagine more than one body-language per state? Or is this an open and closed case of cultural-bias in perception?

Morris explains the obvious – biological explanations usually are – that closing the eyes protects them from harm and stops the fight, for "the victor sees it as a sign of capitulation." He also makes an excellent psychological observation that it serves to reduce "the unbearable tension [presumably felt by the weaker cat]." This, of course, is what his marvelous – though not necessarily correct – metaphor, "trying to blot out . . .," means. Biologically speaking, I think the tension reduction important because it would otherwise result in dangerous indiscriminate biting of third-party cats, but it bears mentioning that the eyes may be more than "fully closed." They may be *scrunched up tightly* the better to stave off the claws; and, this does not always signal capitulation. Equally tough toms engaging in what boxers would call a close-quarters slug-fest or even a grapple, often do it *simultaneously* (I would expect this claim to be backed up by amateur video).

Michael Fox parenthetically captures what Desmond, grazing, missed in a lovely passage on wolf eyes:

> Usually, the wolf elusively avoids eye contact, but in a Mona Lisa way. You always know the wolf is following you with its eyes whenever you are in its vicinity. When you make eye contact it may look away submissively, or even *close its eyes in a relaxed catlike fashion* (not ignoring you but displaying simply that it is at ease in your presence). *The Soul of the Wolf* (1980 My italics.)

usanian jungle book

Had the details of Disney's *Jungle Book* been scripted by *any* Japanese producer, you can bet on one thing. When the previous king of the jungle, Shere Kahn, a huge tiger, acknowledges Mowgli as the new king, he would have either averted his eyes or blinked to end their long eye-contact. That this natural thing was *not* done shows how far Usanian popular culture will go to keep eyes pried open and "looking straight at the other." Did you know that manuals for Japanese tourists sometimes advise them to fix their eyes on the bridge of an American's nose if its too tiring to keep staring into their eyes?

Are Japanese psychologically damaged or strange for having to study to look into "our" eyes? Or is it wrong to judge behavior that is a product of culture, for all is relative? *Neither*, in my opinion. We (Usanians) are strange. Of course, both Japanese and Usanian children may be told not to stare, so we both realize too much obvious eye contact is rude, but please consider the fact that *their* children rarely if ever need to be told to avert their eyes, while we are often taught to look straight into another's eyes, lest our character be doubted. If that is not support for the naturalness of *not looking* rather than of looking, what is? How ironic the strongest support for abundant eye-contact comes, or, came in the 1960's-70's, from gentle souls advocating natural lifestyles. Because they considered not just writing, but *talking* unnatural – a sort of cultural imperialism that brought ecological disaster – they advocated quiet and eye-to-eye communication, while overlooking 1) the fact that we are *already* a high eye-contact culture – albeit less so than the Arabs who stare so much they must hide behind sunglasses to conceal their feelings – 2) the garrulousness of many cultures close to nature exampled by the constant chatter and the overnight marathon blab-fests of the famously gentle and cheerful pygmies and 3) the aversion for direct looks by most of our fellow primates who get *furious* when you eyeball them.

True, the Ecotopian look was supposed to be *loving,* not threatening – but your love could be another's fear, and what if, you, like Thoreau, do not *want* "ultra-reformer" strangers who do "not keep their distance, but cuddle up and lie spoon fashion with you, no matter how hot the weather nor how narrow the bed?" What if you do not want to be rubbed "continually with the greasy cheeks of their kindness?" (*Journal* June17, 1853)

Usanians will not have Shere Khan avert his eyes from Mowgli because we pretend we are all equal. So, instead of the tiger behaving naturally, he gets to keep his pride by having the jungle boy read his mind through his open eyes. No one notices the premise is wrong. We only feel admission of another's superiority is humiliating because our culture insists everyone is as good as the other (unless they are beautiful or strong, for movie stars and athletes are *adored*). For the tiger to have looked away would not have been humiliating. True humiliation is having to eat humble pie for one who you know damn well is *not* your superior. Anyone who has worked for bosses mentally and morally their inferior (most of us who did not inherit wealth enough to be independent) knows exactly what I mean. What our culture needs to prosper is less humiliation, more humility, and the ability to differentiate the two.

staring in reverse

> Nonaggressive cats when staring at other cats or at humans will blink, thereby signaling that the scrutiny is not hostile. In Darwinian terms, once again, cats that did this were more likely to maintain their social relationships and thereby derive the benefits that such relationships provide. Bateson & Turner *The Domestic Cat*)

Primates, like felines, *look aside* as much as they blink. The large white sclera – clearly showing when eyes look elsewhere – suggest this is especially true for us homo sapiens. Cats do not get mad as easily as primates, some of whom immediately attack a starer. Like Japanese, they simply avert their eyes and think "that pushy jerk!" Still, even friendly scrutiny by a stranger gives cats the heebie-jeebies. So, they come over to the one person in the room who is *not* interested in them. They are not being perverse. They are just suspicious of unsolicited looks.

The reverse side of this dislike of being looked at is a less noticed desire to *not* be looked at, which is not, however, the same thing as being overlooked. Understand this and you may quickly make friends with strange cats. As I once put it in an article for a tiny pr magazine for a manpower agency in Japan, written (in Japanese) shortly after getting to know cats, without the benefit of literature,

> If you want to make friends with a cat you need to avoid looking into its eyes as much as possible and show your good intent by closing your eyes a lot (for about two or three seconds)."

The detail is insufficient, but I made a good point: *a* blink is better than *no* blink, but it is not enough. Your eyes should *stay* closed for a while, for that is the proper cat's style. And because it does no good to close your eyes when the cat is looking away or has *its* eyes closed, you must first try to establish mutual eye contact, and then try to be the first to break it off. Think of it like a *staring contest in reverse!* Do this a few times in a row, and the cat is yours!

smiling eyes

A culture's attitude about eyes goes back hundreds if not thousands of years. It is reflected in our respective languages. In English, eyes narrow *in anger;* in Japanese, they do so to *smile* and *express pleasure.* You can say in Japanese, but not in natural English, that a human or a cat "narrowed her eyes (*me o hosometa*) with contentment;" and it is a perfect description of what cats, and, for that matter, humans, really do. Smile in the mirror and you will see. Your eyes close half-way or more. Already narrow "slit" eyes may be completely swallowed up. In the words of the rude traveler Paul Theroux, they have *"eyes that disappear as though they were sewn up"*. Considering the fact people usually smile without intent to fight or take flight, this makes sense. *We have no need to see while we smile.*

Could the uniquely human smile – not just showing teeth – have developed to narrow the eyes by using the raised right and left ends of the lips to push up the flesh below them, without raising the nose and baring the fangs? It is a fact that snarling, where the lips rise over the canines rather than the ends also narrows the eyes – so English is not all wrong about the anger – but that, too, reduces the stare and is not entirely contrary to the smile.

Narrowed eyes also accompany an under-rated basic pleasure of *chewing*. Cats are not as chew-crazy as humans and dogs with their gum and bones. But, they do show great pleasure when chewing dead but still limp prey or soft but springy foods of which my cats' favorite was the tubular fish-cake called a *chikuwa*, and they often purr while doing this, as do kittens, who narrow or close their eyes when nursing. As we have seen, only the cat retains its breast-kneading, tongue-out nursing mannerisms into adulthood. Closing their eyes when they're happy, may well be part of this constellation of psychological neoteny.

We, who close our eyes to kiss, should not find this too strange! Ah, sweet cats, you sit around me with your eyes closed, basking in my presence – as I bask in yours – are you, then, kissing me?

closed is beautiful

> The four charms of a cat lie in its closed eyes, its long and lovely hair, its silence and even its affected love.   – Hillaire Belloc

One sees the fin de siècle mirrored in Hillaire Belloc's cat. Once, our culture admired reticence – at least in the female sex. Now, it admires it in neither. Rather than raising our appreciation for the humble, gentle and meek of both sexes, so-called Woman's Lib has resulted in the universal adoption of Occidental male values of toughness. Where men should have joined women in open-ended clothing, women have joined men in trousers. Where men should have realized that muscles are an expensive adornment (they burn calories like crazy) and not waste time and energy on building them except for joyful sports or practical uses, women want six-pack bellies and buns of steel. Even celebration has become hard and angry. If the feminine had asserted itself, the belligerent fist in the air would never have supplanted the peaceful waving palm. Belloc's was the era of soft beauty, of that delicate sexual act, the kiss. Bram Djikstra makes the psych of that era seem misogynist if not downright *sick* in his *Idols of Perversity* – a book I recommended to a Japanese publisher and helped proof though disagreeing with some of the interpretation – he found flexible hour-glass women (some in the surf remain in mind) to be weak and helpless and called them "broken-back" where I found the voluptuously proportioned lower bodies (especially gluteus maximus) especially when thrust out behind to have an independent power or life of their own. I write this because if we can read our own species differently, small wonder we may not always agree about cats. I agree that there is something perverse in finding consumption charming and drowning erotic, but I think, all in all, we are as sick if not sicker *today*. Or, to put my suspicion into a question: *Are we a better society for no longer appreciating closed eyes, for expecting women to open their eyes wide, rather than have men learn to close them?*

meowing with your eyes

In the chapter on conversing with cats, I print a sketch made of Kuro'ko and our conversation of silent meows. I said *something is wrong* in it that Japanese readers would be more likely to catch than English language readers. By now, you can probably guess what it is. *It is our eyes*. Especially mine: they should not be wide open, for my mouth is drawn in mid-meow, and when a cat or a human meows – or *neows*, in Japanese – our cheeks rise and our eyes cannot help but narrow. That is, meowing back and forth automatically mimics the slow wink we discussed above. Han-chan almost always meowed aloud when I called out his name in a certain emphatic way (*Han! Han!*) or called him an *ii ko (good boy);* and we constantly caught each other's yawn. It embarrassed me, but I think he rather liked the proof of his influence. Who knows but he was faking some of his yawns to see what I would do! (I really cannot complain because despite my belief that it is not good to make a cat do a trick in vain, *I* sometimes faked a yawn to prompt him just for the hell of it).

Unlike Kuro'ko, he did not, however, respond to a silent meow with the same, unless he was too sick to vocalize. He replied, instead, with a slow blink or by temporarily narrowing his eyes. You might say Han-chan had a silent meow, but it came from his eyes.

closing the body

I should add that closing or narrowing the eyes are not the only way a cat can show its trust. One comes to recognize the same in the folded fore-legs of a cat. They also say something more, *"And do not move me, I'm happy right here, thank you!"* Here, for example, is Han-chan:

Because the cat's weapons are not only sheathed but folded under him in this posture – doubly-sheathed, like a rifle with a safety on in a case. That is another reason it bears a strong resemblance to closed eyes. When Han-chan did it, I felt he was simultaneously demonstrating his politest posture to put me at ease and expressing his pleasure to be allowed close to my work on the desk, or close to the dinner table. Strangely enough, here, too, the Japanese and the cat show a parallel! *Seiza,* literally "correct-seat," a formal way of sitting employed by Japanese before their superiors, is done by sitting back on ones heels with the outside of the foot on the ground.

A cat with a lot of *savoir-faire* – usually a Tom – may also fold its front-paws, its main means of defense, under its body, when facing a human he does not trust. I suppose we could say that he *learned* to adopt the strategy of unilateral disarmament for intercourse with humans as other, more foreword behavior may result in a kick or blow from a painful weapon, but never any food. As such, it seems a logical behavior and nothing remarkable. But, we should remember that there is another even more rational choice. *Flight*. Is it sentimental to say these cats show great courage by disarming themselves rather than fleeing?

the eye-squeeze

Patricia Moyes caught "my" wink twenty years before I did. In the "Body Language" chapter of *How to Talk to Your Cat* (1993), she wrote:

> cats have a most attractive way of squeezing up their eyes in an *almost-closed* position when they are especially happy or relaxed. A cat who is lying comfortably, being stroked and spoken to, will keep his eyes in *this half-closed* manner while smiling and purring. However, it is even more endearing when your cat . . . accompanies his remarks . . . with a series of eye squeezes . . .. The eye squeeze in combination with the silent miao is an irresistible combination. (ibid, *my italics*.)

I do not know if Moyes or Morris used the term "half-closed" first, but the "almost-closed" here is closest to what should be called loosely or lightly closed. Those eyes are almost always closed and, again, I feel that is missed because the English-speaking person reserves closed for sleep. Cognitive dissonance is not only for politics. The term "squeezing up" is far from felicitous – and I think better reserved for eyes scrunched up in a close-quarter scratch-fest, but it is food for thought. A dead man's eyes do pop open. So the idea that eyes must be squeezed shut has some logical basis. But experience tells us that we need not squeeze up our eyes to close them. Then again, maybe I am being too literal. Moyes's "squeeze" might be nothing more than a synonym for "narrow" used to avoid the latter verb's association with anger.

blowing kisses

Barbara Holland's paragraph on "Eye contact" in her classic *Secrets of the Cat* is a masterpiece. She even uses the word "close." Not "half-closed." And her "kiss" is sweeter than mine. After telling us we must *look* at cats, and not just pet them while reading the newspaper, for "looking is conversation to cats," she writes:

> "Some cats, when feeling especially fond of you, slowly close their eyes, like blowing a kiss. It's polite to answer. Close your eyes back at him, slowly. Because a cat feels pleasant to the hand, we rely too much on the crudities of physical contact, but as the Egyptians knew, eyes matter in cats . . . . The hand without the eye is an empty message to send back."

cat tails

Down on Words. Not Just Ecotopia. I think it astounding that some environmentalists do not realize that words are the ideal tool for sustainable living as they entertain us with little energy expenditure and are vital for intelligence to survive in a material world favoring beauty and power; and it even more astounding, no, traitorous, that even poets who make a living with words so often put them down to write paeans to silence.

Thoreau's "ultra-reformers." The long passage, I would title *"Beware the Slimy Benignity of the Ultra-reformer Lest You Meet the Fate of Jonah!"* is telling – W. Reich was right, but not all right – and timeless, so I will quote it in full (minus the . . .)

"[1853] June 17. Friday. Another breezy night and no fog this morning. . . . . ¶ Fresh mackerel for some days past. ¶ Here have been three ultra-reformers, lecturers on Slavery, Temperance, the Church, etc., in and about our house and Mrs. Brooks's the last three or four days, — A. D. Foss, once a Baptist minister in Hopkinton, N. H.; Loring Moody, a sort of travelling pattern-working chaplain; and H. C. Wright, who shocks all the old women with his infidel writings. Though Foss was a stranger to the others, you would have thought them old and familiar cronies. (They happened here together by accident.) They addressed each other constantly by their Christian names, and rubbed you continually with the greasy cheeks of their kindness. They would not keep their distance, but cuddle up and lie spoon-fashion with you, no matter how hot the weather nor how narrow the bed, — ~~chiefly~~ wholly —. I was awfully pestered with his benignity; feared I should get greased all over with it past restoration; tried to keep some starch in my clothes. He wrote a book called "A Kiss for a Blow," and he behaved as if there were no alternative between these, or as if I had given him a blow. I would have preferred the blow, but he was bent on giving me the kiss, when there was neither quarrel nor agreement between us. I wanted that he should straighten his back, smooth out those ogling wrinkles of benignity about his eyes, and, with a healthy reserve, pronounce something in a downright manner. It was difficult to keep clear of his slimy benignity, with which he sought to cover you before he swallowed you and took you fairly into his bowels. It would have been far worse than the fate of Jonah. I do not wish to get any nearer to a man's bowels than usual. They lick you as a cow her calf. They would fain wrap you about with their bowels. — addressed me as "Henry" within one minute from the time I first laid eyes on him, and when I spoke, he said with drawling, sultry sympathy, "Henry, I know all you would say; I understand you perfectly; you need not explain anything to me;" and to another, "I am going to dive into Henry's inmost depths." I said, "I trust you will not strike your head against the bottom." He could tell in a dark room, with his eyes blinded and in perfect stillness, if there was one there whom he loved. One of the most attractive things about the flowers is their beautiful reserve. The truly beautiful and noble puts its lover, as it were, at an infinite distance, while it attracts him more strongly than ever. I do not like the men who come so near me with their bowels. It is the most disagreeable kind of snare to be caught in. Men's bowels are far more slimy than their brains. They must be ascetics indeed who approach you by this side. What a relief to have heard the ring of one healthy reserved tone! With such a forgiving disposition, as if he were all the while forgiving you for existing. Considering our condition or habit of soul, — maybe corpulent and asthmatic, — maybe dying of atrophy, with all our bones sticking out, — is it kindness to embrace a man? They lay their sweaty hand on your shoulder, or your knee, to magnetize you." (I hope to publish *Five Thoreaus*, in 2010 and the above will be part of the book of his Relations. The other four books are *Phenomenal*, *Surreal*, *Semiological* and *Ecological*).

Wolf's Eye Avoidance, Revisited. I quoted a passage on how polite wolves avoid eye contact. The impolite wolf, one more interested in unnerving or attacking you, will not only look straight at your eyes but drill holes into them. According to Deborah Goodwin and her colleagues at the University of Southampton, "dogs stop developing emotionally and behaviorally at the wolf puppy equivalent of thirty days" (Temple Grandin: *Animals in Translation*) and the only dog that can manage a withering long stare like a wolf's is a husky, a dog resembling a wolf. So, it would seem that avoiding eye contact and delivering it in a devastating manner may be opposite sides of the same coin. Is it a coincidence that Japanese, famously low eye-contact, also have a formal practice of starring down an adversary, the *nirami-ai* in sumo? Japanese consciousness of the significance of looking or not looking directly at others is also formally recognized in their high-security prisons, where the inmates may be punished for looking at a guard or visitor. Most modern Occidentals I would guess might find this either absurd or cruel and unusual punishment, but it might be worthwhile testing the same at a Usanian prison to see if it would prevent criminals from coming out as cocky as they went in. After all, toughs think their eyes rule the air (Has any boy grown up in Usania without hearing a mean *"What are you looking at?"* coming from a bully?). It is the perfect eye-for-an-eye punishment, is it not? Where we look has long been known to reflect our mental state. Might not the contrary also be true?

The Oddly Quiet Counter-culture & the Talkative Old Culture. Read naive Ernest Callenbach's novel *Ecotopia* for the assumptions behind less-words-&-more-eye-contactism; and read wise Lauren Van der Post on the all-night blab-fests and other verbal delights of the gregarious and garrulous pigmies in any of his books you can find. He is always a treat, so the more of his books you must look through to find it the better.

The Stare of a Cat. Unlike a dog, a cat can stare as ferociously as a wolf, but it tends to do it not to make things happen (scare someone into freezing or running) but about something that has *already happened*. It gives you the eye.

I could not help pegging this drawing in one of Issa's journals on the tail of "Smiling with Closed Eyes," though I got the nostril wrong. Han-chan was still well here, unlike the case with my better later drawings. I probably had music streaming from the 365-channel cable radio for, otherwise, he would be facing me.

the value of self-delusion
Han-chan's Greatest Battle

Fall in Japan is supposed to be the fairest season of them all. A red brocade of hills Japanese who do not know New England claim as their unique heritage burn below a dry blue sky. In love with someone who was married and in love with someone else, I was grateful for the abnormally stormy weather. Every peal of thunder brought me cheer.

"the end of the world"

"Motto! Motto!" (More! More!) I shouted.

"It's all your fault," I wrote her. *"If the harvest is destroyed and no one can enjoy the moon this Fall, it's all your fault!"*

The idea is not exactly fresh. The Japanese and Chinese classical poetry I was reading at the time may not have included much heavy weather, but rain of tears or vice-versa were common; and links between our hearts and the elements are still found in modern song lyrics. What was new to me was that I found myself partly believing it!

a textbook case

Han-chan was not doing so well either. I had no idea who bit him, or when. Most serious cat wounds are like that; you do not notice them until the infection sets in. This was a classic puncture wound. The calf of Han-chan's hind leg was swollen up to Popeye forearm proportions and a silver-dollar-sized patch of hair was missing from a smooth pink inflammation around a pair of puncture marks. My notes:

Han-chan treats his infection as a deadly snake, biting near to it, but afraid to really bite it for fear of pain. Funny enough to make a video of – one method of externalizing pain? [I have a drawing in my diary, but it is awful. The only good thing about it is the bright pink – for once, such a marker has been put to good use – coloring of the inflammation, and that I could not show you here.]

The pink area looked as taut as a female sub-human primate's privates in heat, so I could well imagine the throbs of pain that Han-chan felt whenever he moved and the stinging sear around the edges whenever he touched it without succeeding in breaking through. I wanted to help, and considered sterilizing a needle or razor but, lacking a topical pain-killer and curious in an all too scientific way convinced myself to let nature take its course. No, I am not that cold. There is more.

f__k the vet's "natural"!

So why not take him to the vet? Because I had no car and every slow trip out of the valley – 400 yard-walk+trip by train+more-walk – carried the risk of traumatizing Han-chan. Vets simply do not understand what a trip *means* for a cat with no experience of cars and other traveling. They generally see cats that openly live with people who are allowed to have them, in neighborhoods where cars come close to houses. My apartment was over a hundred yards from the nearest road. Even humans who have never left their neighborhoods can literally sicken from travel. In Bali, there is a word for it *"paling."* The only way to move such cats without risk to their minds (see Tinkerbelle Syndrome pg. 107), is to drug them like you would drug a wild animal (though apparently well wild animals we treat may experience mental problems if insufficiently drugged). But, I was told by more than one Japanese vet that it was "unnatural" to drug the cat and should be avoided.

I do not buy it. Taking a feral cat to the vet for an operation is already unnatural. I do not know if the narcotic dulls the sensual overload and panic response enough to prevent lasting memories, gives the cat time to adjust to the new experience, or, my favorite hypothesis, allows the experience to be passed off as a bad dream rather than developing into long-lasting trauma. Who cares! *It works.*

And for the same reason, or reasons, it prevents moving disasters. After a sad experience with an untranquilized cat who, despite being close to me and the another cat jumped out the window of my new apartment and was never seen again, I as we shall see next, I used sleeping pills to move cats with great success.

I have heard that cats are weak-livered and sleeping pills are dangerous for them. If so, veterinary medicine had better work hard to devise pills that *are* suitable for cats. Take out the nippy part of the catnip and keep the part that gives them the hang-over. Try opium. It is not enough that vets have ways to anesthetize cats in their hospitals. The mental health of millions of semi-feral (*han-nora* in Japanese) cats depends upon the layman having ways to drug and take them to the vet or move them. Even if there are risks, it is worth it. If the cat has an allergic reaction and dies, he dies. Better that than a broken mind where the result is misery, sometimes for the cat and always for the cat's relations and his owner.

I had no tranquilizers on hand for Han-chan, so we stayed home to weather the storm.

moving a king

Before Han-chan's promised battle, let me interject an example of a difficult move that worked thanks to tranquilizers *begged* off a young vet.

One day a cat with ribs like a xylophone, a runny nose, crow-like voice and filthy matted coat appeared at my bay-window. He had the biggest eyes and paws I've seen outside of the zoo and despite his sorry state *somehow* retained his dignity. With his huge tail ramrod-straight and proudly held high at all times (excepting my only photo of him where his gravitas is still present but seems to say, with respect to the photographer, "Off with his head!"), he had a commanding gaze and expected to be obeyed. To our other cats' disgust, we took him in. His inability to bite softly, suggested he had been separated from other cats at a tender age. His favorite activity was walking through the woods with me. He did it in the fearless manner of a dog.

I do not think he realized cats had territories. Or, more likely, he thought the whole world belonged to *him*.

The other cats had been taught not to loiter in front of the apartment, but Ohsama, or King, as I immediately called him, *insisted* upon setting up his royal court there. He moved out to the edge of the tiny front lawn to keep tabs on anyone coming or going. *"See this,"* he seemed to say, *"I own it! Don't forget to pay me my due whenever you come or go!"* Soon, every apartment received a scary note from the real estate agency: "Keeping-a-cat-is-grounds-for-eviction." I think my landlord knew I was the main culprit, but did not want to discriminate against the lone foreigner.

I scoured the neighborhood for someone to take "our" Ohsama. What do you think happened? People tried to give me *their* cats. Unable to jeopardize the lives of my other cats – when poor people are forced to move, animals also suffer – and my writing (moving wastes money *and* time), I gave Ohsama enough tranquilizers to kill a horse, stuffed him in a duffel-bag and took him by train to the Komaba campus of the public Harvard of Japan, the Imperial University of Tokyo, which I walked through three times a week commuting to work.

I lay the still sleeping Ohsama under a low bush in an out-of-the-way woody area, leaving the bag, a dirty tee-shirt and a dirty sock. I took care to pee here and there to further prove the place was under my care, reassured him when he came to, showed him around, fed him his favorite food and spent much of the day with him. If Ohsama had been his normal alert self, he would probably have sauntered away (the closest he could come to what another cat would do, *bolt*) the moment I opened the bag; but this worked like a dream, for both of us. He did make some "I am pissed off" meows, but they were only luke-warm. He was too groggy to figure out what was happening. When I called him the next morning on my way to work, he was still in the area and, still groggy (he slept!) came out of a wooded area. It was hard getting him not to follow me to work, but I got away when he was eating, and the found him on my return that night.

To make a long story short, within weeks Ohsama had other people feeding him and soon even had subjects at his service. Before a month had passed someone I never saw made him a house with a corrugated roof (!) which the grounds people or security soon found and trashed. But even that turned out for the good, as Ohsama found shelter under the Library eaves on the window by the office desk of the chief librarian, an angel who made certain he got medical care I could not afford for my own cats. His water dish sitting on the ground level window ledge said "King" *in English*, and what is amazing – or maybe not amazing for all who knew him – she said he was named without knowledge of the name I gave him, by another woman who helped feed him before he took up residence by the library. Only his nemesis, a mob of crows or ravens (I can never recall which is which), who seemed very jealous of his Highness's popularity, refused to do him homage. Indeed, the only time I have ever heard he ran, was from those crows. I imagine they literally tweaked that priapic tail and the King, unable to drop it down after a lifetime of keeping it up was defenseless. According to the chief librarian, they once forced him into an incinerator, hence the ashes I found on his regal coat.

Ohsama always came trotting out to play when I sang the old country number *"Fraulein! Fraulein!"* graced with an

Emmet Miller yodel on my way back from work. One cold winter night, when I had worked too late to give him the usual fifteen minutes or so without risking missing the last train, I received a Royal Bite on the ankle for trying to take my leave before his Highness was good and ready! All of this, mind you, was ultimately, thanks to the kind vet giving me the necessary sleeping pills for the move.

Han-chan cornered by his own leg

So, there was Han-chan sparring with, lunging at, his own leg. And this was accompanied by those agonized groaning, moaning growls that make cats, unlike dogs with their out-going growls, sound so damn tortured. And, every once in a while, after actually touching the enemy, that is the inflamed member, he would let out a savage hiss, something evolved as a form of snake mimicry according to Desmond Morris (*Catlore*), who, we might add, credits woman's breasts for her buttocks.

Han-chan was not enjoying himself; that much was clear. He was cowardly, as might be expected of any cat who thinks too much, and avoided fights by climbing up things when I was gone and staying there until the bully departed, or calling loudly for pea-shooter (soybeans shot through a long plastic, later copper tube) help on his side when he knew I was around. As mentioned elsewhere, he chased the cat the flying soy-beans routed. What I did *not* say, but you can probably guess, is what happened if the other cat stopped running. He skidded to a stop. If Han-chan's four-paws were car tires, they would have smoked.

But there was no escape from his own leg. He was cornered. After fifteen minutes or so of pitched battle, Han-chan's anger finally surpassed his pain. He gave the enemy a sound whack with one of his front paws. That did it. The pain was so intense that he blew his top and, forgetting fear, *bit* the bastard but good!

You have never seen so much .... let's just say it gives a new pronunciation to the word *pussy cat!* With the wound opened, the pain instantly left with the pressure, and I could help a calm Han-chan with mop-up operations.

life as a head trip

Han-chan, I thought, you have done it again! You have given me a marvelous kernel for thought.

This idea of *mind and body* as an Occidental fiction is, itself a fiction. Anyone who has read widely in cultural anthropology knows there are any number of cultures that are *far* more dualistic than Westerners are. Without any knowledge of Descartes, much less selfish rich Usanians who would freeze their heads until they, like frozen words released from Arctic Ice (an idea from early science fiction), may be resurrected with new bodies of flesh or silicon, people from such cultures say, "You *are* your head." They value singing more than playing a musical instrument *because the voice comes out of the head*, and playing musical instruments more than dancing *because the feet are at farthest remove from the superior part.* In such a culture, to say something *comes to a head* means that it is perfected. (See Sylvia Ardyn Boone: *Radiance From the Waters*, Yale 1986). Odd that we never find anyone lamenting these peoples estrangement from *their* bodies, isn't it?

Deep down, I think we all know damn well we are *not* bodies. We *have* bodies. Of course, our behavior affects our bodies to a degree, as it affects our pets, but that does not make them us. Nor is a body any more you because you happen to have good mind-control over parts of it. Even otherwise astute philosophers get bodies wrong. Alan Watts, I recall, flippantly related how he once put down a pretty girl who complained that the beauty he praised was not her real person by sarcastically asking her whether she was, then, no more than the driver of the taxi-cab that was her body. The metaphor is witty, but wrong. The beauty was *hers*, not her.

To me, Han-chan's behavior shows that even an animal of a far lower intellectual level than a human, and needless to say not under the influence of Monsieur Descartes, would not agree, and even contradict, with the New Age proposition that you *are* your body.

hallucinate and live!

I wish I could have seen inside Han-chan's head. Though anger tends to blur, I like to think he imagined his leg to be the cat who bit it . . . . That *would* be poetic, wouldn't it! Something like taking the hair of the dog that bit you.

At the time, I am sure Han-chan had a fever for I compared him to the other cats in the room. So, could one use of a fever be that it helps you hallucinate to do what must be done to save yourself? Had Han-chan not become infuriated with his leg and gotten into a serious cat-fight with it, how could he have lanced it? How, if I was not there to help – my curiosity could have killed this cat, though I was just about to heat up a needle – could he have saved his leg? Could a feverish hallucination help the proverbial fox chew off a paw to escape a trap?

It is hard to say what happened that night. I have seen Han-chan and his family confronting two tough toms, who had bullied him before, when a remarkable thing happened. Caterwauling Han-chan suddenly turned and bit Kori, his own niece. This tells me that rage itself, in the case of a cat, or at least a cowardly cat, can be relieved by biting, and that can be totally lacking in discrimination – or, worse yet, biting what is easiest to bite, i.e. one's friends, because they won't bite you back ! (since then, I have noticed dogs do the same).
But, on this occasion, note that Han-chan did not take the easy way out and bite his other leg or another cat in the room. For once, he bit the correct object. That is why I think he clearly had to be seeing things.

the paradox of pain

There is an interesting paradox here. Pain serves to remind us – people and cats – not to take our bodies for granted, on the one hand, and highlight the otherness of the body as object (not even a subject, for it won't necessarily obey our will) on the other.

Pain both brings us closer to and alienates us from what is and is not our self.

hypersensitivity and pain

If Han-chan could shake off snow he had yet to step into (pg.82), and cover up catfood before it was even opened (pg.93), you can bet that his cowardice was not only due to the greater physical pain felt by the sensitive being, but by imagining the pain he would receive in the course of the altercation.

While the painful sound of caterwauling has long impressed me, I had always thought of it as psyching-out, a sort of staring contest in sound, with each cat gamely waiting for and hoping to force the other to do an audible "blink," at which the winner pounces and the loser either flees or rolls over into a defensive posture. But, Leonard Michaels' poetic explanation sounds much more suitable for the cat that Han-chan showed me:

> "When threatening to fight, cats whine at each other, a blood-curdling sound, shrill with miserable lamentation. They foresee the ghastly lacerations they will inflict and suffer, and already regret them." (*A Cat*)

Regret for wounds they will *inflict* seems a bit far-fetched, but if the gist of this poetic statement is true, as it may well be, Han-chan is no exception and we must ask whether concern for what *will* happen is a feline trait, as opposed to the happy-go-lucky dog, who, like many of our species puts his trust in providence?

& nothing happened

Next to my note on Han-chan's battle – and a picture too ugly too share – I wrote a *low-ku* in Japanese, the proper way, vertically. There was nothing in it about the battles raging in my heart which I thought responsible for the unseasonal weather. I was thinking of Thoreau:

the rain this fall
even that rooster's craw
has mildewed

Han-chan won his battle; but I lacked the guts to bite my heart. The longing festered, ... and, since I cannot recall exactly when it popped, I think it just slowly dried up.

cat tails

Thoreau's Rooster Thoreau has a dozen or so descriptions of cock's crowing in his Journal, all of which are paeans to it. Here, I may have been thinking of an entry he made on July 22, 1851 including this,

> the rich crow of young roosters . . . hoarse without cold, hoarse with rude health. That crow is all-nature-compelling; famine and pestilence flee before it. These are our fairest days, which are born in a fog.

Original Ending to this Chapter I have excercised editorial discretion to cut the words ending this chapter in the previous draft:

> (It is a good thing this is not a novel, for the metaphors, though actually found in Japanese poetry – love as a swollen pus-filled wound, analogous to John Suckling's love-as-a-fart (found in Johnson's Dictionary), a problem whether held in or not – come from *haikai* and are no more my invention, than 'Caelia shits' (stolen from Ovid) was Swift's – would destroy the plot even if something rather than nothing were to have happened.)

I did not mind it being convoluted and, for most readers full of references they might need to look up to fully comprehend. I think it useful to improve the effect of short sentences and encourage readers who need to read more to do so. The problem is, I am no longer sure what it means.

Konrad Lorenz vs. *Camille Paglia* regarding *the* World's *most* True/False Animal

Cats are very complex animals. Or, perhaps, they are not. It is possible they only *seem* so because especially convoluted people tend to like cats and naturally make them out to be creatures of their own mind, while dog-lovers, being more straight-forward, would describe the mind of a dog in a simpler way. If the cat-lover finds the cat's complexity intelligent, the dog-lover identifies it with deceit. Considering the fact that many of the best writers on dogs also write well about cats and vice versa, my generalization is no more than . . . a generalization.

paglia's cat: "I can never be known."

Camille Paglia, one of the most entertaining aphorists since Wilde, makes the classic old saw of the mysterious cat sing:

> Cats have secret thoughts, a divided consciousness. No other animal is capable of ambivalence, those ambiguous cross-currents of feeling, as when a purring cat simultaneously buries its teeth warningly in one's arm. The inner drama of a lounging cat is telegraphed by its ears, which swerve round toward a distant rustle as its eyes rest with false adoration on ours, and secondly by its tail, which flicks menacingly even while the cat dozes. . . . The cat's ambivalent duality is dramatized in erratic mood-swings, abrupt leaps from torpor to mania, by which it checks our presumption: "Come no closer. I can never be known." (*Sexual Personae*)

Paglia is not putting down the cat. She builds *a case for it* as *the* creature of night, *the* image of that elegant slinkiness known as Egyptian aesthetic, and *the* representative of "the sinuous craft of daemonic darkness", which it "carries into day." Her cats "dwell in the occult, that is, the 'hidden,'" so it is hardly surprising they are unknowable. (Are her cats not what many men think of as "woman"?). While the "false adoration" and "abrupt leaps" are old hat, her claim of ambivalence and "divided consciousness" greatly improve upon the classic diabolical cat that purrs one moment and licks your bones in another. Paglia's cat does both at once.

But I am uncertain how to take her claim that "their 'evil' look is no human projection: the cat may be the only animal who savors the perverse or reflects upon it." As Paglia, herself, clearly savors the perverse (Read her ferocious chapter on Emily Dickinson, 'Marquis de Sade of Amherst'), here, too, I think no insult is intended.

lorenz's cat: the transparent animal

For a diametrically opposed viewpoint, I call to the witness stand the dean of modern ethology, Konrad Lorenz. From his chapter on the cat in his 1953 classic *Man Meets Dog*,

> In the chapter, 'Animals that Lie', I have recounted everything I know about real deceitfulness, that is conscious dissembling, in animals. . . I have never seen an analogous case of duplicity in a cat, although I have lived with these animals nearly as long and as intimately as dogs, nor do I know of any typical behavior of cats which could foster even the erroneous notion that they are deceitful."

Lorenz does not give what may be the strongest evidence of purposeful deceit: dogs have been killed for it. In his essay "Pastoral," R.L. Stevenson writes of a fine sheepdog, the shepherd's most important investment and closest friend, "taken to a dykeside and promptly shot" by its owner because another shepherd saw it skulking through the heather and into a pool where it repeatedly washed himself "over head and ears, and then (but now openly with tail in air) strike homeward over the hills" – the dog was erasing the evidence of his crimes against sheep several farms away. (*Memories and Portraits,* 1906). I could point to simpler lies, one dalmation at my sister Susan's house – where I write this now – makes a practice of barking as if there is good cause to make other dogs run outside when she wants to monopolize food inside. That pattern of deceit may have started by accident – barking brings food – but when I also see her sneak away to eat without letting the other dog hear I suspect she knows what she is doing. Another does not do that elaborate ruse, but has caught on to my signal for hush-hush and seeing me put my finger to my lips will sneak from room to room in a careful manner avoiding the eyes and ears of her rival and gain sole possession of some tidbit.

Lorenz also points out another, unintentional kind of canine deceit. There are shy dogs who wag their tail deferentially and *unintentionally* fool those who don't read fear in the crouched body. German even has a term for such bites resulting from fright: *angstbeissen*. (Here, the appendage one might expect to show the animal's gut feeling betrays us. As we shall see below, that is the exact opposite of the case with the cat.)

Then, coming back to the cat, Lorenz considers *bears*. Accidents with pet bears due to miscommunication are common and, like *angstbeissen*, not so much because the bear is deceitful. It is a result of its being a solitary and unsociable animal lacking "the expressive movements with which other, more social animals announce their inner feelings to fellow members of their species," leaving us with nothing but a mask (Hornaday) to read.

"In the reputedly 'catty' cat," on the other hand, "these expressive movements are particularly highly developed."(Ibid.) Lorenz comes down four-square on the side of what I will call *the transparent cat*.

> There are few animals in whose faces a knowledgeable observer can so clearly read a prevailing mood and predict what actions – friendly or hostile – are likely to follow. The face of the cat portrays so clearly and unmistakably the slightest degree of mental agitation that anybody who is familiar with this animal knows at once how he stands with it. How plain is the expression of trustful friendliness when, with erect ears and wide open eyes, a cat turns a smooth unwrinkled face

towards its observer, and how clearly expressed by the facial musculature is every rising emotion, whether of fear or of hostility. (Ibid.)

the paradox of reading cats

A "knowledgeable observer" may be able to read a cat well; but "facial musculature" does not convey much to the novice, especially through a fur mask. Indeed, my first memory of a cat is one of being scratched by a black cat that suddenly lashed out at me while we were interacting (I can not remember details, except for being utterly surprised) in the hull of a boat my father was outfitting in our backyard. The solid black color did not help me. Lorenz finds the 'wild-colored' tiger cats particularly easy reading because the striped markings on the face highlight changes in expression. In their case, he argues, the slightest changes of mood is plain to see even without the additional information to be had from "subtle change of the body attitude" and the movement of the tail. I find the cat's eyes, mouth and whiskers stand out less clearly against a tiger's (brown tabby?) relatively complex markings, and prefer to study a slightly marked cat like Han-chan. Perhaps, Lorenz can simply handle more visual information than I can.

Lorenz also notes the clear sociality explicit in "the threatening attitudes of a cat" that are extraordinarily diverse for one species, and vary depending on "whether they apply to a human friend who has 'gone to far', or to a feared enemy", are purely defensive, or a warning that an attack is forthcoming.

So why, then, if cats are so damn expressive, especially when they are ready to attack, do so many people get scratched? There is a touch of irony here and a paradox. What this seems to mean is that, for the expert, the cat, being more diverse of expression, can be more accurately read; but for the layman who hopes for a simple snarl or growl, the same riches prove an obstacle to understanding!

Jeffrey Masson writes "What I have always liked about dogs is how directly and intensely they express their emotions." To each his own. Until my mid-thirties, so did I. I was an unabashed "dog person." *Now*, I find intensity (from an adult animal) a turn off. Then, again, maybe I only *thought* I liked directness. I disliked opera from my twenties. In retrospect, that suggests I preferred something more mature or subtle from the start. Having grown up with a dog and a loud-voiced father in a far from gentle or mature culture, I just did not know it. For some things, cats can be as direct as dogs, while humans generally hide behind their persona, but on the whole, when cats are not in heat, they are, cool, rather than intense. They sit back and watch the world through sunglasses. It may take a bit more patience, sensitivity and observation on the human's part to understand what they are up to, but I find that takes less effort than putting up with loud and needy dogs do.

mixed emotions in the cat

> I gave an order to a cat, and the cat gave it to its tail. – a Chinese proverb (according to *Puss In Boots*)

What makes comparing Paglia and Lorenz so interesting is the fact they draw opposite conclusions from what is basically the same evidence: i.e., cats simultaneously reveal themselves through multiple channels.

Paglia, calls it *ambivalence*, or worse: "The twitching, thumping tail is the chthonian barometer of the cat's Apollonian world. It is the serpent in the garden, bumping and grinding with malice afore-thought." (Ibid.) Had Lorenz given more space to the tail, he would surely have described it as *a source of additional information,* "a sure barometer of a cat's mood" (*Florida Cat Owner's Handbook*), *i.e.*, as a *plus* in terms of trustworthiness!

For better or worse, the cat holds no patent on ambivalence. It is just that it is easier to recognize in the cat, for it wears its heart, or part of it, pinned to its tail. This appendage may indeed register discomfort, desire-to-pounce, or whatever, *before the cat is conscious of its feelings* or decides to act on them. When the Roman critic Quintilian (d. ca.100 AD) compares an orator carried away by his own tongue to a lion that "lashes himself into a fury with his own tail, he is referring to this feline predisposition. But, just as often, in my opinion, it marks an *afterthought,* or lingering feelings (and not necessarily malice!). Life, human or feline, is like that. One's mood can either *lead* or *follow* one's thought.

Let's see several examples.

You and your cat play fight. You are pushing your cat to the limits of his patience. Although you are getting in too many whacks, his ears don't go back because he *knows* you are playing, But, if you are very attentive you note a wild high look in his eyes – like when cats are on catnip – his slightly raised upper lip – don't think smile but grin or leer! – and his tail. Twitching nervously, it speaks for his feelings: *"I don't like losing! Time to give this joker my claws!"* This is *premonition*.

You make up to each other after a disciplinary clash, or your accidentally stepping on his tail, and the cat *realizes* that you are back on good terms and *all will be fine* if it refrains from doing anything dumb, but is, or *was,* after all, pissed off. So the tail keeps twitching until his mood catches up with his understanding. This is *afterthought*.

From a book of children's observations about cats: "If she wants some food she will miaow non-stop. If she does not like the look of it, she will flick her paw at the food, then turn and look at us as if it is our fault. Then *she flicks her tail* and walks out really stately. . ." (Exley ed.: CATS; *my italics*) Josephine Healey has the makings of a naturalist, for her detail is impeccable. The flicked paw says "this is shit and we should cover it up!" and the tail has launched what rhetoric calls *a Parthian shaft* – or to put it more colloquially, a parting shot.

Leonard Michaels writes that "when a cat is thoughtful, the tail moves like part of the mind." If thoughtfulness means *conscious* thought, then this movement is but part of the tail's portfolio. I would, rather, put things in terms of Paul McLean's triune brain and say that the cat has a window open to each of its souls, the reptile, mammal and personal. But, I would be careful about assigning one or another brain to the tail. The temptation is to give it the reptile, as it looks serpentine, but it is true that a cat who restrains himself while watching birds through a window fails to restrain the id of a tail lashing up a storm, but I trained

Han-chan to twitch it with a click of my fingers, and many cats enjoy the game of *Can you grab my tail?* where it is flicked into and out of your palm. They do something like it with their kittens. Rightly or wrongly, I like to think of it as a first step in training them to fight snakes.

what is night? what is wildness?

> A cat has absolute emotional honesty: human beings for one reason or another, may hide their feelings, but a cat does not. Ernest Hemingway.

Paglia's prose is bewitching, but I vote for Lorenz and Papa Doc. A cat is honest. It cannot help but be known to all with eyes to see. A creature of the night? For sure. But *what is night?* What is darkness, if not a transparent world, where we can see billions of miles into the space that is obscured by the light of day?

If Paglia did not mean to degrade the cat, neither did Lorenz mean to praise it.

> "I do not regard this inability to deceive as a sign of the cat's superiority. In fact, I regard it as a sign of the much higher intelligence of the dog that it is able to do so."(Ibid.)

There is one unwritten assumption in all this that I find particularly interesting. Everybody seems to find the cat closer to the wild than the dog (except, perhaps, Paglia who identifies the cat with *a type* of civilization, a slinky fluid Egyptian aesthetic at odds with the muscle-bound horsey Roman one). From the "wild cats" chapter of *Puss In Books*, bits of quotes from Kipling to George F. Will:

> "walking by his wild lone
> "a tiger that is fed by hand
> "runs wild with the wind in its coat
> "still only a whisker away from the wilds
> "domestic only in so far that it suits its own ends
> "the wildcat is the "real" cat, the soul of the domestic cat
> "a wild beast as uncowed and uncorrupted as any under heaven
> "the phrase domestic cat is an oxymoron

Even Lorenz, who declared the cat a social animal by nature and nuture also wrote that it is "no domestic being but a completely wild being." So, you wonder: how, then are deceit and wildness linked in the minds of so many people? Do Hemingway and Lorenz associate honesty with wildness and deceit with the world of men, of which the dog is an honorary member, while those who find the cat enigmatic, or even off-putting, think, rather, that the wild is something foxy, while the world of men is tame?

if looks could kill

> After scolding one's cat, one looks into its face and is seized by the ugly suspicion that it understood every word, and has filed it for further reference. Charlotte Gray (in Exley: *Cat Quotations*)

How about Paglia's "evil" look? Cats *do* give people more dirty looks than any other animal I know. If a dog has something thrown at him and looks back over his shoulder to see if he is safe , his look will probably reflect fear. With a cat, it will more likely reflect *anger*. If looks could kill, cats would depopulate the earth. In a culture that believed in the power of the Evil Eye, you would be very careful to keep on the good side of the "spiteful" creature. But we don't believe, do we? Why not be grateful to the cat, then, for letting us know where it stands?

This may seem to contradict what I write elsewhere about my gut dislike for bare passions, but after living a long time in a society where emotions were held in check, I sometimes felt it refreshing to see hate expressed openly. I recall feeling all the more attracted to (this is someone I almost married) the anchor of a morning news show because her hate for a regular reporter coveting her position, lit up her eyes – this was on-air – regardless of what pleasantries were being exchanged. I did not find the anchor a hypocrite, or ambiguous. She had to be polite on the job, just as a cat must act nice to, or at least not pounce on a human. But, unlike most mass media professionals, she could not hide her true feelings. In such a situation, contradiction is honest. As Lorenz points out, it is slander to call cats "catty" in the usual meaning of the term. But to call this anchor *catty* would be perfectly accurate and a compliment in my book.

Besides, if you ask me, most of a cat's "evil" looks are fully justified. They don't just go about cursing people like the proverbial bitter old witch. They do it when someone treats them meanly though they have done nothing to that person, or when they feel someone has betrayed their trust. They do it because they expect better of us.

why japanese came down hard on cat tails

> I would always recommend the budding novelist to buy the tailed variety; for the tail in cats is the principle organ of emotional expression and a Manx cat is the equivalent of a dumb man – their tails are tapering black serpents endowed, even when the body lies in Sphinx-like repose, with a spasmodic and uneasy life of their own."
>
> – Aldous Huxley ("Sermons in Cats" in *Music At Night*)

While it is true that a stumpy tail – for there are no tailless cats – cannot swing or lash about, Huxley is wrong, for they actually exhibit a *more* "spasmodic and uneasy life" than the long ones perhaps because, they tend to have pinched nerves. Be that as it may, they do indeed make poor serpents compared to long ones. Instead, the word maggoty comes to mind. Still, considering the fear and hate of snakes by the Judeo-Christian Civilization, one might expect cats to have been bobbed a long time ago. Oddly enough, it is the Japanese, who do not share "our" enmity toward snakes, who were known for being hard on cat tails. According to B. H. Chamberlain (*Things Japanese*), kitten tails were lopped off because most Japanese cats were tailless, or, more properly "short-tailed," to begin with.

> the habit of only seeing tailless cats has engendered such a prejudice in their favour that, should a litter chance to be born with one long-tailed kitten, somebody will generally take upon himself to chop the tail off to a respectable shortness. (*Ibid*)

Chamberlain further described popular fears of bewitchment by "cats furnished with one or several long tails." I cannot judge the accuracy of that claim, but *most* Japanese cats today are born without full tails. They are not tailless, either. A species of endangered wild cat on Iriomote Island (near Taiwan) does indeed have the tiny tail of a Manx, but the lion's share of Japanese cats embody the sad reality of twisted, kinked and otherwise misshapen tails such as may be seen in the cat sketches of Kuniyoshi. Because Japanese tend to be perfectionists in matters of appearance, the existence of this imperfection suggests to me that some sort of right-to-life Buddhism saved cats with deformed tails from being put down at birth as, I assume, usually happened in the West. In that case, it could be argued that the sorry condition of what may well be the majority of Japanese cats was born of compassion rather than cruelty, and the old horror story must be turned upside down.

Be that as it may, in a society where emotions were kept under cover, the cat's openness, as symbolized by the honest tail would have disgusted people's sensibilities as much as a shaved chin disgusted decent Victorian Era

Englishmen (I read somewhere that a naked adult male chin was considered obscene for its resemblance to the head of an erect penis; which was why Oscar Wilde and co. created a scandal by removing the fig leaf from their chinny chin chins, which is to say shaving off their beards.).

deceit and intelligence

I started a chapter on intelligence but stopped, for it is already treated, in one way or another, in *every* chapter. However, it is worth pointing out the disproportionately large number of *they-do-this-and-that-so-they-must-be-intelligent* stories concern deceit. A socio-biological agenda on the part of the researchers? Perhaps; but, mainly, it is interesting. This is not just true for higher animals, either. Even when the intelligence involved is only a design – the cicada that looks like the alligator, the caterpillar that flicks its horn like the tongue of a snake, etc. – we are enthralled.

> "Everybody thinks my cat is innocent but they are fooled." Haroon Rahman, 10 (Exley ed. CATS and other crazy cuddlies)

Young Haroon and old Camille are not all wrong. Lorenz' generalization is too pat. Even kittens practice deceit, for it is part of play. They quickly learn to run away in such a way that they can double back and pounce on their pursuer from an unexpected angle. Where *fooling* is part of the game, deceit is not "bad," but it is hard to think any animal capable of purposeful misleading in a game would be incapable of doing so under other circumstances. Dogs may practice more complex forms of deceit, but Paul Corey, in *Do Cats Think?* gives us many interesting stories of a deceitful cat who would seem to offer competition to Lorenz' dogs. Let me sum up a couple –

1) Tang slept on the kitchen clock but pretended he didn't; always managing to be down on the floor washing himself when Corey looked in. After his habit was discovered because of the moved hands on the clock, he stopped moving them. But he only gave up the perch after Corey returned home early one day and took a snap shot of him

asleep there, using a flash-bulb! (There is a lot going on and Corey gives the story over a page.)

2) Tang got attention by pretending to scratch the rug. One night, apparently discontent over a food matter, he started to do it and got a swift boot in the behind instead of the usual "Hey you!" Corey and Ruth laughed as he fled, but he soon came back to the same spot and made "an elaborate show of repeating the act." Ruth, who was barefoot, "fell for his ploy," but when her foot came down this time "he turned and grabbed her ankle with all four feet, claws out and jaws wide. He used just enough claws and teeth to get a scream out of her. Then he rolled free and dashed out of the room with his tail up."

After the first of the above stories – and there are more Tang stories – Corey knowingly comments:

> "When a cat behaves as Tang did, he's called "sneaky" and "sly." When a dog does it, Dr. Lorenz credits him with superior intelligence." (Ibid.)

the cat that bit camille paglia

> "There's two sides to a cat, one side is nice and fury, the other side is sharp." Daniel Dass, 10 (CATS. Ibid.)

But what of the cat that bit Paglia while purring? I doubt not that it happened. But I doubt her interpretation of it.

Maybe the cat was, like Kori (pg. 107), disturbed. Though cats normally "never bite or scratch without giving previous unmistakable warning to the offender," Lorenz made an exception for "the case of unreliable or mentally deficient psychopaths – which occur in cats just as in dogs." Or, it could have been separated from its family at a tender age and lacked the ability to gauge how hard to bite another without hurting them, in which case, a love-bite, or nibble, can draw blood. But even a cat with social biting and clawing skills can forget you don't have fur when it is excited and it faces a problem dogs do not have, namely, extremely sharp claws and teeth. Purring only means the cat is at ease and is no guarantee of gentle behavior. Paglia's cat could have been in a happy "you bite me and I'll bite you!" mood. Unfortunately, the best "warning" of such a form of fighting arousal is unintentionally misleading to humans: that "slightly raised upper lip" I mentioned earlier resembles nothing so much as a *smile* and it takes much experience to recognize it.

There are also cats that, like children who throw tantrums without realizing they need a nap, are unaware of tension building within to answer nature's call and bite their owner before they themselves know what they are doing. If you are attentive to their toilet cycle, and succeed more than once in smacking such a cat after it falls into a reverie – a dreamlike state of arousal one can learn to recognize – and is just about to bite you, then immediately chase or lead it to the box (or outside), the cat can learn to snap-out of it by himself. I have saved such a cat from having to go to the pound for repeatedly biting his owner "without warning."

Or, Paglia may have touched a sore spot in the cat's body, a puncture wound not visible from without, an internal cyst remaining long after contraceptive surgery, or even a *psychologically delicate place*. I have known cats (and dogs) tolerant of rough petting who will lash out or attempt to bite anyone who even *tries* to investigate their belly or privates, even if in a purring good mood.)

Then again, maybe Paglia's cat bite was no accident. Maybe the cat knew what it was doing, and was purring in advance for the pleasure of biting someone who was called cats *false*. If a story told by Miami News columnist John Keasler is correct, there is a precedent for this sort of poetic justice. A group of reporters including Keasler were standing by an enclosed inlet with dolphins on Key Biscayne. They were there for a story about "dolphin liberation," but the talk drifted to the psychic powers of the creature. Some were believers, others agnostic, but one was upset by the very idea. "Hogwash!" he said. Just then, a dolphin swimming nearby snapped a tail-full of water in the group's direction. All but one of the reporters got hardly a drop on them. Yes. Only that vocal dolphin-atheist was soaked from head to foot!

envoi

My second cat memory was of another black cat that took to my electrically rigged warning mat. I was very proud of this home-made device placed outside the door of my room (over the garage) in high school, and liked to see how it surprised – no, scared – visitors. Then, the tables turned on me. This cat I did not even know existed took to jumping on it at about 3:00 AM! After being woken up three or four times and failing to nail the culprit – I must confess to throwing things after it – I removed the mat.

That cat obviously got a kick out of bothering me – or seeing me bothered, at any rate – and even risked bodily injury to do so. But compared to the dogs that quietly watch you come by on your bicycle and suddenly rush out to take a hunk from your leg, who could hold such tom(cat)foolery "evil"?

cat tails ~

The Angry (or obviously annoyed/pissed-off Cat Photo. I am holding the very angry but self-controlled (if he were wild, he would bite me) cat, Mikan (i.e., Tangerine) in a photo taken by a Jiji-tsûshin (a top Japanese news agency) for a magazine feature on me. I sit at my desk wearing gloves because I kept the window cracked for the cats and used no heating. It was before I got a Mac (now I have a Lenovo because I like the stub on the keyboard) which forced me to keep the temperature high enough to prevent condensation. Unlike Han-chan, when Mikan suddenly matured, he was fine with fighting it out to mate so I confess that I took him to the same University I took Ohsama, where he could live as a Tom, for that was impossible in my neighborhood as the commotion might get me kicked-out and all my cats would end up homeless. He occasionally came out when I called for Oh-sama and I treated the two of them to competitive hunts. Mikan is shown retrieving a fish-cake in a tree on page 257, that part of a photo from another feature on your author who has, so far, been ignored in the country of his birth. I cut myself from the picture for I looked just too damn gleeful – like a kid – watching Mikan's balancing act.

Growing Up as Toms and Queens
Why Cats *Also* Have It Tough

A tom-kitten has it made *inside* the house. Bigger than his sisters, he enjoys being on the top of the kitten pecking order. But before he is even a year old, the outside world comes drops on him with a vengeance. If there is a real tom in the neighborhood, and, believe me, there *always* is, he will be bullied day and night.

are all young toms buggered?

You read about novices testing their strength by challenging their seniors. *Gallantry.* You know, *males like that sort of thing.* But, hold on. That is only *after* years of what can only be called *torture*; it is only after enough testosterone kicks in to help normally meek males forget themselves in their rut. Unfortunately, toms do not wait to be challenged. They keep a careful note on every young cat in their neighborhood. If it is female, they treat her kindly and check off the days in their calendar as they wait for her to come into heat. If male, they do their damnedest to terrify him and drive him from the neighborhood every time his human benefactor is absent. For months, I could not leave for ten minutes without returning to find little Han-chan up a tree (I'd guess ten times more cats are treed by other cats than by dogs, and they must climb higher!).

The ethologist may call this "territoriality." For Han-chan, it was torture. Ninety percent of his time outdoors was spent in sheer terror. The same could be said for young human males living in many parts of the world. I recall the return from school as akin to running a gauntlet. But we are usually bullied by our own age cohort, or slightly more mature boys, rather than adults, and few of us disappear. Young toms literally vanish. I've lost two during this trying period and still have no idea if they were chased so far they got lost, caught in a tree somewhere, rescued by someone and taken in, or killed by a grown Tom or a dog.

Some young toms adjust to it better than Han-chan. Gutsy and confident in their running and climbing ability, they turned it into a catch-me-if-you-can type of game. But even they had to endure an apprenticeship in the ways of sex. The first time I witnessed it, I thought *"Wow, a gay cat! Do we have proof here of a biological imperative!"* Later, I found it is part of the game. *All* young toms are trod. It would seem to be a natural stage in male development.

Researchers call it "riding up." Cats are not so perverted (perpetually horny) as dogs. They do not grab your leg. But all young male cats I've observed – as a writer I am home alot – were sexually molested by older males. I am not certain if their loud protests were only from the indignity of being grabbed by the scruff of the neck, held fast and trod, or if they actually suffered painful anal penetration, but it was definitely not encouraged by the victims.

As this type of thing also occurs between different generations of related cats, where there is no intention of frightening away the other, it is not only bullying – "assertion of dominance" fails to reflect the pain involved – but may serve as a form of sex education where the young male learns how to do it right by having it done to him! That is, hetero- and homo-elements of sex would seem to come together in a cat's adolescence. The only question is whether having to suffer through such a role is more merciful than what happens to young toms trying to hone one's skills on females and being mauled for one's inadequacies.

*Do those whiskers
make love to whiskers?
Cats in heat.*

*Two w/ whiskers
make love: Catamites?
Nope. Just cats!*

One of these two takes on a vaguely recalled haiku or senryû adds what was only insinuated in the original but human cultures as divergent as those of ancient Greece, Mexico, the New Guinean highlands and, possibly, Japan, had boys cater to the sexual needs of their elders as part of normal growing up. I am tempted to call it *the way of the cat*, but since young cats can not be verbally persuaded that the act they are being asked to accept is for their own good, they have a harder time of it than their culturally malleable human counterparts, who, it would seem, take it in stride.

unforgiving pussies

A young tom rarely learns well enough. During his first efforts at mounting he tends to grab the neck too far off-center and adjust his grip too abruptly – unlike old toms, who slowly adjust yet maintain their grip as carefully as bulldogs – and, even miss the mark entirely and grab an ear. All of this does not endear a young tom to the females, who are not as helpful as older women can be to young men. Rather than meowing "Let me teach you, sonny," they give him a hiss and . . . their claws. Since the young males did not dare give Big Tom *their* claws, they do not imagine the party on the bottom can be so dangerous. They are genuinely shocked. They panic and run, only to be called back again and again by the caterwauling in the air and the drumbeat of testosterone in their blood. Watching them grow sadder but wiser in the ways of love is piteous but very entertaining. If we were not so uptight about sex, we would surely be watching it on funny video shows (in parts of Europe perhaps they do) and, believe me, though you may feel sorry for the young toms, you will laugh until you cry.

At least, they have all their teeth. Some old toms know how but still cannot. I've never actually seen it, but a veterinarian in Japan says that gum alone cannot purchase a secure grip on the queen's neck, so old geezers without teeth get their faces shredded before they get the job done. It is, he explains, a way to prevent unfit genes from being propagated; if you do not worry about the gene pool, dental work is the perfect present for your active old tom!

Even when a young tom gets the grip down pat, he may spend an hour trying to get into the right hole – which he may not rightly know – without success. This is not only because he has to find it without looking and might confuse the anus for the real thing because old Tom might have taken him there, but because it takes a lot of finesse to properly kick-start a Queen. She is willing to be done to, but not willing to help. So the final setting must be carefully orchestrated by the male to keep her in the mood.

"Kick-start" is *my* term, for I have yet to see it properly noted in a cat book. A tom can not just rub a queen over the base of the tail as we do to get a comical rise out of cats of either sex. His hind-leg must scrap down her thigh. While the neck-grip keeps her put, this "kick-start" is what makes the ultimate docking possible. It is so tricky that even as the action recalls a motorbike, the lower success rate makes a child attempting to start an outboard engine the better metaphor for a young tom's efforts.

And, on top of all of this, most of a young tom's sex is attempted when the females are usually not quite ready, as the big toms monopolize the heart of her heat.

little miss popularity

Now, for lament of the little queen, or princess. Young females are perplexed and frightened when strange males suddenly seek them out. At first, they think they are under attack; but soon learn to appreciate the attention, and go sallying out to troll for their favorites.

I could do little to help my young males other than chase off my least favorite toms to let young tom get a turn and, once – this is gross! – pull out a wad of hair plugging up the urethra of a very horny but unaccomplished young Mikan! This tangerine-colored tabby – later to boast chimpanzee-sized balls – had missed his target and dry-humped the queen's back! But, you *can* help the females. You can give them a safe haven. After they give that high pitched scream of climax – pain from the prick's tiny barbs according to some – they want to be left in peace for a while. That is when they will appreciate your chasing off any toms who try to follow as they run inside, plop down on their back, wave their paws in the air and squirm about, in as clear an expression of ecstasy as you will ever see – *Hypothesis: Could cat ejaculation have opium or some other feel-good chemical in it to make the female do this, for such behavior would help the ejaculation get through the cervix!* – then, after fifteen or thirty minutes, when her high is replaced by her heat, you must let her go out to be tailed again.

Toms take years to learn how to be good lovers, but females are into the swing of things by the time they finish their first heat. The next time around, they are as good as their mothers, while their brothers are still working at it.

learning to mother

The real challenge for the young queen is not sex, but motherhood. If her brother must learn to grab necks right, so must she! Her brother grips wrong, he gets scratched. She grips wrong, her baby dies – I exaggerate, or young mothers would lose all their babies in days, but the problem is real. Kittens must be moved for cleanliness (to keep ahead of the parasites), confuse humans or thinking of culling the litter and throw off murderous toms and hungry snakes. Yet, some young mothers have a hell of a time catching on. Mothering requires so many skills!

子を喰猫も見よ／＼けしの花　一茶
ko o kurau neko mo miyomiyo keshinohana

look at the cats	*poppy flowers*
that eat their little ones:	*look you kitten-eating*
poppy flowers	*cat of mine!*

Chewing off the umbilical cords right seems to be genetically programmed, but sleeping right takes practice. Young mothers can squash their babies. That, combined with the smell of blood on the umbilical chord can lead to cannibalism. Once, I heard a cranium crunch in the night. A squashed kitten's calcium was being recycled. Sumner's classic *Folkways* (1906) mentions cultures where dead infants or one of a pair of twins are similarly eaten by the mother. Issa must have witnessed the same, or the murder of kittens by an outsider Tom (which we will come back to soon) though I do not know how often they are eaten.

For nursing, mothers really have no choice. Get sucked or pop! Only a starving mother would hold back. But, without Han-chan's help, Kori's kittens probably would not have had their waste removed as often as it should be (no lick, no poop). And, there are finer matters where experience or lack thereof come into play. Two notes (written in terse poetic Japanese) from my 1991 diary:

mother
has a tail!
first discovery

bite it
and it moves!
second discovery

felix ludens

aroused by her kittens
mother kori comes into play-heat
too strong, she attacks the covers!

At first, the new mother is exhausted. But about the time the kittens begin to play, she finds her second wind. Not only does she enjoy responding to their play, but she provokes them to do so using her tail. In the end, she becomes so excited herself that she sometimes has to take a break from her play with them to expend her pent up excess energy on the bed cover by pulling it toward her with her foreclaws and ferociously kicking it with her hind-legs. (So, could we say human mothers tend to gain weight because our babies do not rough-house enough?)

A cat can get so worked up playing that they are dangerous. More than once, I had to whack Kori for losing control over herself and threatening the lives of her kittens! I would have liked to see if her mother would have done the same thing I did – as cat mothers and daughters tend to assist each other with domestic duties – but unfortunately, she was not around.

the tom's burden

The queen's "plight" is to spend her entire adult life full of babies, milk or both. If she is properly fed and sheltered, it is not a bad life at all. It is a life full of love and play. If she is uncared for and has to go begging and stealing to make ends meet, it is a life of servitude, a slave to her kittens and her genes. Issa's *ku* bear witness to her travail:

> *Used by her kittens,*
> *The mother cat is all*
> *but exhausted.*

haha-neko ga ko ni tsukawarete tsukarekeri

> *A female cat,*
> *Stealing for her children –*
> *Flee, mom, flee!*

onna neko ko yue no nusumi toku nigeyo

> *Let her steal it!*
> *She's crossed the rubicon*
> *for her kittens.*

nusumaseyo neko mo ko yue no dekigokoro

The male's burden is equally heavy, but less rewarding. It does not *have* to be rewarding; males are expendable. So they spend their lives cruelly driven by their twin-pack batteries to roam where they are not wanted. They go into rut as surely as the female goes into heat, but must be far more heroic to satisfy it.

ukare-kite tori oi-makuru o[男] neko kana

> *Still in a rut,*
> *chasing around the hens,*
> *a male cat.*

One could write a whole book on the escapades of a single battle-scared old tom. Issa has four-score or more haiku about male and female cats in heat. Some prefer to stick to the stove and others get going and never seem to stop. The above might be a frustrated young tom or an older tom so excited he is out of control. As there are many men who enjoy war, there are many toms who love hanging out with their fellows in rut, competing by claw and by song for turns with the queen of the neighborhood. Doubtless, some are crying from sheer terror, but most at the eye-wall of the "hairy hurricane" (Shepherd in Prof. Wilson's *Noctes Ambrosiane*) sweeping over the eaves are probably sky-high, fearing absolutely nothing.

Toms on the road average twenty two sprays per hour (Liberg 81 in Karsh & Turner ed. *The Domestic Cat:* 1988). Even a house-trained cat can not hold his spray for more than ten minutes. I remember the extremely conscientious Han-chan's rear-end starting to twitch before he was aware of it. I'd toss him out the window and whatever he landed by would be instantly sprayed and stink to high heaven.

It is, I think, worse than skunk. Hence, all toms are loners. No human with a nose could bear to have one around! I let Han-chan sow a few oats for the experience, but he hated conflict and wanted to stay at home, so I had him altered.

desexing as natural

I was relieved to find Han-chan *delighted* to be rid of the burden. Within days of the operation, and despite more bleeding than I have ever seen after such a cruel cut – and, believe it or not, a wet dream on the day after he came home! – he was as playful as he had been two years earlier, *i.e.*, like a one year-old. The pussies were less well served by *their* operations. The agony and the ecstasy of sex itself cancel each other out; but child-bearing is a different matter: for all of its rigors, most of my cats seemed happiest while taking care of their kittens. Without that responsibility and loving hormones, they seem worse off.

At first thought, this business of de-sexing animals seems unnatural and, unless you have known a cat like Han-chan, cruel. But on second thought, one finds a certain rightness in it quite apart from the pragmatic and ecological problems caused by an abundance of pets. Natural cats are not such slaves of their gonads as domesticated ones. As Michael Fox points out,

> The wild cat, like the wolf, has only one breeding season and males produce sperm only during the season; domestic toms are constantly

potent and female cats have two or more heats
per year (*The Soul of the Wolf* 1980).

Breeding favors perpetual breeders because without the natural territorial (food and space) limits, frequent sex and birth improve the chances of surviving offspring. In other words, we did not deliberately create sex maniacs in our own image but by creating circumstances in some ways perhaps like what created us, ended up with the same. Or, perhaps, I credit us with too much. Is it not possible that reproductive excess drove the dog and cat into the human camp for help . . . Now, if humans breeding themselves into oblivion could only get some help from extraterrestrials . . .

Whatever the cause of our pets being oversexed, the fact they are is significant for we can argue that de-sexing domestic cats liberates them to enjoy the same freedom from desire that, wild cats experience for most of their lives. Fox notes that the wolf bears no resemblance to his dangerous libido-driven metaphorical counterpart:

> Wolves can enjoy mutual love and affiliation without year-round conflicts over and desire for sex. (Ibid.)

Well, Han-chan showed me that so can cats, or some cats, if they are desexed.

an appeal to vets of the world

We live in a world that is not only authoritarian but doubly repressed. Many if not most cats in the world board with people who are not allowed to keep pets.

> "In America, cats make criminals of decent folk. Me for instance. For my rented house, I signed a lease ..... . Countless once loved cats are gassed in the shelters because of landlords. Countless lonely, law-abiding citizens live without companions because of them. Convalescents, the depressed and the elderly . . . . Even more mysterious is why we, alone of the world's peoples, put up with it."(*Secrets of the Cat*)

Barbara Holland's last line is naive. The situation is far *worse* in Japan, where there is a higher percentage of renters and conditions more favorable to the landlord. There, *most* cats, like mine, lived in the shadows. There, where responsibility is usually all-or-nothing (as opposed to Americans doing *what they can* and hoping for the best), these apparently ownerless *han-nora* (half-alleycat) are generally treated very coldly by all who do not know them and many who do. It is not because they are cruel. People in Japan withhold affection and food for fear kindness will bring kittens, loud sex at night, odor and the censure of the neighborhood. Altering the cats *should* change this, but poor neighborhood communication and the inability to discriminate one cat from another means an operation is not enough. People need to be taught that cats no longer enslaved to their gonads are less aggressive and need protection from the sexually driven cats that pass through the neighborhood. With time on their paws, these cats also crave for attention. They need not only help with food but *to be played with* rather than ignored.

One day after a night of caterwauling, maybe a hundred yards from my place, a middle-aged Japanese man with sleepy bags under glaring eyes suddenly appeared at my window shouting that "my" cats kept him awake. After he finally ran out of wind, I pointed out that all *my* cat "friends" were neutered, so maybe he should get to know *"his"* cats, the one's nearer to his house and do the same to them. I wanted to add that *"my cats were right here sleeping with me and scared shitless because of the noise"* but that would have gotten me kicked out (shades of an old ballad, *The Long Black Veil*) for he was related to the landlord. What know-nothing cat-haters forget is that unless *they* are willing to eradicate all the cats for miles around, every square inch of turf will be contested by the local toms *forever*. Want quiet? Do not create a vacuum by doing away with feral cats but keep the neighborhood full of altered cats and help them guard it from encroachment.

As a well-known nonfiction writer who had a chapter in a book comparing Japanese and Occidental relationships with animals, I was once asked to address a convention of veterinarians about living responsibly with pets and semi-feral animals. I started with a demonstration of my pea-shooter (hitting a thin fry-pan hung on the side of the hall) to catch everyone's attention before describing how I got even cats to behave, but my biggest contribution – my purpose for being there – was to suggest that the veterinarians work to pass laws permitting only altered cats the right to wear yellow collars, in order that even people who do not take the trouble to learn who's who in the cat-neighborhood would give these cats the benefit of the doubt and the additional love they need and deserve.

do toms kill kittens?

I cannot recall if they were Kori's or Me-chan's kittens. I do remember doing my damnedest to chase off ugly toms and welcome good-looking ones, for I hoped to find homes for all the kittens I didn't kill, and most kittens born to *han-nora* (half-alley=wild) cats in Japan had short deformed tails and nondescript markings. The fathers included a rare puma-colored cat, and what seemed a cross between a Burmese and a Maine-coon. The result was magical. A puma-colored kitten with longhair – could two of the fathers' sperm have merged? Even longer hair, grey with black tips yet with a touch of tabby design and blue eyes. All in all, three of the four kittens I let live were more beautiful than any I had ever seen.

Then, the dream turned into a nightmare. The closest tom in the neighborhood, slaughtered all but Papyrus, the plainest but quickest cat of the litter (who was found hiding in a hole in my notes) – my housemate got there before me and saw the tom jump out the window. That ugly blotched orange and white tabby tom, who made Han-chan's life miserable, tried to live on my verandah, and was discouraged from mating with my cats, had finally gotten revenge for being shut out. Pliny mentioned such things, but I never dreamed I'd experience them.

Desmond Morris claims the event is "extremely rare" and the killing unintentional. He writes that a false heat on the part of the female sets off the tom, who, rebuffed by the female, attempts to mount and thereby accidentally suffocates the kittens with a "perfectly normal neck-bite." I appreciate his effort to correct the "bad reputation" of the tom as "a sex maniac whose only interest in kittens is to kill then if he can get half a chance" and put the queen back into heat, but only new-born kittens suffocate that easily (mine were already scampering around) and think he is wrong to turn the phenomenon into an anomaly rather than a genetic strategy on the basis of the facts that 1) male European wildcats have been seen participating in rearing the young in zoos, 2) males "should not want to eliminate their own genetic progeny," and 3) "in the wild, ... the chances of a tomcat coming across a female with a litter in her den with her kittens is remote."

In response to 1), and 2, toms could help queens they are closely related to, or mated with, and their kittens while still killing those unlikely to be related or progeny; and, as I have already written, it is debatable whether house-cats come from stock so solitary and tiger-like to make the chance of an encounter "remote."

killing kittens

> "I was six when I first saw kittens drown.
> Dan Taggart pitched them, 'the scraggy wee shits',
> Into a bucket; a frail metal sound,
>
> Soft paws scraping like mad. But their tiny din
> Was soon soused. They were slung on the snout
> Of the pump and the water pumped in. . . .
>
> from Seanus Heany "The Early Purges"

Even if "pests have to be kept down" on "well-run farms," a boy callous enough to call kittens "scraggy wee shits" makes me wince, but killing kittens itself is no big thing compared to what happens when you do *not* kill them. *Then, I am sometimes told, you should not let the mothers have kittens in the first place!* No, that won't do, for two reasons. *First*, all female cats allowed to live should get to experience motherhood at least once. The welfare of the adult cat – a sensitive, conscientious, caring life – far overrides the mere potential of a new-born kitten. If we really believed all creatures had an equal "right to life," we could not kill a mosquito. In our hearts, we all *know* that life for life, more highly developed (i.e. more sensitive and conscious) life is worth far more than the more prolific lower forms. This is not only true evolution-wise, but development-wise. It is why killing a fetus is not murder while killing a doctor for killing a fetus is murder. And, *second*, it is unnatural to let all kittens live. *Someone* or *thing* has to cull the litter. If we do not let Mother Nature do it, the responsibility is ours. Had we not, we would not have so such sweet and beautiful pets. It sounds dreadful, but killing a kitten can improve the future of the world. As Shakespeare wrote (in quite a different context):

> "Let those whom Nature hath not made for store –
> Harsh, featureless, and rude – barrenly perish."

My main concern was killing them as painlessly as possible, while minimizing the mother's trauma by keeping my role secret from her. Planning it and carrying it out felt like committing a crime. I will not detail methods used here. Although I talk up a good argument, no kitten is a "wee shit" to me, and writing about it is painful. I just wish our veterinarians would be of help, rather than giving that crap about how their job is to save rather than take life, or telling you to bring them in to be properly put-down, where the separation from their mother would be torture, or holding out for the slight chance someone might adopt them, while some other cat the same person might have adopted, one older and more deserving of care, is killed.

envoi

Mama cat, the first cat I took in, once left a litter out in the rain to die. I brought in the kittens and put them with her in a cardboard box. They were gone in the morning and still missing when I returned from work. Two weeks later, there was this stench . . . . .she had killed them or let them die and left them in a closet! I believe it was just too soon after her last litter was born and she preferred to nurse her older kittens. I would like to think this natural proof of what might be called compassionate infanticide, such as bravely described in a book about a Brazilian practice of neglecting the baby for the benefit of the older children by Nancy Scheper-Hughes called *Death Without Weeping*.

But, I may be naive. Barbara Holland tells of a cat, who was a good mother, had finished house-breaking her kittens, and one fine day marched out with them in tow and came back alone an hour later. "She ate, she washed, she hunkered down with her paws tucked in and closed her eyes, ignoring the family's shouted questions." Or the cat "Me`ry tells of," who tired of successive litters when they were a week old and dropped the kittens "one by one through a balcony railing to their deaths on the tiles below." I am not sure what to make of her explanation, but it is *very* poetic:

> Any instinctive passion as awesomely strong as the cat's for her kittens may sometimes, from the unwieldiness of its sheer power, tip itself over the edge in a few individuals, and turn itself inside out from love to murder. (Ibid.)

cat tails

Issa's Cannibal Cat-ku. The poppies in the *ku* are a common trope for the little boys sent off to the mountain temples, where many caught cold and died as easily as the poppy petals are blown in the wind (*wind=kaze* being a homophone with *a cold* and *poppies=keshi* with *vanish* in Japanese).

Homosexual Cultures. There is not *one* type. The most noted is a New Guinean culture where all boys pass through a period of growth where they regularly give the adult men oral sex, considered fortifying for the boys who imbibe the substance. Needless to say, these boys grow up to be normal adults and fathers. The more broad-spread largely sodomic Latin-type/s is not justified as good for boys but, rather denigrates the done as effeminate and celebrates the doer as masculine. That over-simplifies the diverse cultural practices of what Burton called the Sodomic Zone, a large waist-band of the world (including the so-called Middle East) but, to return to the subject, the homosexual practices of cats shares one aspect of the New Guinean model, as it is part of the normal process of development, and one of the Latin type, as weak young males are bullied by macho elders. I write this only to make clear that animal (including human) life is far more complex than most people think.

Marking De-sexed Cats.   Collars are said to be dangerous for outdoor cats, but many housecats who spend much time out have them. I do not know. I do know that cutting the tip off one ear is ugly. If ear-tips are cut, *both* tips should be cut.

what japanese call "what's michaeling!"
Do Cats Save Face?

what's michael-ing?

Comic books are big business in Japan. Not thin like ours, but thick as real books, they fill up half of your average Japanese bookstore. Adults read them. The top-selling comic by an individual author (as opposed to the cartoon magazines that are the top-selling print media in Japan – over ten-million circulation for *SHONEN JUMP*) in 1985 starred a tangerine tabby named Michael.

Traditional Japanese names for cats (and dogs) are limited. Tama, meaning "gem," for females (When the name is given to a mis-sexed kitten, his *balls* become laughable), Mikan, or "tangerine", for orange- colored tabbies, Kuro, or "black," Danshaku, or "Baron" for a commanding Persian or tuxedo-cat, etc.. If you would give an individual name to your pet, that is, give it a nominal personality without going so far to grant it the full human status implied by a native name, a foreign one will do. If any cat needs a clear-cut character, it is the star of a comic book. So, "Michael."

More remarkably, the book's title, *What's Michael!*, made it big time in the highly competitive world of slang. You might overhear one OL (<u>o</u>ffice <u>l</u>ady, or female white-collar worker) laugh and tell another, "Now don't you try to '*wahtsu-maikeru!*' me!" Or, you might see a white-collar worker whisper that someone else was a good one for "*wahtsu maikeru-ing!*" Or, perhaps more commonly, you would not hear anything, but just observe someone nodding in someone else's direction and then making *a few gestures* with his or her arms to indicate the same!

Can you guess what they might be talking about?

<u>*Do* guess *before* turning the page!</u>

hint: a little pirouette

He extricates himself from the most difficult situations by a little pirouette.   Jules Henri Poincare (*Puss In Boots*)

Any cat who misses a mouse pretends it was aiming for a dead leaf.   Charlotte Gray (in Exley: *Cat Quotations*)

One reason we admire cats is for their proficiency in one-upmanship. They always seem to come out on top, no matter what they are doing – or pretend to do.   Barbara Webster (*"Creatures and Contentments"* in *Ibid*)

yugao-no hana kamu neko ya yosogokoro buson

the cat bites a morning glory, thinking of something else	out of frustration the cat bites a flower morning glory

the cat bites
a morning glory, taking out
its frustration

harusame ya neko ni odori o oshieru ko   issa

spring rain a little girl teaches a cat to dance	spring rain children are teaching a cat to dance

Issa's *ku* has nothing to do with the behavior in question, though it does connect with the cartoons in another way.

"What's Michael!" ? – the answer!

The quotations and haiku above pretty much give the game away, but it is still worth looking at the drawings that caught the imagination of a nation!

Note, the dance depicted by Kobayashi Makoto is traditional Japanese folk-dance which has a delicacy well-suited to a cat. Hokusai, the greatest graphics designer the world has ever known and Kuniyoshi, who loved cats, depicted them dancing centuries ago, but this modern cartoonist found a convincing context for it! The cartoon reads right-to-left. Three rows deleted for space show the slow transition from missed grab to "I was just dancing."

koshka again!

What's Michaeling is a very complex array of behavior and we would do well to begin a serious discussion with Vicki Hearne whose "clumsy" cat Koshka has just caught her playing with a couple kittens in *his* house. First, he leaps in and physically tried to break up the play all the while "screaming hoarsely that it wasn't RIGHT." Vicki Hearne appreciated his point, but could not allow the behavior, so:

> I batted him in the nose and told him to mind his manners, but Koshka said shrilly that they weren't minding *their* manners, were they? Other more graceful cats would at this point have taken to washing their paws perhaps, or have developed a sudden interest in a squirrel outside of the window while they worked things out. Koshka retreated to the end of the couch and looking depressed and forlorn, alternately meowing and purring at me in a loud and unseemly way. [a paragraph passes, as Koshka goes here and there] .... until he finally managed to be hunting an invisible fly that was buzzing near me and the kittens. Leaping for the fly, he suddenly "noticed" the kittens and began playing with them. This is not a remarkable cat story, of course. (*Adam's Task*)

It *is* a typical affair. *Felidae domesticus*, the species, is what is remarkable; but Hearne's observation is, as far as I know, unique in two ways. First, it is exceptionally complex: rather than directly admitting he was wrong and should have been nice to the kittens in the first place, Koshka would make it look like (or convince himself that?) he was accidentally making their acquaintance! A run-of-the-mill plot – all most of us are capable of noticing – might have the cat about to take a swipe at the head of a rambunctious kitten, then, noticing he was watched, stop in mid-swing and lick his paw, or smoothly redirect it to land elsewhere. And, second, the cat seeks to edit a social faux pas. We are far more used to the physical boo-boo where the cat misses something it intends to catch, or miscalculates the stability of what it jumps on and, embarrassed to be seen slipping up – "when reality punctures their dignity" (Paglia) – the cat pretends it was intending to do something else by doing it. As we have all seen our cats do everything but dance to escape from an ignoble predicament, everyone cat owner in Japan immediately knew the cartoonist was one of them.

what's Michaeling as cussing?

An ethologist might explain away much of *What's Michael?* behavior in the same way playing with prey is explained away as an automatic overflow, or displacement of, nervous energy; I recall reading such an explanation for the most common *What's Michael?* of them all, when a cat misses a prey and immediately takes a whack at the nearest substitute. Indeed, Michael's creator, Kobayashi Makoto, has him bat about a pebble after missing a mouse, before discovering that he really wanted to dance when he notices he has been observed missing that bird.

The violent "overflow" – the biting of the morning glory or the batting of the pebble – could be translated into everyday language as follows: *the cat is cussing with its paws.* I use such words with purpose, for they help us to realize that if the cat is an automon, then, by god, aren't we all!

But, many of the cat's coverups are not at all violent. Some seem almost aesthetic as they pivot a misstep into a proper sequence. The dancing is, in that sense, an accurate metaphor. Moreover, as Han-chan will show us in the next section, the amount of physical energy expended can be miniscule, hardly enough to displace any energy, while the cat is need not be worked up at all.

a cover up? let's test it!

The other day, Han-chan initiated a handshake, as he sometimes does to get attention. I started to reach out in return, then something happened. I cannot remember if I reached out the wrong hand (we always shake right with right and left with left.), or the teapot called [me away]. Whatever, I withdrew my hand right when Han-chan's lifted his up. With hardly a blink, he began licking it. Come to think of it, it is the

> *same thing he occasionally does when responding to my initiation of a handshake with the wrong paw, which I refuse to take.*

There is no question that cats erase their mistakes. It sure looks like they are trying to save appearances. But, is it possible it just *looks* that way because their behavior streams along so seamlessly that the breaks are automatically covered up? There is no need to press the point. This is something that can to be tested. Cats divided into three groups – one where they are tested singly, another where they are with a sibling or cat-friend, and another where they are with their master – could be put into situations rigged to make them slip-up in one way or another, while provided with ample means to *What's Michael*.

If the cats prove more fastidious at covering up when they know they are being observed, we shall know once and for all that they take their image seriously. If, on the other hand, no difference is observed, it will not prove the energy overflow explanation is correct, either. All cats are athletes and all athletes are perfectionists when it comes to motor movements, so they may be faking out *themselves*, attending to their own peace of mind. You might say they are making their misses *retrospectively right* in the same way a musician will turn what would have been a miss into harmony more interesting for being improvised, rather than stopping for corrections, which would ruin everything, and will do this whether or not there is an audience.

<u>a hypothesis: associative movement</u>

Or, *What's Michaeling* may be not be art, which beautiful or not is something "made" by definition, but the natural product of the thought process of a cat's mind.

> *Today (the very day after I wrote all of the chapter but this paragraph), I played a game of grab-it-if-you-can with Han-chan. After a few incisive grabs that succeeded in snaring the piece of fur on a string (which he then licks and bites), he connected with air. At that time, he was on his back on the futon, and the miss left him with his arm over his head. So what did he*

> *do? He stretched his arm out yet further, and yawned as if that were the only reason he had his arm over his head in the first place. (my notebooks)*

Since missing was not uncommon in our games, and no other cat was watching, Han-chan had no particular reason to be embarrassed. Besides, I sometimes stuck my finger in his mouth when he yawned – something Japanese do to teach children to cover their mouths – or mimicked him, simply because I liked to kid him, so this particular action was probably not a conscious "cover-up." Not plotted at all.

Could it not be something like the chain of associations instantaneously born in our dreams where physically discontinuous action may be tied together by a common mood, or the inverse, where unrelated moods are strung together by seamless action, and words pivot from one context into another as they do in Japanese poetry by pun?

In other words, the cat may be a somnambulist – though less a sleep-walker than a walking-dreamer – a creature to whom life is indeed "nothing but a dream." And if you are in a dream, you are all there, which is to say, in the present. If you are present-minded, or living in the now, would it not make perfect sense to constantly renew the meaning of your movement so that no mistakes would be possible? Or, could the continuous flow of association be seen as never-ending rationalization expressed in action rather than words? Thanks to cats, I find myself suddenly wondering if the mark of human waking thought – as opposed to dreaming thought – is not so much its being logical as its being discrete, *i.e.,* stopping and starting.

<u>saving *whose* face?</u>

When Hearne proceeds to hypothesize what happened to change Koshka's "clumsily expressed aggravation into graciousness" so quickly, her remarkable story grows even more remarkable. For she does not attribute it to Koshka saving Koshka's face, but to "that typically feline interest in and focus on my pleasure, which is to say, on my interests."

Cats may be obstinate when it comes to performing for performance sake, but when it comes to real life, *they aim to please*. As explained elsewhere, I strongly agree. And this, Hearne further suggests, they will work out in a manner that leaves their dignity intact. Like Koshka, if they have to, they will do the right thing, "accidentally." *What's Michaeling,* then, applied to the limited case of social faux pas, is how they save their face *and* yours. Or, I think I would prefer to put it like this: wishing to please us, they are forced to act in ways that they do not want to, and never wanting to admit to being forced to do something, they pretend it was their idea from the start.

a paradox of saving face

> A cat lives mainly by its instincts. If it makes a mistake in judgment, it remains dignified and never looks like a fool. Leonard Michaels (*A Cat*)

The only problem with the saving-face theory is that nothing gets a cat more laughs than when it is caught in a cover-up. Missing a prey does not necessarily make a cat look like a fool, but biting a morning glory does. (And can anyone explain to me what living by "instincts" has to do with remaining dignified?)

no one likes being laughed at

George Romanes found his terrier "evidently much annoyed" when ridiculed for missing a fly. "To see what he would do," Romanes "purposely laughed immoderately every time he failed." After a series of failures,

> He became so distressed he positively pretended to catch the fly, going through all the appropriate actions with his lips and tongue, and afterwards rubbing the ground with his neck as if to kill the victim: he then looked up at me with a triumphant air of success" (*Animal Intelligence*, in Jeffrey Moussaieff Masson: *Dogs Never Lie*)

Masson wonders whether "Romanes may be transferring some of his own deviousness onto the dog" but agrees "the dog's behavior, if the report is accurate, displays a remarkably sophisticated awareness of human thought processes and emotions. Romanes was humiliating the dog and the dog did not wish to be humiliated."

Romanes was lucky he didn't try that on the wrong dog. Dogs may be toad-eaters compared to cats, but they are not without pride. Most dislike being laughed at every bit as much as cats do. Many growl, and some actually bite for being made fun of. So it is not surprising to find dogs covering up to save their face.

No fancy experiment is needed to prove it. Millions of dog owners have seen their dog fetch the wrong stick when they either couldn't find the correct one or found it difficult to reach. As in the case with cats, this could be interpreted as saving the dog's face, the owner's or both.

The biggest difference between the cat and the dog would seem to be in the method of the cover-up. I can not remember seeing a dog switch meaning in mid-activity or a cat pretend to save the meaning of a failed activity as the dog described by Romanes. So which is more false? Which more clever? Which more entertaining? Which more endearing?

cat tails

Let's Michaeling in Issa? We saw a clear case of Let's Michaeling in the haiku by Buson. Issa, who wrote two generations after Buson, might have another (*tanpopo no atama hari-tsutsu neko no koi issa*) :

the loves of cats
lead to fisti-cuffs: hair flies
like dandelion

my cat in heat
makes dandelion heads fly
between bouts

whacking off
the heads of dandelions
cats make love

Issa may be thinking about the expression of frustration, a temporal coincidence or speaks in metaphor but I believe my last translation the most likely, for one of his better-known *ku* speaks to the violence of the loving cats' leave-taking 猫の恋打功=切=棒に別れ　けり *neko no koi bukkirabô ni wakare-keri* 文化9年十月.

Hearne's Koshka story. The quote is a bit long to do without permission but I hope the author's estate and publisher will appreciate the publicity value. I think Hearne's chapter on the cat in *Adam's Task* is so well written that it deserves to be included with *best essay* collections and hope continued exposure will get it there if it is not already and keep her writing alive.

Psychological vs. Darwinian. My mother sent me a copy of Jeffrey M. Masson's *Altruistic Armadillos, Zenlike Zebras* as I was wrapping up this book. In "About the Author" I saw a title I wish I had read, *The Nine Emotional Lives of Cats* and, thanks to Google Books, was able to read some on-line, including:

> "I have seen cats pretending not to be mortified when they are. When you scold a cat, she has a tendency to begin washing herself, paying zero attention, quite on purpose. If she leaps and misses a ledge, for example, she also starts to wash herself, as if it were of no consequence."

Masson was judging from a tiny sample of cats, or he might have realized pretending to wash is but one way cats pretend away things, but what a fine word: "mortified" is! And, it is true that the cat does not always pretend by morphing one movement into another but more simply acts like nothing happened. Continuing,

> Humans, when they fail, feel humiliated. . . . Is this the same feeling cats have? It is hard to say whether the need to maintain dignity is a form of self absorption or if the self absorption is merely a ploy to maintain dignity. The origin, though, at least in cats and possibly in humans, too, is an old survival mechanism: not to show another predator (us, in this case) that they are weak. This is less a feeling than a strategy.

One can sense the author-as-psychoanalyst in the "self-absorption" which puzzles me here. I think he means one must strut one's stuff and exude confidence to remain on top of the game, which would seem to be Darwinian, survival of the fittest. *However*, comparing (evolutionary) "strategy" and feelings is apples and oranges. To say it is *less* one than another is as wrong as it is common and is exactly what Vicki Hearne so eloquently challenged in *Adam's Task*.

Elsewhere, Masson mentions a friend's cat that, laughed at for missing a fly, examined her paws and left the room, because "cats do not like being laughed at" and "like elephants, great apes and dogs" interpret laughter as "hostile, not humorous." This is true and, I would argue, for more animals (such as our raccoon). It also fits into the larger saving-face strategy. Should we define a human as the only animal that can laugh at itself?

no relativity in aesthetics
the Beautiful Animal

*To respect the cat
is the beginning of the aesthetic sense.*

erasmus darwin

We inherited the cat from the Egyptians, but as we discuss elsewhere, mousing alone can not explain why *they* chose it. *That,* I believe, is simple: *because cats are beautiful.*

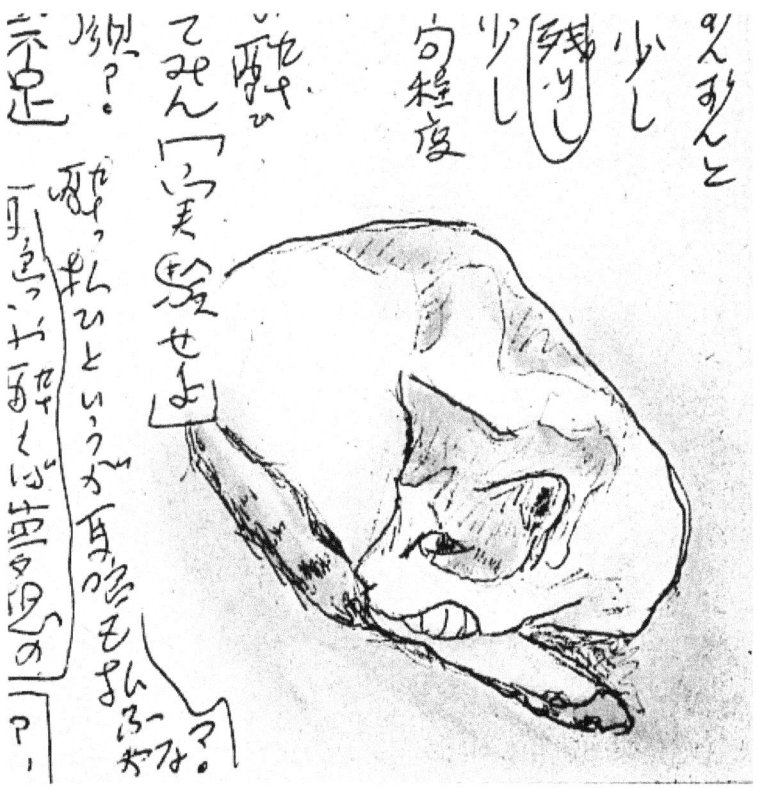

why beauty crosses species

The official line on animal beauty is this: *a toad is beautiful to a toad* and *a horse to a horse*. Interspecies comparisons are meaningless, if not prejudicial. Now, that may be true from a hypothetical objective point of view; but from *ours* it is false. Discrimination is only natural. All animals may be equally beautiful in the eyes of their Mother, Nature, but not in the eyes of her children, who are, in many cases, not even satisfied with themselves; and this is a good thing, unless you prefer life to devolve into mud and melt back into a primal soup because, without ideals – something desired that is far from average – a species' looks quickly crumble. No matter abnormally large males are hopelessly vulnerable to predation by birds, the female moth *wants* them for her mates! (Stanley Gooch has expressed this most beautifully I forget where). If she did not, her descendents would end up the size of gnats.

The ante-Darwinian belief that species, or races, sought to maintain their God-given types may contain a kernel of the truth; but that conservative truth is not without irony, for to hit a target, we must aim above it – or, in a wind, to one side or another. To aim at the mean is often to miss it. Ideals are not only needed to drive evolution forward, but simply to hold it in place. Without taste, which is to say abnormal or perverted desire, life backslides. Yet, idealism, by which I mean the literal pursuit of the ideal, consciously or not, is not without risk. The moth that goes for hunks of her own species cannot help seducing the larger males of a different variety.

And, the above is hardly the extreme case, we can find this idealism even goes so far as to favor artificial creatures: drawings with nothing but two large eyes preferred over mothers, man-created calls attracting more duck or deer than the real thing, . . .

None of this is new. I point it out merely to put the question – *what are the aesthetic qualities we like in ourselves that might explain our weakness for cats?* – that will be answered in this chapter within a natural frame.

the ape, the horse and the cat

First there is *poise*. That, writes Paglia in her brilliant masterpiece, *Sexual Personae*, is what attracted Egyptians to the cat. Compared to our *"hunkering, chattering, chest-beating, buttock-baring"* cousins, the apes, cats are sophistication itself, *"arbitrators of elegance"* (Ibid). Why, she claims, they even *"have a sense of pictorial composition: they station themselves symmetrically on chairs, rugs, even a sheet of paper on the floor."* I am unsure about this last point, for I have only seen such symmetrical positioning by a dog, a very proper – you could even call him square – male dalmation, but some cats do indeed *pose*, and that is 80% of poise.

I tried and tried and tried but have failed to catch Kōri-chan's seductive poses (according to Yoko, mind you, not me!). It is true. She crosses her legs (!) beautifully. Demurely. Sweetly. I can't draw that.

Moreover, Paglia writes, "the cat follows a code of ritual purity, cleaning itself religiously." I have a different theory for *why* cats keep so clean, but I will grant that when a cat *is* clean, it usually practices preventative hygiene, trying not to touch anything dirty; and that might help explain the symmetry Paglia saw and I have my doubts about: they center themselves on new or freshly cleaned things to avoid being polluted by whatever is old. But, let us skip these fine points: apes throw shit; horses drop it; dogs eat it and cats *bury* it. Which acts in the more attractive way, in a way a civilized human can identify with?

Yet, as Paglia brings to our attention, our paragon of Western civilization, the Greeks, *"did not care for cats."* They admired citizen horse, *"an athlete proud and serviceable"*, rather than this *"law unto itself,"* with *"its despotic air of Oriental luxury and..... indolence... too feminine for the male-loving Greeks."* The *"slinkiness"* which was appreciated by the aristocratic Egyptians with their own elegant costume turned off the broad-shouldered wrestlers of the Aegean.

Though I recognize the trope, I do not see luxury and indolence as oriental or female. And a female cat, especially when it has growing kittens will work themselves down to the bone...

why cats keep clean

A racoon will even wash a sugar cube – not good if you have put the medicine in it – before eating. And, worse yet, it will wash food in the tub of water it has defecated in. *Instinct*. Racoons *must* fish for crayfish before eating them. I knew an Indian woman who never felt like eating until she actually touched her food. Well, a raccoon must do more. It must play with it.

Such foreplay to work-up the appetite is understandable enough from a biological point of view, but why do cats invariably clean themselves directly *after* eating? (as shown in my "quick sketch(es) of an old cat after a good breakfast on the last page)

The behavioral explanation is far too general. We are told that since cats lie in wait for game rather than chase it down like a dog, a smelly cat would starve. This may be true, but after a cat licks itself it is more likely to fall asleep than go hunting. Then, again, it is a mark of fitness. While a dog can prove how tough he is by stinking to high heaven, a cat, by keeping exceptionally clean, may prove it is in good enough circumstances (by being well-kept or being a skillful hunter) to lick alot. But, from what I have seen of cat mating practices, this is hard to buy.

Cats themselves only know that they prefer smelling things to smelling like things. They would keep a clean olfactory slate. But, that is not what I think impressed the Egyptians about the cat's cleanliness. There is something that lifts it above a racoon's toilet and, for that matter, our own. Oddly enough, what I am about to reveal is overlooked by all who have written about cats – everyone I have read, at any rate – so please take careful note of this simple point. For once, I will italicize myself: *The cat who is loved makes an enormous effort to clean himself, to improve his looks, while the abandoned cat quickly turns into a pigpen, who only licks his chops and his behind.*

Unless you have an angel looking after your cat – someone who not only feeds the cat but plays with it, keeps its litter clean and sleeps over – when you are away, chances are that when you come back from a trip, you will find your cat looking horrible, and the cat will only work at cleaning him or herself up after you prove your love and are forgiven your absence. That is why Paglia, despite her fine eye for feline aesthetics, has it backwards when she writes, *"when it is dishevelled, its spirits fall."* That is why another who has written on cats, James Gorman (l.s.), is dead wrong to call a cat *"the ultimate narcissist,"* from *"the time they spend on personal grooming."*

Since licking and love go together in rearing kittens and good food triggers a lick-fest – not to miss a molecule of it! – there are abundant psycho-somatic grounds for developing a link between contentment and vigorous licking but, still, to see how far this link has come in a cat is to know that here, for once, cleanliness *is* next to godliness! The cat does not pretty up to snare the loved one, but because love makes him do so.

pretty is pretty, ugly is ugly

Paglia's aesthetic theory is fine as far as it goes – far indeed, for it gives the cat, a fusion of Apollian sleekness and Chothian slink, credit for being *the* "model for Egypt's unique synthesis of principles." Paglias attention to kinetic elements – the movement of a cat – appeal to me, for our culture largely ignores beauty in motion. We talk of a woman's *proportions*, whereas the Mende of Sierra Leon (West Africa) begin to train girls to *move* their buttocks from infancy. To them, a large rear without functioning independent suspension is a fraud (Sylvia Arden Boone: *Radiance from Still Waters*). Why, most Usanians – and Japanese, for that matter – cannot even differentiate between the comically reptilian sway of hips thrown from side to side and the beautiful bobbling up and down of *rumps* (one wonders if the Mende word for the rear is not only plural like our "buttocks" but more obviously – a plural-indicating conjugation of an accompanying verb?) that represents the ultimate development of mammalian locomotion!

Be that as it may, I have a feeling that even if cats were plump rather than sleek – and some are – and moved no more than adult oysters, they would still be loved by all for their pretty features.

Take apes, for example. They do not only act ugly; they *look* ugly. As Bacon wrote: "it addeth deformity to an ape to be so like man;" but even without this disadvantage, we would find their faces so grossly constructed as to be laughable, and their buttocks, especially the female's, with a running sore for a mons veneris – or should we call it a hypertrophic labia majora? – on its rear, utterly disgusting. Even cows, with their relatively bony butts have better looking privates! (One wonders if a pretty face preceeded and brought about a pretty vulva or vice versa!). Even if apes could be trusted around the house, a culture attentive to beauty would probably not want them around. And, if I am not mistaken, all cultures until ours have been by-and-large honest about our bias for beauty.

kind of beautiful?

The horse, does better. Its almond eye may be too heavy-set (eye-shadow rnight help), but it is recognizably beautiful. The body looks fine, at least from a distance, through the impressionistic lense of a cave artist. I can see how the chest, with its well-defined muscles would appeal to brute power-worshipping cultures. And I imagine that when odor was considered the deepest part of bodily beauty, even the horse's crude practice of shitting in motion could have worked to its advantage, for the fragrance proved that the horse's beauty was more than skin-deep. Up close, however, the parts appall. The nose like pollen magnified a million times, the gas-taut stomach and knobbed, sinewy legs are hopelessly ugly, and even the high courtesian rump admired by Monseiur Ponge is too hard to turn me on (though it might appeal to Usanian women who work out to gain "buns of steel"!). An equiline nose pleased the Greeks for whom sniffing food was more godlike than chewing it, and a nosebone flowing straight from the forehead was considered divine. Still, was it *ever* a compliment to look like a horse?

Dog physiogomy varies too much for a simple description; but *all* are crude products compared to cats. Proper breed features are betrayed by yucky rims remain about the eyes, cheap rubbery noses, lolling tongues and saliva slivering over gloppy gum. Petite dogs? Unlike cats of similar size, they shiver with anxiety, their eyes bulge. Neotony has not really completed its work. Sure, a large dog with droopy folds looks *personable* – but *beautiful?* Sure, softly twinkling eyes and glossy fur draw us to puppies. A teddy-bear is cute, too; but is it *beautiful?* We don't judge those we love, so our dog becomes beautiful in a *comforting* way, but that is not Beauty with a capital B.

Moreover, the dog's oafish appearance is underlined by its behavior. If cats, like Japanese (according to Miss Eliza Scidmore (1890), comprise *"a nation of poseurs,"* the dog is *a country of clowns*, or to use the words of R. L. Stevenson's rarely cited – I've yet to see a citation, at any rate – essay on "the character of dogs,"(*Memories and Portraits*) the dog is *"far more theatrical than the average man."* As a servant of the tyrant man, he is marked by "vain-glory" which men miss because it is not expressed in words. To know what dogs think, he recommends the autobiography of Hans Christian Andersen, *"thrilling from top to toe with an excruciating vanity, and scouting even along the street for shadows of offense."* Stevenson wonders whether currying favor is the true business of dogs, where their true joys may lie outside, or whether they have, *"like the majority of men . . . foregone their true existence and become the dupes of their ambition."* Whether they chose to ham it up or do so because they cannot help it – I incline to believe the latter – such a oafish existence is not conducive to beauty of expression.

Pic. Note how composed old Han-chan is. Head is a bit too large.

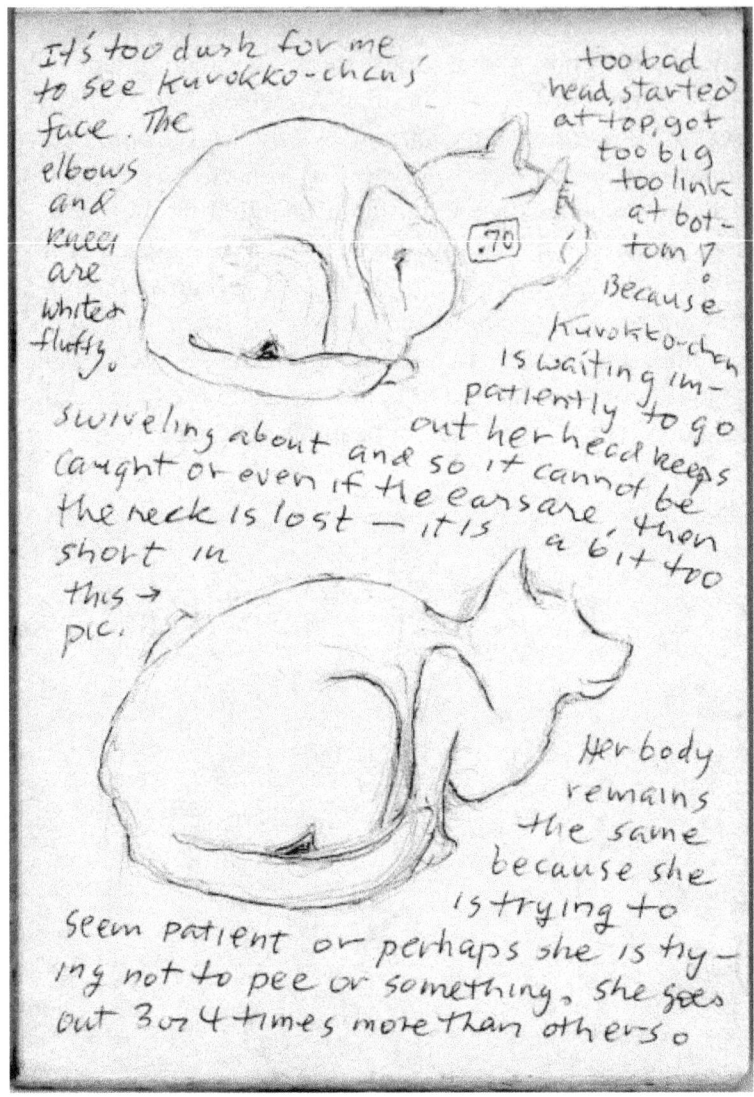

"the smallest feline is a masterpiece"

Even Leonardo da Vinci, who, true to classic tradition and his man-loving heart, was abnormally interested in musculature at the expense of softer and more beautiful forms, knew a masterpiece when he saw one. That was, I think, because he was into detail. He probably saw them less as "sculpture walking around the house" (Wanda Toscanini Horowitz) than as "living adornments" (Edwin Lent) whose "function is to sit and be admired" (Georgia Strickland Gates: last four quotes from l.s.).

Pardon a copy of a copy of a weed I once tossed upon a copier. As people and civilizations mature, we find not all beauty is animal, nor even cultivated. But we will stick to animal beauty in this book. Old English spoke of "parts" – a *wo/man of parts* was well endowed in three ways (body, mind & purse). In Japanese, likewise, we have *jôhin,* or *shina-ga ii*. Restricting ourselves further to our countenance, how do our "parts," then, compare to the cat's?

The nose. Even the finest of our hair-filled knobs are closer to dog snouts than the "tiny, cool, exquisite nose" (Leonard Michaels) of the cat. A blind sculptor can make a human nose, but a cat requires the detail work that goes into a violin bridge, which I have noticed, it resembles.

The whiskers. Look how neatly they are arranged in little rows, usually three clear ones sprouting the lion's share of the hairs. Surprisingly, some dogs boast rows, too, but they are less perfectly arranged and the distance between the whiskers makes them too sparse to be beautiful in themselves. Ours? God must have closed his eyes when he sowed them! A sketch showing rows as dots is lost and will have to wait for me to literally get my things together.

The eyes. "The diameter of the human eye is about 10 percent of the head," while that of our gods (i.e. sculptures) varies from 11 to 20 percent, writes Julian Jaynes, who sees this as proof the idols "spoke" down to our ancestors. Well, the cat has eyes of a godlike proportion, more obvious when open then when closed. I find the most beautiful human eyes – I refer to the shape of the whole closed or open – are those with a soft s-shaped lid found in about one in a hundred Mongolians – beat the cat's and predict that within decades, wide eyes that are vertically narrow (slits) will be considered as beautiful or more beautiful than "round" ones. But most cats' beat most people's. As for their luminescence, I have seen the light they reflect, reflected as if from two narrowly focused pen-lights in turn upon a misty plate-glass window!

The ears. Our ears may be our most extraordinary feature – their resemblance to sea-shells is marvelous and, well, compare them to other apes! – but thick as cardboard. A cat's are paper-thin. The thousands of straight hairs on the inside are wrought fine, each coming to a tip so tiny it might serve for nano-engineering. I have written a number of haiku (in Japanese) on them. Here's one in translation:

> *smelling the plum*
> *every hair stands out*
> *in my cat's ear*

The plum blossom itself has delicate "hairs" – that can pun for nostril hairs in Japanese – and I had a branch blooming in my room.

The mouth. A cat's mouth – except when yawning – is hidden. We only see a hint of bottom lip. The tongue is only twice the size of a cherry petal, a far cry from our thick slab of meat. While large eyes attract more conscious attention, a small mouth and nose probably appeal to us just as much. Look at cartoons. The facial proportions of the heroes and heroines are closer to a cat than a human. Japanese researchers, citing the proportion of composites made from traditional pictures of "beauties" (*bijin-e*) say that these traits appeal more to Japanese than Occidentals, because they are more neotenous (source?). Perhaps.

the ugliness of man

If man could once freely boast of *our* species' beauty – today, even a conservative would be ashamed to do anything so unrelativistic – he could also lament *our* ugliness. When Montaigne (citing Ennius, quoted by Cicero: "How similiar the simian, ugliest of beasts!") writes "those that resemble us most are the ugliest and most abject of the whole (beast) band; for in external appearance and shape of the face it is the apes," *he is not using apes for a metaphor of the disadvantages of similiarity, but for secondary evidence that men are ugly!* "By many animals we are surpassed in beauty [Seneca], even among the terrestrial ones, our compatriots."

He finds us wanting, superficially – "I think we had more reason than any other animal to cover ourselves" – and, to our very core. *Celia shits!* We had better not snoop in boudoirs, he writes, for:

> whereas in many animals there is nothing that
> we do not love and that does not please our

senses, so that from their very excretions and discharges we derive not only tidbits to eat, but our richest ornaments and perfumes." (*Apology to Raymond Seymond...*)

But, Montaigne cannot help but feel attracted to some women more than to other animals with their "wool. feathers, fur, silk," or last mentioned scent. He hastens to qualify: "This dissertation concerns only the common run of us, and is not so sacrilegious to include those divine, supernatural and extraordinary beauties that we sometimes see shine among us like stars under a corporeal and terrestrial veil." This is a fancy paraphrase of the old philosophers, who admitted that all their theorizing on beauty meant nothing before a beautiful woman who was, after all, a beauty, *period*.

to be a god, or to worship one

So what should "the common run of us" do? Should we find someone uglier than we are, who will think us beautiful and love us? Or shall we find someone lovelier than we are and love this being though our love may not be reciprocated? Would we worship, or be worshipped? In other words, do we go for a dog, or a cat? Here is a librarian speaking for "bookish types," real "picky people" who "know what an honor it is to be chosen by someone just as carefully selective as we are" –

> When a cat first makes your acquaintance, she circles around you warily ... If you summon her with a *"Here, kit, kit, kit,"* she will pause and think before she moves ever so slowly toward you. . . And when she gets within touching distance, you still have to prove yourself by the delicacy, the hesitancy with which you touch her. Only when she really trusts you will she climb into your lap.
>
> And you'll feel like a god has chosen you. Marylaine Block (*My Word's Worth*)

In other words, cats attract because they play hard to get. *"And you feel honored just to have been chosen to serve."* Unlike a dog or horse, who willingly work for us, with a cat, "you are the one doing all the work."

Ah, now I see! In a culture, like ancient Egypt, where royalty probably had servants to wipe their butts – apparently true for most ancient civilizations – the cat would have given them the rare satisfaction of experiencing the other side of life without going incognito.

One can imagine the proverbial powerful politician, bringing a real pussy home to feed and get scratched by, rather than sneaking off to a cat-house to get tied up by a woman.

delicacy is beautiful

The best description I know of what we might call *the discerning cat* comes from Roger Caras. A cat is a creature of "most refined and subtle perceptions." Dogs – and, remember, this is coming from a dog-lover extraordinaire – lack this "delicacy" of "actual touch." No, we all fail in comparison, for the cat has "the most refined sense of touch in the natural world." His cat reminds us of the nineteenth century aesthete:

> "As a man who has tact exercizes it on all occasions for his own satisfaction . . . a cat will walk daintily and observantly everywhere, whether amongst the glasses on a dinner table or the rubbish in a farmyard." (l.s.)

Cat-haters can ask, what about the godaweful loves of cats? Is caterwaulling the music of a refined sensibility? Indeed. What about the loves of *our* aesthetes? Our Oscar Wildes? Our Bauldelaires?

Do moments of gross abandon contradict character? Of course not.

Delicacy. The cat's fine nerves do match its fine features. It will not pull frantically on a leash. It will not splash and slobber half of its water on the floor. It will not wag its tail back and forth like a windshield wiper oblivious to the havok its happiness creates. It knows that staring is impolite. That large eyes are the more beautiful for remaining closed most of the time. The cat generally behaves itself.

When I see the calm and gentle expressions on classic Egyptian faces, I wonder if it might not rather be this demure aspect of the cat, the animal that, to some of us, seems more quietly appreciative of the good life than most humans, rather than its "nocturnal stealth," haughtiness and "pagan sacrifices," as Paglia calls "a neat pile of mole guts or mashed mouse limbs on the porch" that won it the love of a civilization.

(The picture above, scribbled into a journal of haiku poet Issa, almost makes Han-chan indelicate if not gross, but note, if you will, the tiny fiddle-bridge nose.)

beauty for beauty's sake

If Egypt loved the cat more than Greece, it is to Egypt's credit. It tells us that the Egyptians were not ashamed to worship beauty for beauty's sake. Greek aesthetics were fatally flawed by rationalization. Fluid beauty – such as that found in cave-art – was derailed by lumpy things called muscle. What is useful is beautiful? Like hell it is!

If the Greeks really did not appreciate the cat (I have not checked Paglia's bold pronouncements, so I write "if"), then their taste, the taste we inherited, may not be as good as we assume it is. Maybe, then, it behooves us to pay more attention to other artistic traditions; not as primitive art, but as civilized alternatives to the ugliness – the doggy, horsey muscularity – the high(?) culture of the Occident takes for granted.

cat tails

Cleaning Up for Love. While editing this chapter, I thought of a reason for cats keeping clean when they feel loved. Could it not tie into the hunting? A cat tends to hunt more when it has either kittens or a master to present its game to – which is generally the case when a cat is feeling lovey-dovey – and, as pointed out, lack of body odor facilates successful hunting.

Cats with Dangerous Tails. Since pronouncing cats careful and dogs careless, I have come to know a cat whose tail is a walking disastor. Boogieboo as I now call the cat I first called Miaomiao, with whom I now share the terrible isolation of living without transport in the woods with no-one but four cows, two dogs and one sister who is a nice enough person but absolutely matter-of-fact and not someone I can enjoy a lively conversation with. Seeing birds fighting at the feeder by my window, he is do eager to referee that his tail knocks over glasses, takes water from his bowl and throws it across the desk upon me and the monitor and even dislodges the venetian blind panels. I bet most cats that grow up inside learn to control their tails, but it is hard for a cat to learn to do once grown.

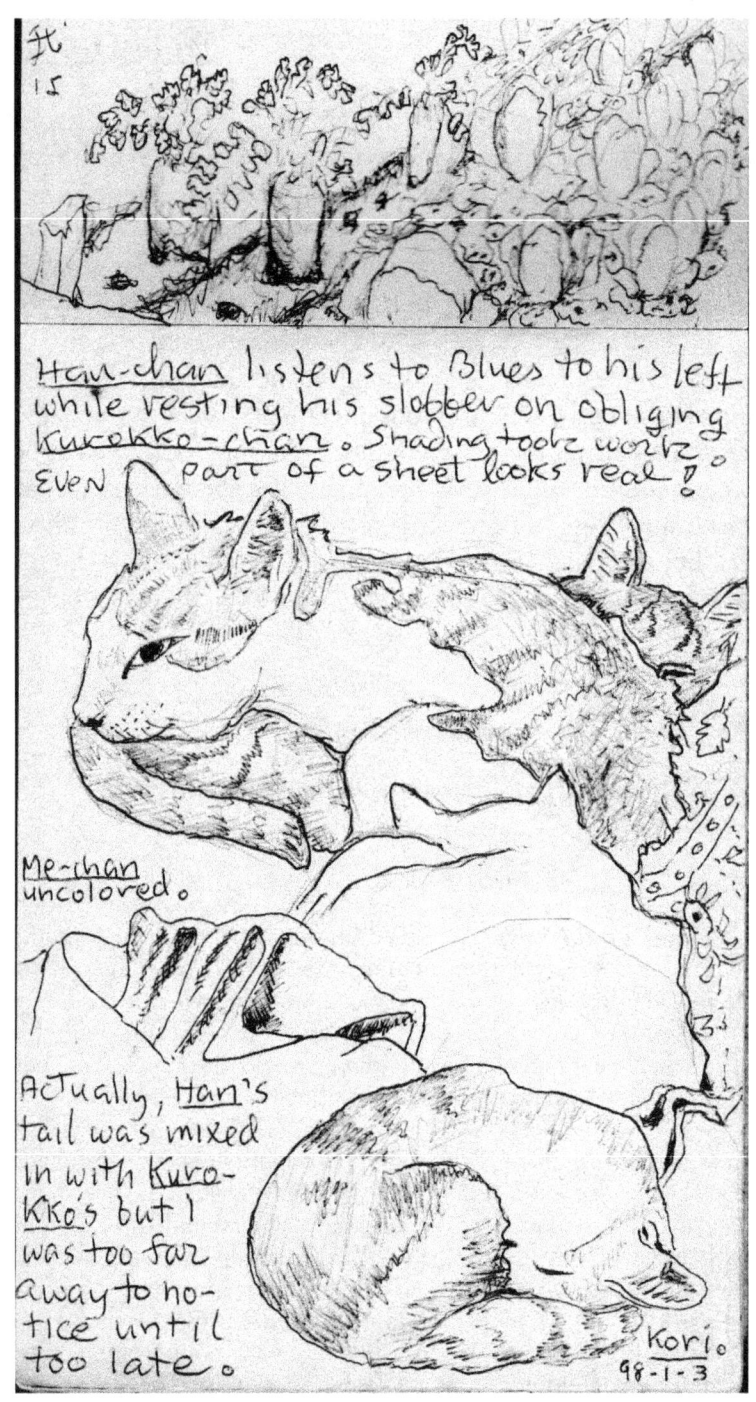

Han-chan had already contracted his fatal disease. You can see his weakness in his ragged coat, but something of beauty is still found in this portrait.

<u>how dreams help cats cope with life</u>
Han-chan's Dream

the dumb things they do

It is the 'dumb' things animals do that tell you how smart they are. Mary Catherine Bateson tells a *Gregory Story* about an alleged slow learner tested by a rat runner:

> .... the ferret went through the maze systematically, going down every blind alley until reaching the reward chamber, where he devoured the haunch of rabbit. The next day, returned to the maze, he again went down every blind alley but ignored the tunnel leading to the reward chamber. As Gregory said, "He'd eaten that rabbit." (*Peripheral Visions* 1994)

It takes intelligence to recognize the same, for recognition requires interpretation. It also requires sympathy, for correct interpretation depends upon putting oneself in the other's shoes. Or paws.

must be a bad dream

Let me relate a story of my own. I call it "Han-chan's Dream." The main text is straight from my notebook (but parsed), written on the day of the incident. The numbers refer to the sequence of events as marked in the drawing –

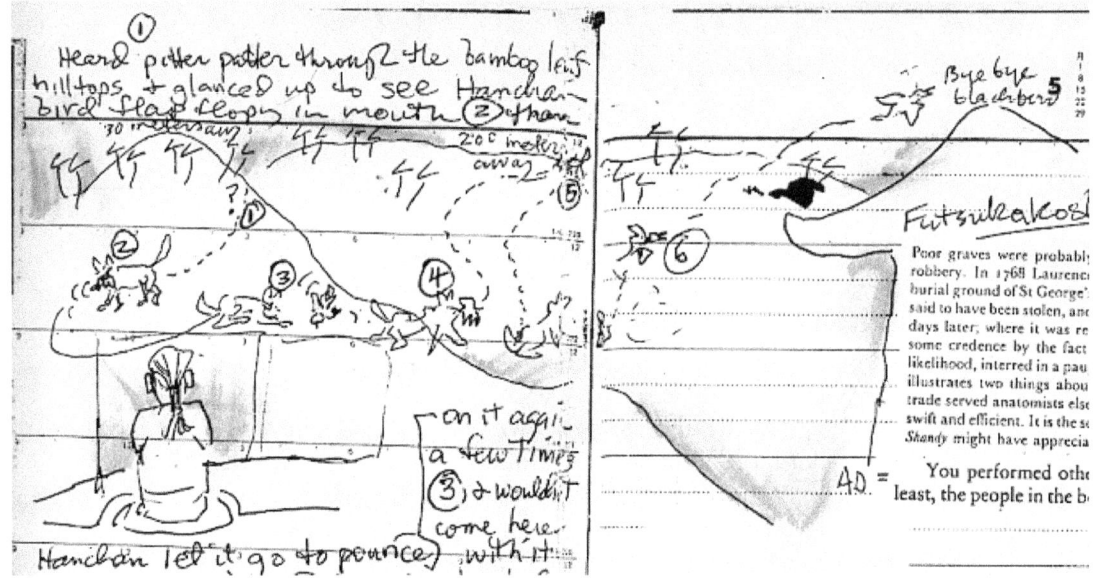

1) Heard pitter patter through the bamboo leaf hilltops & glanced to see Han-chan bird flap-flopping in mouth

2) Then Han-chan let it go to pounce on it again a few times

3) & wouldn't come here with it when I called but

4) Decided to hunt for someone else to show it to (?) because he was vocalizing thataway & he trotted all the way to the top of the Eastern Mount

5) Announced himself(?) & returned to the Valley to play with the bird that from the looks of it before my window 3) had <u>at least</u> a broken wing and even as Y[oko] was watching, suddenly fluttered through the bamboo brush and picked up speed & quickly flew off

6) & Han-chan believing it must be a bad dream retraced his tracks (even to 3) for a few minutes before wandering off to I-know-not- where & Y & I felt glad to know that Han-chan <u>can</u> hunt, though Y thought that losing the bird was very Han-chan-like (wouldn't have happened to Riko) & I wonder if a lucky bite of Han-chan's reset a pulled shoulder of the bird's or what – All of this took 5-10 minutes!

why birds are sweet

The bird that got away was an *onaga*, or "tail-long." The dictionary calls it a magpie, and it does indeed chatter. But only when it is not shrieking like a banshee, which is most of the day. In fact, the only time I have ever known one to be quiet for even a moment was upon the above-mentioned occasion. Even an *onaga* knows a dead bird is silent. The beak on the head dangling from Han-chan's mouth – it dangled so loosely I thought its neck was broken – moved not an iota.

No wonder Han-chan was fooled! I knew how easy-going Han-chan, by far our worse hunter, must have caught the bird. You might think that with all that signifying going on, the *onaga* would have no call to come to fisticuffs. But no; they incessantly wrestle in the treetops with such tenacity – playing chicken? – that they end up tumbling down plunk upon the ground.

Han-chan discovered this years earlier. Well aware of his ineptitude as a hunter, he stopped paying more than cursory attention (pricked ears) to the denizens of the upper world. Except for *onaga*. When they fought, he followed. I do not know if "little birds in their nest" ever "agree" as claimed by the didactic children's poem in the century-old McGuffy reader; but if adult birds do, it is thanks to the likes of Han-chan, who are perfectly happy to perform the little appreciated task of removing quarrelsome genes from our skies. (Now, fifteen years later, I have a desk by a window with a bird-feeder a foot away and the cat I let watch has learned to remain calm except when birds quarrel, when he forgets himself and lunges at the window. Ornithologists, take note: it is cats that make birds so sweet.

framing the question

> "It is my conviction that cats never forget anything. That is a fact of cat psychology. One always has to bear in mind that a cat's brain is much less cluttered with extraneous matters than a human's."(Paul Corey: *Do Cats Think?*)

I should like to give a paragraph to every line of Han-chan's Dream (which might have been the name for this book had a I a name or a major publisher for the book). One about Yoko caught between pride for our pet predator and pity for the prey. One about Riko, the calico witch and super-hunter, though she gets her time on the stage in the chapter about hunting. One about the importance of showing off one's catch in a cat's life. One about Han-chan the poor hunter not because he was stupid – as described in the chapter *Do Cats Love?* judging from his ability to perform more tricks than any cat I have known and his (what can only be called) foresight, he was extraordinarily intelligent – but because he was a hopeless klutz. Here, we will examine the central theme, broached but not developed in item 6):

"Han-chan believing it must be a bad dream."

Why did I come to that conclusion? Because I *knew* Han-chan was no dummy. Having clearly seen him stare after the flown bird with the body-language of a child with a broken kite string, and knowing how much that rare catch meant to him, I could not believe he forgot what happened; but there he was, frantically searching for the bird he watched fly-off from that same spot, 3), five minutes earlier.

I remembered a mother cat searching over and over again for the kittens she *knew* were dead and gone (they were killed by a renegade Tom). She was no dummy either. There had to be another explanation. And, as I pondered, it came to me. And then it hit me: *dreams!* Cats reduce trauma incurred by a shocking experience by a unique form of escapism: they pass it off as a bad dream.

Paul Corey's poetic generalization might hold for the long-term, but short-term memory, as we discuss in the *"What's Michael!"* chapter, may be another matter, with cats conveniently forgetting many things. But changing the narrative to rewrite the immediate past might be called editing rather than forgetting. I bring it up here to develop the idea of turning better-forgotten reality into a bad dream by way of contrast. Unlike the little embarrassments a cat may edit out to unconsciously avoid frustration and, possibly, consciously avoid being laughed at, this is serious business. The cat is not worrying about appearances. The cat, or its inner wisdom or whatever, is trying to prevent shock that could bring with it health-damaging stress.

animal dreaming and consciousness

The ancient Greek philosophical essay *De Rerum Natura* has a wonderful detailed passage on the manner in which all animals' "devotion and inclination" are reflected in their dreams. Anyone who has lived with animals has, with Lucretius (99-55 BC ?), observed something of them.

There are studies reporting an increase of rapid eye movements when an animal is in a heavy learning situation suggesting dreams re-enforce memory and serve for repetitive practice. Others have more generally suggested that dreams keep our brains limber (ready to jump up and go in an emergency), or are the sleeptime equivalent of off-line sorting work done by the unconscious brain when we are awake. But strangely enough, I have read nothing about what dreams *mean* to animals *when they are awake*.

Coming to terms with our dreamlife must be part of the growth process of all animals who dream. For mammals, that apparently means all but the tiny echidna when it sleeps outside of the limited range of temperatures when it dreams. I remember my three or four year-old sister waking up from her nap tearful and indignant over my eating her ice-cream cone. She made such a fuss that my parents berated me before coming to their senses – no such ice-cream was in the house. I have no doubt that something similar happens with cats as I have seen young cats jump up out of sleep and dash outside. This type of thing is very amusing if the third party is a human with a sense of humor, but it is not easy on the dreamer. Sooner or later, dreaming makes it inevitable that we learn to tell reality from illusion. All mammals are naturally propelled into consciousness, if consciousness is knowing we are awake.

dog dreams

After writing the above, I discovered the "Dog Dreams" chapter in *Dogs Never Lie About Love*. On a BBC radio program, the author was asked if *"dogs remember their dreams during the day?"* If they do, Jeffrey Moussaieff Masson writes,

> there is no reason to believe that they do not think about the dream . . .Indeed it is not impossible for the dog to remember a particularly intense dream from childhood. A dog could be haunted by a dream of long ago, just as we can be haunted by a childhood dream.

He also describes something I have seen many times. One dog licking the face of another having a bad dream, He did not think the lick was *"just empathy,"* but *"that Rani knew, from her own direct experience, that Sima was having a bad dream, and was attempting to relieve her anxiety."*

Assuming a dog remembers and recognizes dreams, how much credence do they give to them? Normally, I would bet that they give them little if any, so that a dog, like a human, could only be haunted by a dream that was seen before he or she was old enough to wake up and discount it. To my mind, that is the neglected half of childhood trauma and explains why memories can be so treacherous.

The cat lying on my desk as I write this additional paragraph is not a particularly interesting dreamer, but the other day I noticed he was *drinking* while asleep. This was not like a kitten nursing but like lapping water. So I put some water in a bowl and woke him to see what would happen. Sure enough, he immediately started lapping up the water. I wonder what Boogaboo thought about *that!*

other realities

> A cat doesn't look at itself when you hold it up to a mirror. . . . That's because a cat believes it is invisible. A cat has to believe this, because when stalking, it has to be invisible in the eyes of its prey.   Leonard Michaels (Ibid.)

Mirrors. It is commonly accepted that only people and apes recognize *themselves* for certain, as proven by removing a sticker from the forehead or something found on ones person through the mirror.

I am not yet convinced. What if other animals just don't mind the sticker? What if a live bug were pasted upon the sticker so it could not be felt but could be seen to move? Kuro'ko-chan, the shy cat who preferred exchanging silent miaows to acoustic socializing, was quite the mirror cat. She enjoyed watching *me* in the mirror and when my hand crept toward her ear from behind, she damn well knew it was *her* ear, for she turned up and back to face it. (And I am now – this *now* being an earlier rewrite in 1998 or 9 – living with a dog I caught watching a mirror to see me approach her while pretending not to. I was surprised she reacted quickly when I crept up behind her line of vision, until I glimpsed at a mirror and our eyes met there.

With studies of self-consciousness taking the lion's share of our attention, less romantic (?) aspects of consciousness are given short shrift. Consider, for example, how a kitten strongly reacts to itself in the mirror – sparring, hissing, and trying to psyche itself out in the usual raised back crab walk manner – yet, before long, learns to pay no attention to the images in the mirror (or television, for that matter). A friend who had never seen a kitten react or check out what was in back of a mirror told me that the lack of reaction by cats in front of a mirror shows 'just how dumb' cats are.

Dumb. There is that word again. That, as Bateson realized, is where the opportunity lies. Think about it. A cat has *learned* that *appearances may be deceiving*. Like dreams, things in mirrors and on television, need not be taken seriously. The simple fact that an adult pets – cats or dogs – can pass a mirror *without* giving it heed should tell us something. Cats – and dogs – *are* conscious in the sense that they can tell apart the world that matters from those that, for all practical purposes, do not.

While it would be difficult to determine whether experiencing a mirror and a television while young help a cat discover his dreams do not matter, it should be easy to compare the reactions of kittens to *mirrors* and *televisions*, with the purpose of ascertaining whether familiarity with the one influences ones reaction to the other. The experience might be titled: "learning to learn about reality."

hypothesis: the imagined "bad dream" as a cushion

Pardon the repetition – I jumped the gun and gave away the game pages ago – but when I wrote in my notebook that Han-chan believed the bird's escape *must be a bad dream*, I was not using a figure of speech. I think that is precisely what happened. Han-chan could not handle the shock of losing his prize so he told himself, *"Nah, it must be a bad dream! If I return to the place I was before the unthinkable occurred, I shall find everything as it was!"*

I have long been interested in dream interpretation. Not the Freudian or pop-psychology revelation of the inner-self, that is micro interpretation of individual dreams nor even the vocabulary of signs that had Danish Scientist-Poet Piet Hein chuckling about how the fact all things are concave or –vex pretty much assures it is all about sex, but in the nature of the associations which have much in common with the pivot-puns and link-verse associations in Japanese poetry and the macro-interpretation of the significance of dreams found in comparative cultural anthropology. Some people believe dreams express the *desires of others.* (Were I a Yamami, and my sister appeared in a wet dream, I would, by this logic, have to chastise *her* for incestuous thoughts.) Some people believe dreams to *predict things* to come. Some hold dreams to be *a separate world we visit* at night. Others say they express *our own true desires* or real character. Some hold them to be *prescriptive,* blueprints for the reality we *ought to* make. Chinese and Japanese sometimes even believed in *opposite dreams* (*gyaku-yume*) predicting the opposite of things to come and had spells recite spells to turn the predictive nightmare into an opposite dream.

But, strangely enough, I cannot remember ever coming across a theory about dreams being *useful for denying the past*. Songs and poetry around the world are full of people escaping, or wishing to escape from harsh reality to sweet day-dreams; but how often have you heard someone attempting to deny reality by turning it into a delusion, a bad dream? That would seem to be the prerogative of cats, or at least of one cat I knew, Han-chan.

This may be a tiny observation, exciting only because I know so little of the research of others. But it was what made up my mind to write a book about the animal intelligence demonstrated in the person of the most sensitive of all cats, Han-chan.

An alert Han-chan a couple years earlier than most drawings in the notebook, before he became ill and still looked his age or younger. A different rendering is found in the the chapter on beauty,

envoi

Now, I write surrounded by dalmations. A couple weeks ago, Ashton, the male, found an endangered tortoise. He would not let me release it, so I brought it home. I would have loved to keep the tortoise around, like the Timothy Turtle whose periodic appearances livened up Gilbert White's *Selbourne*. But, the dalmation kept trying to shuck the poor animal, so I crammed it into a plastic box so tight he couldn't get his muzzle in sideways. He spent the day in my room, literally drooling – mouth to carapace – over his catch. That night, as my sister fed the dogs, I snuck the tortoise away and released it in a property she judged safe. Then, I carefully washed my hands to remove myself from suspicion and watched to see what would happen.

Poor Ashton. He was a picture of misery. He looked five years older – thirty years older by human standards – and even threw up. As my sister put it "How would you feel if you lost your most valuable possession?"

Sure enough, Ashton returned over and over again to the spot he last saw the tortoise in the box in my room. Since, he didn't actually see the tortoise go, as Han-chan had seen the bird fly off, he was not necessarily telling himself *"This must be a bad dream!"* But something about his persistence makes me think might be the case. Chances are we are talking about a mammal, rather than a feline phenomenon. Think about it. *We* humans can cope with tragedy by looking into the future and imagining better times. We can survive on a pie in the sky.

◎At this very moment, eight years older than when I wrote the past paragraph, still penniless, possessionless and personless (no mate) – again helping to care for old Ashton who, now senile, will poop on the floor if not taken out every few hours, living in a god-awful place where one can not even enjoy the simple pleasure of eating out and socializing without driving miles (and that I would not do even if I could afford car insurance and a portable phone (to call the AAA) etc. not to mention a car and gas, etc.) – that *hope* is the only thing giving *me* the strength to keep writing.

◎◎ Luckily for me – now, over two years later, Ashton is gone, but I am still here in what amounts to solitary confinement that makes the months I worked on a small freighter in my 20's seem like a holiday – *hope* that I may eventually be out in the world again and sharing my dreams is all that keeps me going. What is a less farsighted animal, an animal without the ability to construct castles in the sky, to do? How do our cats and dogs cope with sad circumstances and blunt the shock of loss, if not by telling themselves *it must be a "bad dream"?*

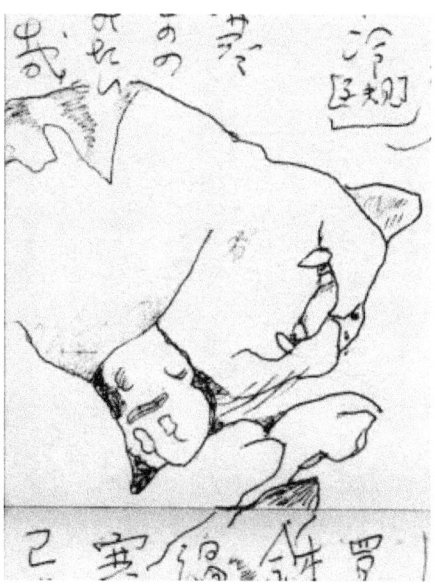

 cat tails

1. Gregory Stories. *Gregory Bateson* a thinker identified mostly with cybernetics was a philosopher and a wizard for straddling old-fashioned positivism and what might be called the New Age. His science stories – generally about things encountered in his own work – generally lead to parodoxical solutions reminiscent of the mystic Sufi who were as much wise-guy as wise-man. He was married to Margaret Mead of anthropology fame and Catherine Bateson is their daughter.

on cats, snakes and chickens, or
the Mouse Trap & *the* Snake Trap

In a *Celebration of Cats*, Roger Caras notes the invention of the silo around the 16th century BC "coincided with the first appearance of the domestic cat." The silo drew rats, mice and wild cats, the last of which was soon adopted.

> "You might say the better mouse trap had been invented . . . It probably bit and scratched, back that close to its wild origins . . . . but . . . it purred when it was happy."

The ferret and the mongoose also caught mice, but, apparently, only the cat "caught our fancy." There is no question that purring mouse traps are irresistible to many of us, but how well do they work? In *The Snake* (1964/87), John Crompton suggests the answer is "not very well". He gives three reasons.

two better mouse traps!

1) Many cats mouse, but most are not eager to take on rats:

> *I even saw one of these [from a guaranteed ratting mother], with her kittens, waiting until the rats had finished before they went up to their food.* (Ibid. brackets mine)

2) Cats are not thorough exterminators:

> *Cats cannot go down mouse and rat holes and eat the babies. Snakes can and do. ....[frequently whole litters of mice and rats are found inside the snakes]. This is what counts in pest destruction.* (ditto)

3) Cats do not properly dispose of their prey:

> *Another advantage of snakes as rodent officers is that they swallow their prey. They do not leave it lying about to go bad. I once had a terrible smell . . .* (ditto)

That is to say, if we were serious about rodent control, we would raise and keep *snakes*, not cats. Indeed, Crompton introduces us to a shopkeeper in South Africa who got three snakes (after learning that cats could not handle the job), which he "shut up in his bedroom for a week so they would get used to him, and then let them loose in his store" where "he reckoned he saved £100 a year by the absence of mice", and, if I may add a point of my own: 4) Snakes may not be much fun to play with, but they do not require any upkeep or go into heat and disturb our sleep. So, unless you are not cat-lover enough to pardon their transgressions, or you live in a house with thin flooring and walls, and think the squeals of the baby mice and their desperate mothers as the exterminator makes his creepy rounds in the Chinese "squealing season" worse than the mice running about your walls and ceiling, consider a snake.

What it all comes down to is this: Thousands of years ago we may well have thrown away the best mouse trap we ever had!

cat as hunter-retriever: a hypothesis

So, why did we adopt the second best mouse trap? *It purrs*. Perhaps. We like to know we are appreciated. It also might have helped put meat on the table. Caras writes "I'm not certain why, but it has been suggested that even before the New Kingdom and the silo, cats may have been used as retrievers. He calls that a "bit of dubious intelligence;" but provides the reader with a painting showing two cats in a 'hunting scene,' one is lying down observing things while the other is sitting in the air with its head back, possibly grabbing at a wing, which the museum boldly titles "Cat retrieving ducks, Egyptian.") Why *not?* Otters were used for hunting and fishing up to modern times in Egypt, Iraq and elsewhere. If no bugles, horses and guns are involved – that is, if hunting is quiet and takes place in the cat's own neighborhood, I think many cats would love to cooperate.

And we should remember people once ate the things cats naturally bring back by themselves. Rabbits (Where they abound, cats prefer them to all other game.), rats ("urban-venison" as Chinese call them), birds and other small animals were eaten by people in many cultures. Before refrigerators, the fact a cat's game is usually brought home alive (rather than rotting or shredded as is all too often the case with dogs), would have been important. If we were truly delighted whenever our cats brought something home and shared the favorite parts with the hunter, the cat might well have brought home a continual stream of game, as it does for its kittens when they are in training.

> *After turning off my Mac [I changed to a pc with a clit on the keyboard after mac gave up its trackball for a pad] and getting settled into bed at 2 AM, sure enough, Me-chan brought in a large bird, which I threw out the window, only to have it brought in again and have to throw it out a second time. As I fell asleep, I thought I had the last word. But I did not. For as I write now, again in the morning, I see it: a chunk of bloody bone and a cluster of wing feathers big enough to make a duster of lying on the tatami.*

So, our explanation for why we adopted cats may be wrong. We may have offered them a refuge – protection from bigger animals and other cats – in exchange for fresh meat for breakfast and, only later, when we became dependent on grains, appreciated the cat-as-exterminator.

the cat & the serpent: another hypothesis

Cats and snakes do not only compete for the same food. They fight *each other*. Caras mentions cats killing snakes, but only *as an explanation for why Egyptian cosmology features a cat and serpent fight*:

> As vermin-killers, cats were expected to deal with cobras, which they often did very effectively, largely because cats are intelligent animals and cobras are particularly dumb, even for snakes. In Paraguay today cats are used for hunting rattlesnakes, which is far more impressive than dealing with cobras because rattlesnakes are both faster and smarter than their hooded Asian counterparts. (Ibid.)

Crompton portrays cobra as dangerous prey, if for no other reason than their skillful use of their eyes to mesmerize and the uncanny way the cobra's mate comes for vengeance, so that is saying alot about the rattle-snake! Be that as it may, we might consider the importance of snake-killing for the domestication of cats. Rodents may not have been a problem for primitive cultures where little food was stored and rats would have themselves been food. In anthropological accounts of primitives, the danger of snake-bite is a constantly recurring theme. Whether the snake itself is feared, or the snake that bites someone regarded as the embodiment of a sorcerer is beside the point. It is feared, and rightly so, for in such a society, *everyone knows of someone who has died of snake bite.* In a book on descendants of the Maya, Robert Bruce compared the poisonous snake in primitive society to the automobile in ours (As it turned out, Bruce would die in a car wreck before the book was published!) Snake-control could have been *the* original excuse for people to keep cats.

Wet young Egypt was probably full of serpents (and not only the relatively docile cobra). If the cat was better at killing them than the rat-snake, its prowess in this area might have been appreciated as much as if not more than its mousing. When you think about it, snake and cat go together; the mice that draw one draws the other. The two animals are in competition. Consider this *cat, snake and mouse story* told by Crompton, who was asked to look after a pet snake for a farmer in Africa who went away on leave,

> It was a mole snake, about three feet long, and soon made itself at home in the camp. In fact, I frequently found the cat asleep on my pillow, and the snake asleep underneath the bedclothes. The snake was more attached to the cat than to me, and the only unpleasant-ness between them was when the snake (its name was Ghoo) once swallowed a small mouse the cat had brought in to play with. The cat bit the snake, which retired into a corner and sulked for the rest of the day.
>
> *(Ibid)*

It would seem that two different types of living mouse traps might get on each other's nerves – com*pet*itive exclusion may have operated in the pet world, too.

snake *versus* bird

If the Egyptian cosmology features *cat* versus *snake*, the Aztecs feature *eagle* versus *snake*. This agrees with Crompton's studied opinion that *"of all snake enemies, birds are the greatest."* They are well-armored and can spot them from overhead. *"A bird does not need to be an eagle to cope with snakes"* he writes. Nor is speed necessary. He describes "the most talented" secretary bird, a study of slow motion. *"Interposing an outstretched wing, rather like a matador with his red cloth"* for the snake to strike, the bird bides its time, until it can "rake the tiring snake to pieces" with its long legs and talons" and eat it "with sedate enjoyment". Ditto for the turkey. So, if snakes are better for catching rats than cats, birds are better for catching snakes. Are snakes your problem? Maybe you need a bird.

Crompton gives no examples of snake-guard-birds, but I recall reading somewhere about chickens brought out to the field to route serpents when weeding. It may have been in Sylvia Arden Boone's *Radiance from the Waters*. The use of birds as protectors is not specified, but suggested. Among the Mende of Sierra Leon:

> Birds are friends; snakes are enemies. Birds are light and life; snakes are night and sudden death. Birds are melody and sweetness; snakes are silence and poison. Birds help bring babies; snakes steal them away. A bird and a snake together suggest internecine strife; they are natural enemies – when they meet they fight. The snake bites the chicken's legs; the chicken pecks at the snake's head and eyes. Together they depict life as a battle.

The bird, then, is to the Mende what the cat was to the Egyptians.

> "In America we tend to anthropomorphize our "four- legged friends," especially dogs and cats. Mende reserve their affection for birds, and it is ordinary bird behavior that they regard as "almost human." (Ibid.)

They walk upright on two legs, eat a mix of cereals and animal protein, build homes to cohabit in and raise families, and can talk and sing like no one else but us. Moreover, they have one over us. By flying up in the air, they can spot someone coming long before we can. That is to say, they are so far-sighted they can see the future.

A very un-chicken chicken hypothesis

And "the supreme bird", the bird of birds and most popular pet of the Mende is the chicken! They have the run of the town, the run of the house, and are carried into the fields by women "for company during the lonely day". Boone offers no specifics, but I think it a good bet that even when a chicken did *not* attack a snake, it would raise a ruckus, and that is enough for, once alerted, a human is more than a match for a snake. In fact, I'd guess that might be one of the things that attracted the chicken to *us:* it can count on humans running to help protect it from predators, including snakes. When you consider the autonomy of the African honey-guide bird, who learned to take people to wild honey combs for a reward of the spoils, such cooperation could have developed naturally.

The only specific mention of a snake-guard chicken I know comes from a work of fiction that sits in Japan with the rest of my library that poverty has kept me exiled from, for 11 years now. Luckily, I pasted copies of some parts of Bernado Atxaga's great Basque story-telling novel, or novelized stories, OBABAKOAK, into my journal:

> Grandfather was very afraid of snakes and that was why on very sultry days there'd be five of us, the usual four plus Frankie the chicken; but there was a problem because Frankie didn't like walking in front and so couldn't kill any snakes that might threaten us.
>
> 'Frankie! Get in front!' grandfather would shout.
>
> But Frankie was a very stubborn chicken and wouldn't obey him and grandfather would get furious.

> 'Frankie!' he would yell at the chicken, 'I didn't bring an expert with me to have him bringing up the rear.'
>
> That's what grandfather thought, that snakes are evil things that kill birds, frighten horses and steal the milk from cows, but that they'll have nothing to do with chickens, because chickens are experts at killing snakes.
>
> (transl. Margaret Jull Costa)

Is it not possible, that the egg was only half of the story? That the chicken was also appreciated as a snake guard? If so, where does this leave the cat who cannot lay eggs?

The Chicken, the Cat and the Mouse

Thoreau was a great enthusiast of both cats and those clucking creatures with feathers and thin toenails. His *Journal* is full of entries applauding their healthy throats, their voices capable of vanquishing all bad spirits and illness. Sometimes he mentions other aspects of their singularly robust nature. My favorite entry is on July 6, 1852 and concerns "a chick's stout legs."

> If they were a little larger they would injure the globe's tender organization with their scratching.

But that is nothing to *this* book. We want to see the entry of Dec. 4, 1856. It concerns the relationship between said fowl, a cat and a mouse (only the snake is missing!):

> Sophia says that just before I came home Min caught a mouse and was playing with it in the yard. It had got away from her once or twice, and she had caught it again; and now it was stealing off again, as she lay complacently watching it with her paws tucked under her, when her friend Riordan's stout but solitary cock stepped up inquisitively, looked down at it with one eye, turning his head, then picked it up by the tail and gave it two or three whacks on the ground, and giving it a dexterous toss into the air, caught it in his open mouth, and it went head foremost and alive down his capacious throat in

the twinkling of an eye, never again to be seen in this world. Min, all the while, with paws comfortably tucked under her, looking on unconcerned. What matters it one more or less mouse to her? The cock walked off among the currant bushes, stretched his neck up, and gulped once or twice, and the deed was accomplished, and then he crowed lustily in celebration of the exploit. It might be set down among the *gesta* (if not *digesta*) *Gallorum*. There were several human witnesses. It is a question whether Min ever understood where that mouse went to.

So chickens do not only guard us from snakes, they – the cocks at least – *like* mice. But, they don't catch them. For *that*, an owl would make the ideal pet. I am tempted to start on owls for I am told "owl" was the first word I said and my father told me stories about his pet owl and how the hair of the mice was coughed up in round balls . . . But I do not want to turn this book into a zoo.

Snakes, Cats & the West

I occasionally read claims that the drop in the population of cats after they were persecuted as witch-familiars resulted in the rise of vermin and the flea-borne plagues that wiped out more than half of the population of Europe. *Well. That will teach you to mess with cats!*

In a history seminar on the National Public Television (NHK), a Japanese professor argued that, no, it was the persecution of the *snake* rather than the cat which allowed rats to over-breed. While Mesopotamia, China and other older civilizations worshipped the snake, the Judaic-Christian tradition hated it, and tried to wipe it out of culture and nature, pari passu.

After reading Crompton and considering both the difficulty most cats have with large rats (as opposed to mice) and the time line – for the Inquisition post-dated the first rounds of disastrous plagues – the Japanese explanation seems the more convincing one. (I also cannot help wondering whether cat fleas were totally innocent!). But it may be the persecution of all rodent controllers – snakes, cats, owls, and foxes for a start – is what got us into a situation so bad that we needed the help of a Pied Piper.

There may be a flip-side to this ecological disaster. The great reduction of the Western population was a tragedy for all involved, but it played a vital role in the industrialization of Europe, for the demand for labor rose over the supply encouraging the use of machines, while "our" greater immunity to plague and small pox and measles, etc., permitted us in turn to decimate other populations we came in contact with and ever-so-easily over-run the world, which was a tragedy for the decimated and eventually got us to where we are today, which is depressing to think about and caused me to add a page between the postword and index in one of my books called *"Writing at the End of the World."* It is hard to concentrate when I think my future readership may be heading straight for an iceberg, or rather, whatever will replace icebergs after they are melted and our species has no more chance of making it to the next millennium than a snowball of passing through hell. Yet, as long as the deckchairs have readers upon them, I guess I do want to be read, and so I tell myself that if enough people read me maybe this or that might change, or, so I once thought, but now just do not know.

cat tails

The *gesta* (if not *digesta*) *Gallorum*. Thoreau puns on France's ancient name and the Latin annals that touch upon its gestation. Who knows if that name (Gaul) and that for a rooster (*gallus*) are of the same etymology. And who cares! Good wordplay needs no research or citation. Its proof is in the punning.

a brave little cat and a big smart snake
The Battle of Blue Boss & Zoro

I had yet to read Caras or Crompton. Cats and snakes never crossed in my mind until they did so literally in front of my window. I call what happened that Spring of 1988 *The Battle of the Blue Boss.*

It all began when I spotted a plain-colored six or seven foot snake just outside my window that I later learned was an *aodaishô*. As the color *ao* is used to describe both young leaves and the clear sky, the dictionary fudges, and translates the *Elaphe climacophora* as "a blue-green snake." Green evokes a wispy viper, but the Japanese name has two more characters, *dai,* or "large" and *shô,* the "chief" part of *"shôgun,"* ("chief-army"), a word, which, thanks to a novel of that name no longer must be translated. This thick-set, powerful blue-gray rat snake looked every bit the generalissimo, or boss of the forest floor.

I could not help wonder how my cats would respond to him. I had a roomful, including a litter in a cardboard box in the corner belonging to a first time mother, the one-year old Zoro, named for a dark patch resembling the moustache of the screen hero and for having the fastest paws of *any* cat I've known. Before giving it a second thought, I dropped her out the window and in lieu of pointing tossed a pebble upon the fallen bamboo leaves nearby the snake.

how rattlesnakes got their rattle!

The Blue Boss immediately saw Zoro, but she only saw his tail. It began to slide and Zoro's eyes almost fell out of her head. It had her mesmerized. As the big snake slowly began to stretch out the front half of his body in order to flank her – though neither the cat nor I yet recognized what he was up to – the tail slapped back and forth on the leaf-covered ground. As the Blue Boss stretched to nearly his full length and started to turn toward the cat, the tail began whacking back and forth between a small tree and a survey post. The noise was loud and rhythmical. It riveted the cat's attention. So *that's* what the rattlesnake's tail was all about and how it evolved! I had always assumed the idea was to frighten away a large animal and save the snake from dying together with its victim. But, seeing this, I realized it probably evolved less as a warning than a distraction, or even a lure!

Though thrilled at the discovery, I began to worry for Zoro, still stalking the tail while the head stalked her. That Blue Boss was so damn cool about it. He (as Zoro was female the snake became male.) even flicked his tongue – lit up a cigarette, so to speak – something I thought would catch her eye immediately. It did not. Second by second, he drew the circle tighter, until it seemed to me that Zoro was almost within sure fire-range.

like a pink sponge!

As a boy, I caught and kept a snake now and then; but watching this Blue Boss, began to feel something I never felt for a snake before. Respect for him as an individual with the presence of mind to have survived numerous encounters with cats, dogs and tanuki. He must have outfought or outbluffed a number of them every year, for a dozen years or more to have gotten that big. *This snake knows what he's doing.*

It was no accident Blue Boss appeared. He was probably attracted by scent Zoro's tits left on the ground or the *she-has-babies* odor of her scat and was hoping to find some tender kittens to eat. This was, after all, the start of the Baby-gobbling Season, the time when all the animals in the woods rush about gobbling up each others babies in order to raise their own (Or, if you prefer to think in symbiotic terms, you might say trading babies, something reported to have happened toward the end of World War II in China when two starving mothers whose babies died at almost the same time agreed that it would be easiest if "You eat mine and I eat yours.").

Pretty soon, Zoro would be bringing back little mice for her kittens. Unless my curiosity got her killed first!

I had wanted to see what would "naturally" happen; but it was no contest. If I didn't do something fast, Blue Boss would sucker her. I had no idea how much damage a large snake neither poisonous nor the size of a python could do. But Blue Boss looked so cool, so confident that I knew it had *something* up its sleeve. I tossed another pebble, this time in the direction of the snake's *head*, not to hit it but to catch Zoro's attention. *It worked*. For the first time, she saw the snake's eyes and jerked back in surprise.

What followed was the same thing we all have seen on TV when they show the mongoose and the cobra, except that the cat's feinting was done with the paw rather than the snout. Zoro would try to whack the snake's head at arm's length and the snake would counter with a lunge at her face. The timing of the two combatants was so skillful they always seemed to brush each other and yet you felt little fear they would actually draw blood. I thought of the harmless back and forth dance of Japanese sword practice. Since it was obviously Zoro's first encounter with a large snake, I felt she must have had assistance from instinct. (Later, I was to discover that even house-cats with no experience with snakes will whack down and/or bite knotted ropes flicked about in play *just behind the knot*.)

Zoro had always been an exceptionally gutsy little cat, and now she had what might be called the mother's advantage; but still, I had to hand it to her. The Blue Boss's strike was too fast for me to see its fangs; but that mouth looked *huge!* It was like a foot-long, shocking-pink sponge. With every lunge, the flying sponge reached within a hair's breadth of Zoro's face. Her entire vision must have been bright pink!

the Battle of the Blue Boss: Useless Brothers!

The battle raged for an hour or so, interspersed with far less glorious showings by Zoro's brothers. The orange tabbies (one half-white) trotted over with *a Hrmphf, I'll show you what to do with a snake, Sis;* but after a single close call, the attractive orange tabby brother Shimo was afraid to land a blow any closer than a meter from the snake, and Nora, his heavier deformed-tail brother shot backwards like a squid, hitting a thin bamboo about three feet in the air, from which he bounced off and flew over a concrete wall. He didn't return to the next day and, for days, remained so jumpy that it took him five minutes to de-mine every square meter of ground before daring to cross it (and Nora means Alley-cat as he was not just ugly but the boldest brute of the litter!).

Even granting that Nora might have confused the impact of the bamboo with being attacked by the snake, and suffered the pain of a claw broken on the concrete wall, that jump back itself was nothing like the slighter bodied Zoro's well-measured movement. The contrast between the brothers' poor performance and their sister's brave and skillful performance under fire was amazing to see.

the forced draw

Outside, the shadows were growing. *If this goes on much longer someone is going to get hurt.* My scientific self said "wait and watch!" Snakes cool down and get slow, so Zoro may bat the Blue Boss until he's punch drunk, then bite his neck. Or, even if he had been feigning, with no intention of actually biting, there was the possibility the Boss, knowing time was against him, change his mind and bite out of desperation. Then again, if the snake lunged by feel, while Zoro needed light because, unlike a mouse that made noise when moving, the snake struck through the air, she might be in danger. Either way, I had to stop the fight. I knew I would feel bad if either valorous gladiator were seriously hurt or killed.

But how I hated to do so! It was like walking out of the theater and missing the end of the best movie you've ever seen. Had they naturally encountered one another, I might have told myself, *"But they started it."* Unfortunately, I knew I was responsible.

I went outside and tried to shoo Zoro away from the snake. The Blue Boss began to move away, slowly. He did not seem afraid of me, just observant. That snake was *cool*. Zoro was *not*. She was not finished fighting, not by a long shot. Oh no! I thought, I come out to stop the fight, but if

I'm not careful, I'm only going to get someone hurt and I will have ruined a good experiment for nothing.

I tried to pick up the snake with a stick to carry it to a hole I'd seen about fifty feet away. I remember thinking, *this snake is a lot heavier than I thought!* Then, he was off like quick-silver, down a crevice near the edge of the concrete wall guarding the apartment building from the annual siege of the bamboo army. Zoro ran back and forth sniffing frantically, digging here and there, alternately giving me dirty looks and appealing for assistance. And I was thinking, *Cat, you better thank your lucky stars I stopped that fight! That snake could have been gone any time. If he didn't go earlier, you can bet he didn't think he would lose! And, remember, he has lived ten years to your one.*

At any rate, Zoro taught me *some* cats *do* make good snake fighters. Crompton wrote of a farmer's cat in the Transvaal who brought back a snake almost every night. It even killed poisonous snakes. But in the end, the cat came home one night with his head swollen and within an hour *was* a great snake-hunter. After seeing the Blue Boss in action, I must agree with Crompton's conclusion:

> The truth is, however clever a cat or dog may be [his best snake dog was killed by the cobra's spouse when he celebrated his victory too fast] there is always some snake who is cleverer, and one day the two will meet. (*The Snake*)

zoro's revenge

I believe it was the very next day, but it might have been a few days later. I did not take notes. What happened was so traumatic, I knew I would recall every detail. I woke up in the middle of the night with a snake on my chest. My cats had *never* brought a snake home before, and they knew I did not like them playing with their catch on my futon while I tried to sleep. Since the snake alone would not have woken me, I must have been treaded upon by a cat. Half-asleep, I made a grab for the culprit, and felt instead something cold and slimy. It was only a two-foot garter snake but, believe me, it was shocking to find it in bed. *My God, Zoro, if there were poisonous snakes around here, you could have gotten me killed!* As odd as my life sometimes seems, I no more believe things happen to me alone than that this planet alone has intelligent life. I could not help wonder *how many cats have unwittingly assassinated their owners in this way since cats were first domesticated.*

I pickled the snake in *Shochu* (a distilled liquor) and added another snake a week later. After that, thank goodness, either snakes got scarce or Zoro cooled off, because the snake-kill fell to one a month. If Han-chan, who was still a kitten, was to repeat his uncle Nora's snake phobia, Zoro's granddaughter, Kori, also exceptionally nimble, grew up to carry the banner of the anti-snake crusade that I unwittingly instigated. She did not, however, begin by taking on the Blue Boss. A note from late-1989:

> *Koriko, world's greatest worm hunter – though most cats won't touch them if you rub them in their nose. Grandmother Zoro's great obsession for snakes wormed its way into her brain.*

She took me back to my childhood when for a few years we had a beagle who lived to hunt ghost-crabs!

blue boss returns

A couple years later, my notebook shows a Blue Boss encore.

> *Look out & hear BAM! It's Sabi* [an alleycat] *and the SNAKE* [the drawing shows it coiled up by a small palmetto, and I assume the sound was made by Sabi's paw slapping the floor of the woods]. *They only keep an eye on each other, but snake moves so slowly I think* [it must be] *shedding. Sabi lost sight of* [the] *snake* [according, to the picture and my memory, climbed slowly up the palmetto and, completely unobserved, inched across a stem to a large bamboo, all the while keeping its tail moving ever so slightly in place, in front of Sabi on the ground at the foot of the palmetto, but not

making a racket with it as it did two years earlier. Then it, too left the ground] & *[Sabi] sniffed* [the] *ground where* [it] *laid & finally* [looking up] *noticed* [the] *tip of* [the] *tail, sniffed & whacked it fearfully. Snake at once changed to this* [drawing shows it off the ground resting partly on the palmetto, with its head reaching well around the bamboo observing the cat] *& Sabi lost sight & all interest.*

I apologize for the absence of the picture. It is in a notebook not present at present and was not reproduced because I made the mistake of coloring in parts of the picture. But, please bear with me for there are a number of interesting observations here. First, the seasoned tom did not make much of an effort to engage with the snake though, I recall he had a large appetite and stole food. Second, the Blue Boss – either recognizing his opponent's greater size (Sabi probably weighed twice as much as Zoro), or that active defense would not be necessary? – did not attempt a full circle trick, although I first thought he might when he peeked unobserved at Sabi from behind the bamboo. Third, Sabi lost sight of the Blue Boss though I could see him. *So long as your movements are slow enough, you can be invisible as far as a cat is concerned; and the Blue Boss acted like he knew it.* Fourth, the snake's subterfuge was delightfully complex.

This may sound contradictory, but I like the serpent all the more for discovering that he really can be devious. If deviousness is, more than anything else, a way to avoid unnecessary bloodshed, it behooves us to think of a snake as a pacifist par excellence. That would help explain why the blood-thirsty *Old Testament* so hated them!

doubting the blue boss

William Cuppy once made fun of people who claim the same Robin visits them every year.

> Robins appear to be responsible for an interesting nervous affliction, in which the victim believes that any Robin he sees is the same Robin he saw last spring and that the bird

returned from winter quarters especially to visit him. This may go on for years.

Not having caught the Blue Boss and dyed his tail red – and observing at a distance – I can not swear that Sabi met the same snake. Assuming it was – and that is what I assume because snakes that large are not a dime a dozen in an area as heavily peopled and petted as this one – this second prelude to a battle that never was proves the Blue Boss is no single tactic general, but a master strategist. And if it was a different snake, it would just go to prove that *all* big Blue Bosses have their wits about them. Either way, it would explain how the "blue" snake became a *daishô,* or a military leader (I made it a "boss" for the alliteration).

This might be true for rat snakes in general. Crompton, the best story-teller of all nature-writers, tells of a naturalist who flushed a small rat snake, and raced it to its hole – where the naturalist already knew it would go – winning the twenty-yard race "by a neck, arriving just in time to cut off the snake's retreat." What happened? "The snake did not pause but shot up from the ground and sank its teeth into the naturalist's cheek, thus showing not only how fast it could move but how high it could jump." Now, *that* was a snake who could think on its feet!

cat tails

What became of Zoro. You might think I would have more to say about Zoro, but not long after she fought the snake, I had her spaded and not long after that convinced an old couple living about a hundred yards down the path to feed her, as their old crippled cat had finally passed away. Every day when I walked down that path for the next seven or eight years, Zoro leaped from fence pole to fence pole alongside me for maybe fifty feet running (Maybe I will post the picture at the paraverse website as it looks best in color). Eventually she caught cat AIDs or something and was too weak to do it. After weeks missing her, one day I saw her lying partly upon the path. I understood how sick she was and sat with her for fifteen minutes, then, good-byes said, crying, continued to work. Her owner told me he found her a day later lying neatly composed but dead in a nooky of his workshed off the ground where a dog could not reach her and she probably did pass away on the day we met. I like to imagine the Blue Boss is still living and remembers her.

between phobia & paranoia
Seeing Snakes

A dark thing lies on the leaf-covered floor of the bamboo grove where nothing lay before. Han-chan's ears perk up and his hair bristles when he notices it. Then he gives it a careful whack with outstretched paw. One thinks of the proverbial ten-foot pole. *Once! Twice! Thrice!* Sure enough, it is only another husk that fell off a sprouting bamboo. Han-chan was afraid it might be a snake.

is it in the genes?

When Han-chan was at a most impressionable age, his mother had a marathon battle with Blue Boss, a large snake. As we saw, she thought she beat it, too. On the other hand, one of his uncles who was also involved in the battle was so afraid of meeting up with that snake again, that he began to see snakes everywhere. He thought every fallen bamboo shoot covering was a snake, just as Han-chan was now doing, or seemed to be doing. Since Han-chan had not behaved that way before, I can only guess he met up with the same snake who refreshed his memory. If so, he was lucky to be alive.

To watch a grown cat move through a bamboo grove at the pace of a man crawling across a minefield, mentally defusing each potential snake he came across, only to immediately encounter another was a hilarious sight. If I could get wealthy enough to buy a video camera and go back in time – the one about as likely as the other – I would post it on the internet and share it with the world. A paranoid dog is not much fun to watch as most of its energy goes into barking, but a paranoid cat is a study in quiet stealth, cautious but too curious not to actually touch the feared object. *That* curiosity does not kill the cat, but watching it in action, idiomatically speaking, kills us.

It was little better inside. A navy-blue and white patterned large plate, brown felt gloves, the tail of a shirt protruding from the sheet on my bed . . . . all of these were interrogated by the family's herpephobic.

han-chan in the bathroom

The funniest episode occurred in the bathroom. The only thing that Han-chan likes as much as a serving of raw tuna, is a ringside seat for my bowel functions. At the sound of the seat coming down, or even earlier, Han-chan dashes in. No. Make that *slides in*. He is in such a rush that he must slide to a stop on the linoleum floor of the kitchen-hallway. The only comparable slide I have encountered comes not from real life but from Rudyard Kipling, who imagines sweet Dinah, his deceased dog, almost knocking Saint Peter from his chair as she slides through the Pearly Gates to greet her master. Having experienced Han-chan's slide in the WC, and seen how one of my sister's dalmations likewise desired to be present for every bm, I cannot help but wonder whether Kipling's image was born as he sat upon his own porcelain throne.

It is bad enough to have a dog staring at you as you eat. But a cat as you shit? At first, I did not appreciate this attention; but Han-chan meowed so piteously and scratched the door so frantically that I eventually came to do all my business with open door. And to tell the truth, when you are experiencing foul weather from the nether end, it can be very soothing to find your troubles are at least making *someone* very, very happy.

We all know the bathroom is the ideal place for singing; well, it is perfect for purring too. Here is where I first discovered Han-chan's purring was tri-part – from mouth, throat and chest, each of clearly different tone. I have yet to hear more than two (the number of strings on a horse-head/mongolian fiddle) from my other cats. Perhaps it was not just the acoustics. Could this have been the only place Han-chan got high enough to purr that way!

My 1992 notebook looks at the matter from an ecological perspective.

Han-chan hanging out by toilet – How to save trees/paper. Let your cat clean your ass. He/she'd love to do it. Only problem is it would no doubt be worse than Mexican toilet paper.

snake in the bathroom!

The episode. It happened on a Fall day. All the previous summer, I wore white or light grey socks of a glove-like variety, commonly worn by Japanese blue-collar workers. The toes are divided to keep skin from skin and prevent skin disease, so they are generally called either "ringworm (*mizumushi,* or "waterbug" in Japanese) socks," or "military socks" (*gun-soku*) – for the military around the world has always been plagued by ringworm – and avoided like the plague by all fashionable people. My main reason for wearing them was because the divided toes made it possible to wear wool socks in the winter without getting cracks under the toes, let me wear *zoris*, i.e. sandals with a strap between the toes, and tug at the toe bar on my home-made variable pressure one-string fiddle without getting cut by the piano wire. (Maybe I need a picture of the last, for I am the only one in the world who does it.)

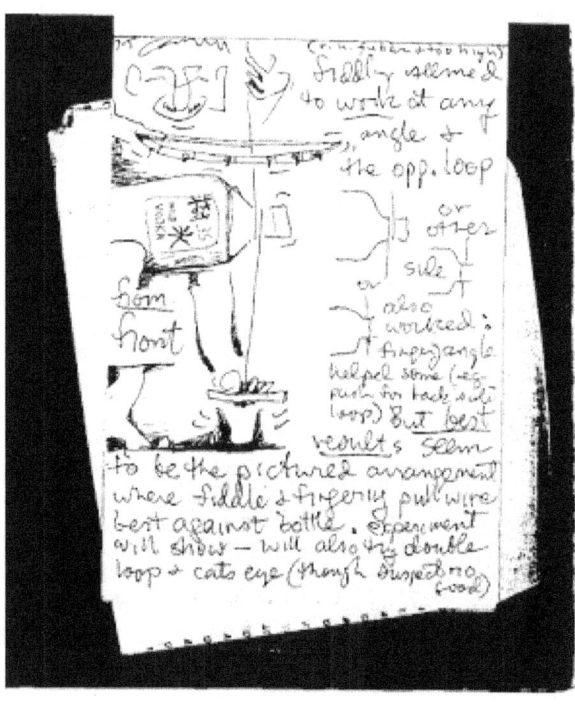

On the day in question, I had put on a pair of warm dark grey socks of the normal toeless variety. Han-chan skidded into the bathroom as usual, climbed onto the doorsill and begun to purr.

Then, he *noticed*. His hair suddenly bristled and he stared intently at one of my feet. I guessed what was happening and could not resist wiggling a toe, just a bit. Han-chan jumped backward off the doorsill into the kitchen, from where he proceeded to investigate by the same fully extended arm-whack process described above. It took several minutes for Han-chan to satisfy himself beyond all doubt that the object was no more than my foot. By that time, I had laughed silently, so as not to disturb his investigation, into tears.

why cats (and people) see things

Imagination in the strictest sense of the word – sensing something that has not come in through your senses, or at least not fully assembled – is hardly a precious skill reserved for artists and poets. No animal could live long without imagining where it will put its foot next or where its prey, or if it is prey, the predator, might head next. And that states it conservatively. All knowing starts with imagination. Han-chan has been traumatized into giving too much benefit of the doubt to possible snakes, but the process of seeing always begins with a supposition. We *imagine* we see something before we *know* we do, and imagining means *making choices*.

I am borrowing something here from *Faces in the Clouds* (Oxford University: 1983), a book I scouted for translation into Japanese. Stewart Elliott Guthrie pointed out the obvious but little discussed fact that all animals are, in a sense, animists who cannot help but animate the world around them. *It is a common perceptual strategy for survival because one is better off mistaking a boulder for a bear than vice versa.* This has nothing to do with seeing what we – humans and other animals – *want* to see. Piaget's animism-as-wistful-thinking is only part of the picture, for, as Guthrie points out, people "often imagine they see what they fear." *There, you see, just like Han-chan.* It is simply that, "as the art historian Ernst Gombrich puts it, *perception is betting*" (italics mine).

We bet on the safe side: for *snakes* over *socks*, *bears* over *boulders*, *men* over *bears*, and *gods* over *all*. And that, to sum up a pleasant four hundred pages is as good a natural explanation for religious belief as any I know.

There are, however limits to this strategy, as for any other. One must not be too quick to see boulders as bears or bamboo husks for snakes. A perceptive facility that sets unreasonably high odds upon erring on the side of safety can immobilize its owner. Luckily, after a couple weeks, Han-chan lost his religious fanaticism. He no longer saw snakes everywhere.

cat tails

While Han-chan's Temporary Paranoia was amusing and the idea of an evolutionary explanation for a tendency to find higher life in things is interesting, what really fascinates your author is the differing ways we treat the process of perception. It seems to me there is a continuum of awareness. On the one pole, we have people who do not mind making mistakes and understand that even a mistake can be right in its own way as part of the process of perception. They tend to be attentive to what they sense before they know it to be a fact. Like people who enjoy dreams, or even jot them down, their positive attitude sensitizes them to something we might call *working*, rather than *final* thought. On the other pole, we have people of a literal bent, who dare not guess and hold guessing against other people because it makes them "wrong," and are seldom aware of what they imagine before they come to the conclusion we call recognition. All who dwell in possibilities – all dreamers – find the latter bore us to death.

To better reflect the puzzling process of perception, movies need to show more things ever so slightly morphed to reflect the focusing of the mind's eye than they do now. At present, there is too much instant recognition on the one side and utter fantasy on the other. That is to say, reality is both over and under-wrought (Movie directors, please note that this is not quite the same thing as the fantasizing you present.).

Kipling's Image Here are some stanzas from his poem, *Dinah In Heaven* (touching, but I still prefer cats):

> She did not know that she was dead
> But, when the pang was o'er,
> Sat down to wait her Master's tread
> Upon the Golden Floor,
>
> There was one step along the Stair
> That led to Heaven's Gate;
> And, till she heard it, her affair
> Was -- she explained -- to wait.
> . . . .
>
> She left them wondering what to do,
> But not a doubt had she.
> Swifter than her own squeal she flew
> Across the Glassy Sea;
>
> Flushing the Cherubs everywhere,
> And skidding as she ran,
> She refuged under Peter's Chair
> And waited for her man.

– how and why cats play with their prey –
the More *they* Die, *the* Higher *they* Fly

Research by Leyhausen cited in *The Domestic Cat* show cats do not hunt from hunger. They *"frequently . . . depart to hunt immediately after a full meal containing meat."* Mother cats are by far the best hunters with 1.6 hours per successful capture versus 11.2 for non-mothers. Was the difference only because mothers carry home more of their catch? *No.* They also travel faster, switch spots more quickly after an unsuccessful pounce, and pounce with a higher efficiency – 3.4 pounces per capture versus 12.2 for non-mothers! And, *move over testosterone!* – a hormone, folliculin, "increases the readiness of female cats to catch prey in the laboratory."

nutritional balance and hunting

This suggests cats may *go* hunting for fun, but only hunt *well* when they must. If a sexual heat precedes conception, a *hunting heat* follows birth! I doubt folliculin explains everything. Might not nursing cats *also* possess heightened senses to help them hunt? Though the extraordinary olfactory sense of pregnant and nursing human mothers is usually attributed to the need to take care of what they eat in order not to poison their progeny, that, too, may have to do with *finding* food as well.

If cats hunt immediately after being fed it may be "meat" *incites* cats to hunt because it increases their need for other foods without which animal protein goes to waste. The body's need for calcium can drive even a vegetarian deer to munch a mouse. Most of our leftovers and canned cat food, are deficient in many trace elements found in the innards and brains of little animals. My cats, *whether mothers or not*, were very attentive to their nutritional needs. When they ate much tuna red meat (The scraps are cheap in Japan) they ate more eggs than they usually did and went crazy for tiny dried fish, even risking getting whacked by climbing forbidden shelves to reach a pack. Cats are indeed picky eaters but not simply to be picky. They do it for balance. That goes for the mouth-feel, or as Japanese call it, "tooth-response" as well. After soft canned food, give your cat some crunchy dried food for desert, if it is low-fat, add a slice of butter and you may see less hunting.

If food has little to do with motivation, Turner and Meister write, then farmers who have traditionally underfed cats "to make them better rodent catchers" (Ibid) may be making a big mistake, for it will only weaken the cats or encourage them to stray. I would guess the choice is false. It is not feeding or not feeding, but *what* is eaten that counts; and the best way to motivate cats would be to feed them full meals missing key ingredients only found in whole prey.

anxiety and hunting

Another incentive to hunt I have yet to see cited is *anxiety*. If I am correct, packing for trips, or the Holiday Season with the different visitors, party noises, and people moving, etc. costs the lives of countless mice, moles and skinks. It does no good to punish a cat for bringing home game either, because that only makes it feel more insecure and sparks another rampage. Some cats respond to family quarrels – whether between the cats alone, or involving me – by tearing off into the woods and coming back with dead bodies. Social tension can be worked off in the hunt, playing and killing. Then, the body may be presented as an offering of peace. I think it no coincidence that Kori-chan, my most anxious if not paranoid cat caught more mice and moles than the other three cats combined!

Presumably, cats insecure about their lodging who went out and brought back gifts for their human hosts were less likely to get thrown out, lose their health and reduce their reproductive fitness; but evolution needs a tendency to work on: the tendency to hunt when anxious was already there. Where? In motherhood. Just as birds cannot bear the open mouths and squawks of their relentlessly hungry young, mother cats may be *launched* into the woods by the squeals and rough-housing of their kittens. That is to say, when home tensions build to a certain point – and it need not involve kittens – *mom is gone*. But not for long.

why bring it home?

We have already hinted at one reason for bringing things home: *appeasement*, of kittens or, by extension, other cats and their "deputy kitten" (Leyhausen), us.

Or, maybe it is not to get in our good graces, but to *teach us* how to hunt, as mother cats do for their kittens. This last reason, given by Elizabeth Thomas in *The Tribe of the Tiger,* is amusing to consider. If your cat brings you dead things, it believes you are as incompetent as a kitten less than a month old. If, on the other hand, you are presented with live game, she is treating you as a kitten over a month old. There is hope for you yet!

But, as Turner and Meister point out, male cats, who "have nothing to do with raising their offspring" (a dubious assumption: see pgs 47-8), also bring home prey, albeit not so frequently as females. They guess, 1) "the cat brings home prey that it usually doesn't eat but doesn't know what to do with", or 2) it may "conceivably be related to the early domestication of cats and their being used to retrieve game hunted by their domesticators." With respect to 1), let me add that a tom who is not the neighborhood Alpha, might want to bring his prey home to play with or munch under his host's protection. With respect to 2), while I think it likely cats did not only retrieve but brought home game naturally to show off, people may have found that meat welcome enough to have favored those who brought it and influenced their character through their genes as has been done longer and more obviously with dogs.

But, whatever the cat's sex or neighborhood ranking, houses are ideal for playing with a catch. Look at it from a cat's perspective. First, you know the area better than your prey, so you can allow it more leeway, more play, without losing it. Second, even if you do lose the prey, it is nearby and will usually be found again either by you or your family. Third, you may play in comfort protected from rain and without worrying about dogs or other large predators. And fourth, you will have an audience, a witness to your valor – and this brings us to what I believe is *the* single, largest overlooked factor in cat behavior.

the show-off hypothesis: bringing home trophies

> Round with *cock'd tail,*
>   and round triumphant walking,
> So carefully her treasure
>   holding, watching,
> And proudly purring,
>   'This is all *my catching.*'

> A description of "kind old Mother Cat" bringing her kittens "a dead bird, or mouse, or rat" in a poem having nothing to do with cats: *Ode to the Blue-stocking Club* by the magnificent underrated Peter Pindar (fl.1780's, a.k.a. John Wolcot).

Sibling rivalry has a tremendous influence on cat behavior. By sibling, I mean both kittens of a litter and those born by the mother cat's daughter within weeks of her own and raised nearby, if not together. If kittens grow up playing together, they also grow up competing with one another. Sometimes a fast growing male may pick on a smaller brother or sister too much, but usually they enjoy the competition. Here is a 1988 note:

> *Hanshiro climbing screen – 3x squirt paws before [he] stop[s] – after once, eager to try again, 2x still eager. Also, if one [kitten] fails, the other little cat insists on doing the same [thing].*

I can only vaguely remember this incident, where I used a squirter on the kittens to train them quickly enough to save the screen, vital for keeping mosquitoes out. But I vividly recall another time where a kitten tried to jump from the stairs to a concrete wall and tumbled down between the gas tanks. I had to rescue the kitten for it was wedged in place meow-ow-ow-ing piteously. I assumed that this would discourage another kitten who was watching from trying the same thing but, *no*, this kitten made a point of trying the exact same thing, and succeeded. Maybe I was just imagining things, but I can still remember feeling I saw *that* kitten flash a victorious glance at the other kitten, saying *Hmmmph! Did you see that?*

When kittens bring back things, their siblings' reaction is never far from their mind. I don't know how to justify *"Look what I brought/caught! Heee, Heee, Heee!"* in evolutionary terms, other than to suggest that a sense of competition drives young cats to try harder, to push themselves to the limit, and thereby improves their survival skills as a group. If people used to wait to see how kittens performed before culling them, it might also have favored the individually fit. Before we got involved, did they grandstand for Mama Cat, who let the best hunter remain home and chased off the others? Who knows!

Can you remember what Han-chan did with the bird that flew away (pg 204-5)? He carried it all around, calling out *desperately* for someone to come and *see*. To have caught or happened upon something big and have nobody to show it off to is *torture* for a cat. The voice used to call everyone is a low rhythmical attention-getter with a little curlicue at the end meaning "Come on!" It is basically the same as that used by a mother cat telling her kittens she has something for them. All cats know what it means, and if they are awake and well, go to see. Even if you are not especially interested, because, for example, the cat in question has been bringing back nothing but worms recently – you are still *obligated* to go and look. That is part of cat etiquette. Next time, *you* might be the one meowing for attention.

It is not enough, however, for the audience just to look. A socially attentive cat makes a visual feint or a half-hearted grab for the prey. This allows the triumphant hunter to exercise his or her most ferocious growl. Within minutes, the hunter will usually let the other cats play with his prey; but, first, he must be indulged.

When there is a family of related cats, you, the owner/host may not be the only, nor even the main reason a cat brings home game. The day of Han-chan's Dream was a fluke. As a rule, when Han-chan called, the other cats came on the run. I was only shown things as a last resort – better to show a human than no one! I did not like my cat friends to kill the all too few wild animals remaining, but had I wanted to cook and eat what they caught and encouraged them, I think I could have had a steady stream of gifts until the woods ran out of animal life.

cats, very sharing animals

Cats are as likely as dogs to vocalize for dinner. This is not simply because they are impatient. It is proof of a strong instinct to share food with all of one's relations. Han-chan, who rarely hunted – he was very secure as the only cat equally loved and respected by all – always meowed loudly when he got a treat. It was a different meow from the one used when he brought something himself. The tone was somewhat obnoxious, as if he wanted everyone else to think he was forcing that food out of me for them.

Sometimes I had food I hoped to give to Han-chan alone. If he kept quiet he could have had it all to himself. I'd tell him *"Hush, Han-chan!"* But he never did. He made enough noise to be heard a hundred yards away and all the other cats came running.

why cats play with their game

Psychologist Susanne K. Langer provides a scientific view of why a cat plays with its prey:

> The belief that the cat follows the act of catching the mouse (which may include sub-acts of watching, stalking, muscular preparations, building up tensions for the crucial leap) with a playful act in which the mouse becomes a toy is universally accepted. Yet . . . it is . . . more likely, the cat is protracting the hunt which is too quickly successful, by repeating the final phase in a telescoped fashion, letting the mouse just start to run away and retrieving it without killing it until the impulse with all its contributories is spent. (*Mind* – an Essay in Human Feeling; Hopkins 88)

This is wrong for several reasons. *First*, the hunter is not the only one who plays with the mouse. Others may join in, though they were lounging around, or even fast asleep a few minutes before. They are hardly spending an impulse built up while hunting! *Second*, if the weather is pleasant and the cat in an, oops, playful mood – a successful catch can make a cat *very* happy – the play can go on for a long time. You can see the cat is not simply running down overheated nerves, but building them up and running them down over and over again, like a multi-orgasmic person. If it is hot, the cat may even take breaks between bouts of play. *Third*, play is indeed a protraction of the hunt, but hardly in the sense suggested by the psychologist. The hunt *itself* is not just a sequence of acts but play, a game. This does not make it any less important to the cat, who is too enlightened, to paraphrase Piet Hein, to take *"play for play/ and earnestness in earnest"* in the manner of the square, who proves thereby he can *"neither of the two discernest."* And, finally, if you are going to reduce play to nervous impulses, *why start with the hunt?* You might as well take it back further, to the *anxiety* I mentioned earlier.

how cats play with their game

Let us return to *hunting* later, and consider the nature of cat *play* itself for a while. For it is a fact that the cat does not just let the mouse – or, for that matter skink – "start to run away" and then retrieve it. A cat's play with its game is much, much more complex and interesting than a "telescoped hunting" explanation suggests. Here are a few rhymed translations of 5-7-5 syllabet Japanese verses of mine, one of which accompanies a drawing which I will not reproduce as it is even more of a cartoon than these words:

play/prey	mercy on mice!
the more it dies	*the more it dies*
the higher it flies	*the more me-chan tries*
– red mouse!	*to keep it alive*

The more the mouse gives up the ghost the more frantically the cat tries to give it a semblance of life with the result: no mouse is so revived as a dead one! A live mouse can at most jump six feet. A dead one has been known to fly ten or twenty. If this is reliving a hunt, it was a hell of a hunt!

I joke. But, to tell the truth, it hurts me to watch the poor mice tortured so skillfully. As you may gather from the *Little Red Mouse* chapter, I like mice and I am reminded of the venerable Flower Doctor in Okakura's *Book of Tea*:

Flowers, if you were in the land of the Mikado, you might some time meet a dread personage armed with scissors and a tiny saw. He would call himself a Master of Flowers. He would claim the rights of a doctor and you would instinctively hate him, for you know a doctor always seeks to prolong the troubles of his victims. . . . . He would burn you with red-hot coals to stop your bleeding, and thrust wires into you to assist your circulation. He would diet you with salt, vinegar, alum, and sometimes, vitriol. Boiling water would be poured on your feet when you seemed ready to faint. It would be his boast that he could keep life within you for two or more weeks longer than would have been possible without his treatment. Would you not have preferred to have been killed at once when you were first captured? What were the crimes you must have committed during your past incarnation to warrant such punishment as this?
(Okakura Tenshin: *Book of Tea*, 1906)

are cats cruel?

It is not "just that cabbages don't scream so loud" (as one Buddhist vegetarian humbly qualified his preference). It really *is* worse to hurt a mouse than a mouse-ear, as it is worse to hurt a mouse-ear than a microbe; and, so long as we are noting the relativism of real (not artificial) morals, as it is worse to kill an adult than a baby and a baby than a fetus and a fetus than a cytoplast.

There is no denying that cats kill and play with a thinking and feeling creature. Yet, it is wrong to think the cat cruel. The cat's victim may experience torture, but the cat must identify enough with its prey to imagine the fear and pain to be a torturer. The cat does not. A cat just wants to play. This is shown by the outlandish way cats treat the bodies of their long dead prey. They do not need an *actual* response, just an *unpredictable* one. The adept cat throws the body with such perfect abandon it loses track of it. That is the idea. It has learned how to guarantee for itself a surprise landing or, sometimes, no landing: my cats' prey occasionally ended up in a tree or falling close to another cat who might or might not be a good enough sport to give it an equally free toss.

One also wonders why the cat is singled out for approbation. Dogs may tear their prey to pieces as soon as they catch them (savagery has its merciful side) – but we forget that the cat catches its prey quickly, whereas the dog may noisily hound its prey for hours, or even days, before putting them out of their misery. Read Margaret Cavendish, the Dutchess of New Castle's seventeenth century verse, "The Hunting of the Hare" where a hunt is witnessed through the eyes of a terrified victim! Not only does it let you feel what it is like to be hunted by dogs, but does not forget that the cruelest of the cruel is neither dog nor cat but the primate we know best.

It may seem counter-intuitive but, excluding the proverbial wily old fox, a hunter himself, who may actually enjoy making fools of the two and four-legged parvenus, there may be more torture in the chase than the post-catch play. A chased animal must keep its wits about it if it is not to be caught, while a cat-handled animal soon gives up and is out of it. I fainted once as my nerve canal was finalized on a generator-powered old belt-run drill after the power went out and discovered that when I came to my nerves were blunted – the pain less. The dazed eyes and silence of the victim-turned-toy are sad to witness, but they speak of far less pain than would be experienced by a fully alert prey. The cat's method of handling its "toy" helps. They tend to grab mice as they do kittens, by the nape of the neck to incapacitate and more easily carry them. Hopefully, the mouse's last memory is being carried by *its* mother.

On the whole, Nature does well. Most mice taken are young. They have received and given less care (*investment* in the cold word of science). No one depends upon them. That is good. But, bad things happen. Every time a mother mouse is captured – unless she is captured precisely because she was in shock due to losing her brood to a rat-snake – we have a tragedy. The mother, desperate to fulfill her responsibility to her family, dies hard, and her children die lingering deaths unless adopted by an older child of the mother with children of her own. Even then, without the help of the more experienced mother, both broods are endangered. If you are concerned for rodent happiness, do not criticize cats, learn about snakes and keep the right ones around to assure that young mice are sacrificed first.

We hear of willing victims. Yes, looks are exchanged, and a clearly psyched-out prey is more likely to be pounced upon; but this does not justify it morally. If anything it is better to be struck down when feeling hope or rage than when giving up. No bones about it, life on Earth is tragic, and no philosophy of acquiescence to fate or the greater good can change that one iota. We only find life bearable because we are capable of feeling only one side at a time. We can read a short story of Seaton's, or see a documentary film on a mouse or rabbit family, and pray that none of the wee heroes and heroines are devoured, and then turn right around in the next story or scene and pray that a Mama coyote catches one of the same so her children do not starve. Taking sides is what keeps us sane; and if we can take sides enough, we can even be happy.

play as primary

We must stop thinking of play as a secondary thing, a spill-over from the real world of making a living. After all, from the point of view of the individual cat, or all of us, for that matter, *play came first*. And, this is not only true for learning motor functions. It holds true for our social selves, our culture as well. Edward Albee's remark about "pornographic playing cards" in *The Zoo Story* hits the mark:

> *When you're a kid you use the cards as a substitute for a real experience, and when you're older you use real experience as a substitute for the fantasy.*

I once observed that the man with his beloved car is more childish than a child, because the child at least knows that his toy is a toy, while his father is completely lost in the game of playing an adult (if you read Japanese, see *Hannihonjinron* (1984, but I recommend the third edition or later), which has a whole chapter on the relationship of play and the creation of a sustainable lifestyle). Who is to say, then, that in the manifest lives of animals – as opposed to genetically set biological priorities – it is not hunting which is a spill-over from the realm of play, rather than the vice-versa? Or, to put that more poetically, who says animals *ever* grow up?

two types of make-believe

When a kitten paws at something containing an irresistible sound, such as rough fabric strummed by a fingernail, for the first time, it is just reacting. Certain noises make it itch. The whacking paw is the scratch that brings relief. This is *not* so much play as pure reflex. True play happens later, once the kitten learns to *seek out the itch*. But, even seeking an itch, or stimulation, is not a very high order of play. It requires no make-believe and involves a low degree of freedom. A kitten unraveling a ball or batting at a cat-teaser – as Japanese call stalks of grass with heads that resemble furry caterpillars – is fun to watch but not at all surprising. What impresses me is what cats do better than any animal I know of – and that includes us – is to play make-believe. *They practice to fake themselves out*.

When it comes to playing make-believe with *others*, dogs are cats' equal if not superior. They bluff anger and pretend to various serious behaviors. Sometimes a dog's nip may become a bite, as an intended light scratch by a cat may puncture skin, and get really upset with their playmate, but on the whole they are playing and they know it.

But left alone, the contrast couldn't be greater. Dogs can play by themselves a little. They can gnaw on bones and tear shoes to shreds. They can dig holes if the tiniest smell gives them an excuse to do so. But, unless they are free to follow their nose into trouble somewhere, they are liable to get bored. Even a dog with a big backyard, including shrubbery to hide in, will howl or feel like howling if left alone for long. People can identify with that, for many of us are the same. We climb the walls unless we are entertained. Cats also get bored and are happy when a playmate of whatever species returns home. But they do better than dogs because they are masters of playing alone.

More on how cats do it, below. First a general remark on what this asexual onanism means. To me, it is the ludenesque equivalent of the perpetual energy machine. A particularly ludicrous example is described in a book by playwright Betsuyanagi Minoru, *Dôgu-zukushi,* or, following Leo Lionni's book on fabulous botany, *Parallel Tools of Ancient and Medieval Japan.* The device takes us back to the metaphor with which I opened this section. Betsuyanagi's simple yet absurdly clever invention is an elegant rake-ended scratcher with the tip dipped in essence of poison ivy. The idea, of course, being that this way you'll happily have an itch for every scratch *and* – pardon, Ogden – a scratch for every itch, as well!

news for unamuno

We saw how cats throw prey up so high and haphazardly as to enjoy the pleasure of not knowing where it is likely to fall. The more remarkable thing is that the game does not require real game and the cat has more ways to momentarily make it scarce. A cat may take a crumpled piece of paper, a doll or piece of hard food and knock it under the table, then choose not to follow it under the table, but, rather, *pretend the table leg is hopelessly in the way so that he has difficulty seeing the object and has to strain desperately to reach it, by batting around the right side of the leg with the right paw and the left side with the left before throwing himself under the table like a great crime-fighter in a movie firing pistols from both hands as he slides on his back across a room.* I do not believe a dog will do this. A dog will go after the object or not go after it, but it will not make it more difficult to go after or chose the difficult way to get it.

Eventually, the effort of fighting under the heroic (?) conditions of this self-imposed handicap will drive the cat to such a high pitch of excitement that he will *slaughter* that clever piece of paper or doll. In *Man and People,* Spanish philosopher Unamuno got it wrong when he wrote,

> The animal is pure alteracion. It cannot be within itself. Hence when things cease to

> threaten or caress it; when they give it a holiday;
> in short, when what is other ceases to move it,
> the poor animal has virtually to stop existing,
> that is, it goes to sleep.   (trans. R. Trask)

Perhaps, only man – or some men! – can *"virtually and provisionally"* withdraw from the world and take *"his stand inside himself,"* or, *"to use a magnificent word which exists only in Spanish . . . ensimismarse* [be inside himself];" but I think our philosopher exaggerates when he categorically claims that *"the animal lives not from itself but from what is other than itself".* What about the cat? Have we not seen that when *"what is other ceases to move it"*, the cat, at least, is both capable of, and liable to, move the other to move itself?

cat versus dog: the eye, ear and consciousness

> Sometimes she casually sticks out a paw to wash
> and then she forgets completely what she was
> going to do with it. So she waits a few minutes
> and then puts it down again.   Lucy Miranda
> Ward, 8 (*Cats*: ed R&H Exley)

Why should cats be more liable to games that involve fooling themselves than dogs? I would guess it has something to do with the different priorities laid on their respective senses. While some cats have such a fine nose for certain foods that they may occasionally out-smell a member of the dog family (more than once my cats found a piece of food stuck to a leaf or tree bark that the *tanuki* had sniffed about for but failed to find!), dogs are far more dependent on their noses than cats, who are as likely to discover prey – or predators, such as dogs – by ear or eye.

The eye and the ear observe what takes place *at the moment*. To depend on them heavily is to live in the here-and-now. Every second may require a major adjustment; the cat's object is constantly moving about. The house-cat may be an awesome predator, but it is also prey – it can be attacked by a dog even as it hunts. So it must keep its senses and plot open for change at any time. Considering this, I cannot help wondering whether the ability to change story so smoothly that it looks like the cat is trying to fool you – what we examined in *"What's Michael!"* – fools the cat himself. Preoccupied with the present, would a cat not find itself in many "Now *what* was I doing?" situations – as eight-year old Lucy observed – except that the cat, like the author lost in his work, might not ask that question? Put in a negative way, a poor short-term memory may be what permits *feline ludens* the luxury of deluding itself, of enjoying make-believe even as a grown-up. A cat, could then be said to enjoy life by virtue of being spaced-out, a scatter-brain. This is not to say the cat is crazy – schizophrenic. The cat does not straddle two different plots, but creates a singular plot that happens to tie together in a different way than our waking one does.

cat vs. dog: the nose & consciousness

A good sense of smell that can read in the air the type of thing we must see printed in clear intaglio on the snow fits an altogether different mindset. It may be described in many ways.

Myopic. The idiom "looking as far as ones nose" is doubly apt when the nature of the nose is considered. A nose is not only literally shoved up close and right into the thick of things, but even past them. Placed in the front of the body, it is not only *near*-sighted but reverses the vector of vision, for it is *hind*-sighted.

Primitive. Is this sense the most or least primitive? Because smells, unlike sights and sounds, are rarely neutral, the olfactory sense does seem immediate and crude despite the nose having been judged superior to the mouth by location and its sense as noble as the visual by Mediterraneans who admired organs with bridges connecting them straight-away with the crown of the head.

Sophisticated. Eyes see straight. Ears hear around walls. Only noses smell through the fourth dimension, *time*. If to be stuck in the here and now is normal reality, a powerful sense of smell might be considered *metaphysical*.

It is a fact:

*Dogs see yesterday
today, by smell;
We but remember it
sometimes all too well.*

*To them,
This so-called past
is just as present
as starlight present
light-years past
appears as stars
to us at last!*

*We,
beyond reason,
trust our eyes,
our precious sight;
Likewise, dogs
believe
their noses
always know what's right.*

*By canine art
the past and present
end their long divorce;
Sniff by sniff,
the subtle scent
is scented to its source!*

*Traced back;
Or is the hunt, perhaps
the other way around?*

*What once was here,
fast-forward chased;
Until, haunches caught
by patient hound,
the past, held fast,
is in the present found!*

I wrote this doggerel after reading G.K Chesterton's poodle on the hopeless noselessness of man, who sadly lacks the noodle to smell as well as he, Quoodle, can, and the detailed description of training and working with smelling-nose dogs in Vicki Hearne's *Adam's Task*.

An animal that keeps his nose to the grindstone, or the trail, benefits by persistence. Sticking to the plot through thick and thin. Good hounds have been known to run themselves to death rather than betray their nose (The benefit? The same dogged determination may already have earned him the admiration of men and pleasure of siring offspring.). With little cause to fear predators, dogs can afford to be single-minded. So, they are. This in no way implies they are dumb. You might just say that they are more together than cats are. Thanks to their noses, they walk the line. They do not lose track of things as easily as cats do; so, for better or worse, they are less capable of fooling themselves.

cat vs dog reconsidered

One could provide a quite different evaluation of the significance of the various senses and the nature of dogs and cats. Instead of calling cats "spaced out" for forgetting what they were doing a moment earlier and thus demonstrating Paglia's *"erratic mood swings,"* we could call dogs "spaced out" for being oblivious to everything but a line of scent if I dare so call the marvelously complex smell-scape Hearne describes in *Adam's Task*. By this definition, cats could be called attentive, if not cool, for being so aware of everything going on around them, while the dog complimented for being more "together" might be belittled as a possessor of a *one-track mind.* Then again, we might call one animal *"spaced-out"* and the other *"timed-out."* The dog, attention focused on the time-line of scent, is oblivious to what is going on here-and-now in space, while the cat, attentive to the here-and-now of the space around him, is oblivious to the passage of time. Regardless, your author seems to be blessed with more than normal capacity for being spaced-out in the single-minded manner of the dog and timed-out in the scatter-brained manner of the cat. Sometimes, he wonders if this is why he gets along so well with both of these animals.

cats that cannot play

We all know that most cats grow more jaded with every year. So do most people. Otherwise "the average Tokyo child" would not need *"411 toys that cost a total of*

$1,530" (AP:1993) and adults would not need to travel so much. By age six or seven, Han-chan no longer cared to bat things hanging from a string more than two or three times in a row. The same thing went for ball play. Sometimes when I cleaned the room and all 100 square feet of *tatami* were opened up, the aging cats would get exhilarated enough to play a game of soccer, reminding me of old times; but usually they were not interested.

Only animals never failed to hold a cats' interest. You cannot get bored with living things because they keep fooling you. But at the same time, hunting can be tiring on an older cat. So they choose to sleep – or, rather, to dream? – a lot. The exception to the "only animals" rule is movement, sound and smell sufficiently stimulating not to require active make-believe on the part of the old cat. They are no longer willing to give life to a ball or string, but if the object is not visible and does not stink of plastic, the cat is willing to *suspend its disbelief* and play along.

If you have a jaded old cat, here is how to make its ears perk, eyes light up and set-off a kittenish pounce if not a helter-skelter race: Get a thin and smooth stick a yard or two long. If there is no bulge at the end, attach something to the end to make a bump big enough to make noise and a wee bulge when the stick is moved between a sheet and blanket – blanket, bed-cover, newspaper, whatever – but not so large as to catch and make it hard to move the stick, or too obvious to the cat. A wine bottle cork does fine. The noise made and the bump seen should be just obvious enough that the cat's attention is not drawn to the stick itself. (gently pull one edge of the blanket in your hand to increase the tension and lift it if the stick rubs too much). The devise can be moved back and forth, around and directly under the cat. The subtlety of this mouse-under-the-leaves effect lets even the experienced cat feel like it is matching wits with something alive. And, in a sense it is. The cat is playing with *you*.

But why indirect? Your cat *knows* it is not allowed to bite or claw *you* hard enough to really have fun. Of course, it wants to play with you, but has long since learned how easily you get hurt (and possibly angry) as a result, and knowing even innocent play can escalate to trouble, doesn't even start. Sometimes, he might forget, or pretend to forget, that the hand on the other side of the newspaper, or the knee on the other side of the blanket is yours, and make a vigorous pounce. This is usually fine; but now and then the barrier does not prove sufficient insulation and you get hurt. That is painful to the cat even if you do not strike back. As he ages, such traumatic experiences make him forget himself less and less. Now you have a safe, but not exactly exciting cat. This device allowing the cat to let go and strike freely proves a Godsend to such a cat.

But, be warned: if your cat has not freaked out like a kitten for a long time, please be careful not to overdo it at first. I do not want to get sued for giving your cat a heart attack!

multiplying toys

But, one toy no matter how good is insufficient. Your cat, old or not, needs toys that move in the air and on the ground, or any surface, as well as its favorite, ears-only movement below it.

For toys in the air, for some cats paper planes do well, especially if they come bearing catfood or scrunched up balls of cat food or balls of whatever size and/or weight the cat is comfortable with. Other cats prefer a a thick rubber band attached to a long string. At present, I use a black intertube-like rubber, a half-inch across about a foot-long if cut and extended). I can swing it in the air around the cat or better yet, hold the end of the string in one hand which also extends as if one were holding a slingshot, while the other hand pulls back the huge rubber band which released, shoots where you aim it, *i.e.*, at, over or near the cat, unless your cat is into fetching, in which case, it may be shot away from him or her. A cat with sharp claws will pierce the rubber so the first band will rapidly tear through and become a strip (still usable) but a smart cat will quickly learn to pull the band to his mouth and remove it from his claws and holding it between his teeth, if he waits just long enough, shoot it back to you. For ground-moving toys, balls within balls is probably best for creating irregular movement that continues for a long time, though irregularly shaped balls are also fine (but hard to find).

Toy *use* also matters. Even a dried stalk of some weed will keep the cat eager to attack it if you can creep around a corner and surprise the cat with it Oh, to play with a cat who enjoys such a game inside of a labyrinth! Of what I am not yet sure, but I bet it would make a fine experiment!

why just chimps?

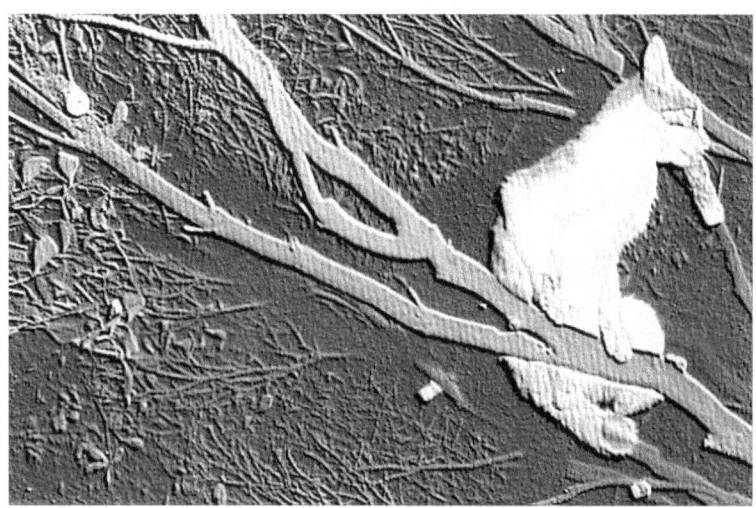

Professional trainers dole out tidbits minute by minute, hour by hour. That is ideal for most pets – not just official working breeds – enjoy challenge-and-rewards. We who are not trainers can spare only minutes a day for our little friends, need to devise ways to give them maximum play/training/working time. I recommend going out if they are in the house or in if they are out, to prepare a difficult hunt, hiding some things for the nose and making some visible but hard to reach. Here you should be able to see four *chikuwa* (tubular fishcakes) and one of two cats competing in this hunt. Chimpanzees at zoos are now encouraged to fish for ants. Our pets deserve the same, with details changed, as suitable for the respective species.

cat tails

Margaret Cavendish's Verse about the hunting of poor Watt the hare is also one of first deep ecology verses we have. Here are its last sixteen lines: *When they[men] do Lions, Wolves, Beares, Tigers see, / To kill poore Sheep, strait say, they cruell be./ But for themselves all Creatures think too few,/ For Luxury, wish God would make more new./ As if God did make Creatures for*

Man's meat,/ To give them Life, and Sense, for Man to eat; / Or else for Sport, or Recreation's sake,/ Destroy those Lifes that God saw good to make: / Making their Stomacks, Graves, which full they fill / With Murtherd Bodies, that in sport they kill. / Yet Man doth think himselfe so gentle, mild, When of all Creatures he's most cruell wild. / And is so Proud, thinks onely he shall live, That God a God-like Nature his did give. / And that all Creatures for his sake alone, / Was made for him, to Tyrannize upon. – The entire poem, properly parsed, is in *The Faber Book of Vernacular Verse*, ed. Tom Paulin)

~~~~~~

Play and Motor Functions. While young animals may hone motor functions through play, according to Temple Grandin, the old idea of it as a simulation of the real thing, for mastering proper fighting or hunting may be insufficient if not wrong, at least for some species. Playing first teaches an animal to play, which does not mean to win but how to win and how to lose – very important as no animal can always *play* a dominant role – and to handicap oneself so as not to lose weak playmates. She describes the "general hypothesis of play" of Czech animal researcher Marek Spinka, who thinks that play's primary purpose is teaching "young fighters to handle novelty and surprise" (*Animals in Translation*). This would be fascinating to consider together with dreams, which serve to reinforce what is learned. It is said that animals dream more after heavy training sessions. One wonders if the same is not true for play sessions.

~~~~~~

From *"A Cat's Garden of Verses"* by Robert Luis Stevenson:

Whole Duty of Cats

A Cat should never kill a mouse
Until he's chased it through the house,
And shown it to another kitten
Before its little head is bitten.

Stevenson's *"should"* is absolutely perfect for talking about the way cats expect other cats to behave. Found in Henry Beard *Poetry for Cats?* (1994)

~~~~~~

Cat Noses. Once I essayed into dog vs. cat, I found myself unable to get back to the cat's olfactory power. While cats may not do much tracking with their noses, they may be seen throwing themselves upon the shoes of visitors, the stinkier the better. That suggests that cats do like to read scents, though they do not necessarily care to follow them. They prefer they are brought to them. If you have a cat or know someone with a cat, *be sure to bring something sniffable when you visit*. A dog will sniff your tire or pants for signs of other dogs, but a cat wants to know *everything*.

when cats bring us things, illustrated
The Last Year Killed Twice

Life beats death. Usually, I am unhappy to find the presents or trophies cats bring home. Like telegraphs, they usually arrive when you are on the phone, eating in bed or worse. Studies cited in *The Domestic Cat* show that, contrary to the general belief, most kills do *not* occur at night. Technically, it may be true that dusk and dawn harvest the lion's share but 5 AM, "dawn" for an early-rising biologist, is *night* for most of us and, worse yet, the time when sleep is deepest. My cat friends and I lived in a tiny one-room apartment. My *futon* covered half of the floor – what my books left us. Any game chased and tossed about the room ended up on top of a very light sleeper, me. As I burnt my candle at both ends to begin with (asleep at two and up at seven) I did not care to have it trimmed in the middle too.

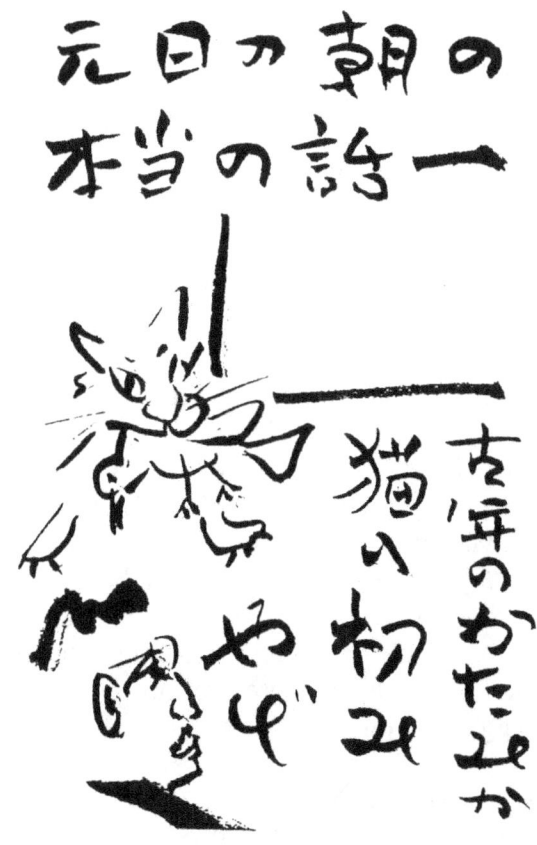

so poetic a kill!

Year of the Dog

a memento mori of last year?
the cat's first gift!

There are exceptions. I thought it was simply marvelous to be woken up on the first day of the "Year of the Dog" by a cat with a big dead *onaga* (Lit. "Long- tail": magpie?). *Why?* Because this noisy bird was far from endangered and the timing was poetic. The last year, that is the one that died the night before, was the "Year of the Bird". Here, my first gift of the New Year was its *memento mori!* I sketched the scene together with a verse on a postcard and sent it to someone after copying it (pic. next page).

and more poetic yet!

I think it was Meg, possibly Kori, I forgot to note *which* cat was so poetic. But, more amazing yet, I would soon get *another* large bird at the end of the same Year by Japan's "*old* calendar," that is to say on "the day before the calendrical beginning of spring; the beginning of the natural year," according to the old luni-solar calendar. We will not get into calendrical complexities here. Suffice it to say that today the second New Year occurs about two months after the first, Gregorian one, and is when you throw hard beans from the window shouting *"Out with the Evil!"* and over your shoulder into your room shouting *'In with Wealth!"* (On TV, I once saw a home video of a family that took the occasion to have an annual bean fight. How heart-warming to see such barbarian behavior in this tame culture! I wonder if there are any Usanian families who have egg fights on Easter?)

The last year killed twice. Kuro'ko-chan scatters
a large dove on Setsubun! (Notes)

There is nothing like a room full of dove feathers. Dove feathers are mostly down, and down won't stay down when you try to sweep it up. It rises up and over the butt of the broom and, floating in the air, refuses to sit in the dust tray. You keep finding it in your room for *weeks* to come.

That, too, was sad and reminded me of killing and eating morning doves as a boy. But, again, I was able to console myself by waxing poetic. Behold, I told myself, the lingering remnant of the previous year! Now, both calendars are covered!

riko the hunter: take 1

I can not remember why I wrote a long note like the following *before* I made up my mind to write a book on cats. Perhaps, Riko's hunting skill impressed me. Even Yôko, too sweet to harm a flea, would gush over with admiration for Riko's doing *what a cat is supposed to do*.

> With something like sparrow wings dangling from her mouth, our great hunter, the terror of the bamboo grove, Rico the [spayed] calico waited anxiously outside the window, meowing as best as she could with a mouth full of feathers; and I said *chotto matte-yo* [Hey! Wait a moment!], and quickly spread newspaper over the *tatami* and then opened the window – *Dozo!* [Please (come in)!] In sprang Rico onto my desk, then onto the newspapers, as was proper [I trained the cats to do *all* messy stuff on paper – when they couldn't get out the window in time, they almost always managed to puke on newspaper], & I hauled out her lazy cousins Hanshiro [Han-chan, about a year old at the time] & Wakamaru by the scruff of their necks & placed them in front of Rico to see. To see what a real cat, a cat of the old generation can do, even in a cold winter drizzle – and Rico growled a bit to show the importance of her trophy & then lay back squirming in delight , . . . & let the youngsters play with her prey for 30 minutes or so which reduced the fluff on the bird's body to the extent it increased in the air & on the newspaper, until Rico [deciding they had

helped her enough?] took it back & crunched it down – all of it, even the feathers . . . . she left the little head with the black on the top & black on the bottom and white in the middle – something like that I can't remember, but it was cute & then it was lost as I talked to Stork-valley Truth-one [a literal rendition of a friend's name] on the phone. The lazy cousins [Rico was their great aunt] were using it as a football. I thought, as it is a "head," it probably ended up on or around the "bed," and advised Yoko to be on the lookout, or at least not shocked should it turn up

there; but she quickly spied it near my feet at the left rear foot of my stool, which just goes to show that rhyme is not a good guide to finding lost objects. And I thought the head would look fine mounted, but, having no time, deferred & Yoko handed me a plastic bag but I, instead, threw it back to Nature out the window.

riko the hunter: take 2

Another note from two years earlier. Riko was always hunting or playing with catches. Can you guess what her most common catch – and the most common catch of all my cats – was?

Riko brings skink. No tail. . . . loses under book-pile. I find & Riko & Sa-chan play and show to Shimo, who monopolizes –might eat? – & carries outside. Riko steals back & Shimo whines & looks & looks & Nora-chan comes & mad search about turns into play [not involving skink]. Then all cats played outside & only Riko on verandah with skink for 1/2 hour & sometimes calling [calling for others to join her] & at last [they] came back, but skink was no longer moving & only Riko could (in her head) continually tease it back to life.

> Riko pulling up small branches on dying pine & releasing, Pooin! to enjoy falling needles & just pulling them off with her mouth.

My best memory of a tail is one that outlived its purpose. What happened was so interesting, I cannot remember if the unfortunate was a lizard or a skink:

ato-no-matsuri
(too little, too late)

a skink tail
fools a cat – the skink
lies dead

Here, the usual translations of *ato-no-matsuri*, "shutting the stable door after the horse has left" or the doctor coming after the patient dies doesn't keep the tail alive.

riko the hunter: take 3

A 1989 entry with a drawing of "Riko eating bird outside window in the rain," observes that birds are often brought home "during or just after rain." Why so?

> 1)Birds like rain and get careless [playing around]; 2) Birds hide out from rain in low easy-to-reach places; 3) Rain hides sounds and smells so cat can sneak up better; 4) Birds slip and fall in the rain; 5)Birds with colds drop in the rain. [6) Birds get cold and drop in the rain. (Not only does rain mean a sudden drop of temperature but brings on hypothermia by its wetness).] (notes)

The bird did not impress me. But the methodological way Riko prepared its innards did. I wonder how common it is:

> *She munches up the body good, like a butcher*
> *with a wooden mallet moving back and forth*
> *from neck to legs, like on a blues harmonica &*
> *then chomps for good & in end little is left.* nb

I had planned to use my drawing, but it adds nothing to the description and is pretty damn ugly, so let us skip it.

riko the hunter: take 4

I reply to Yoko re R's bad eyes, that's why she catches only moles instead of mice & that very evening R brought in a rat-sized mouse! nb

I'd forgotten about Riko's poor eyes; but I can remember not being too surprised about that mouse because I had on numerous occasions, unfortunately not recorded, learned that cats always contradict what you say about them. One more is recent enough [when I was writing the first draft of the book] to be retrieved from the memory: I just told a friend about how Kuro'ko-chan was the sweetest cat in the world when, to my embarrassment, she savagely attacked Kori-chan and chased her out the window and into the bamboo grove! I am afraid that unless a feline researcher can prove me wrong, this is a perfect example of a claim that is impossible to prove. (The picture below shows Meg the mother of Rico, eyes wide open to hear the magpies shrieking outside. The whiskers actually curved straight forward but I could not manage to draw that.)

riko the hunter: take 5

This is my last note entry mentioning Riko. Here, there is no question about the "gift" coming in the middle of the night!

Han-chan trying over and over again to rape his pregnant sister Wakamaru-chan. And whopping him. Outside, rain. Riko brings home a mouse at 2.30 AM. Yoko only goes *"Huh?"* Plays with mouse. Eats mouse (after growling for audience). 15 minutes later gets sick. I clean it while Yoko sleeps & find head neatly on newspaper. 3:15 – 4:00 AM. Boy in room above cleans noisily. 4:30 to bed. (notes)[pic]

Pardon the information about Han-chan before his operation! Evidently Han-chan's sister exuded a smell while pregnant that he found exciting. Back to the subject.

dead animals as art

I do not know what it is about these dead animals or parts of dead animals that attracts me to draw them. You have already seen a bird head and a mouse head. Both might be considered natural gems, the crown-piece of these cute little creatures, so fresh the eyes still glistened. The head, more or less round (without indented areas or joints) stands alone as an objéct – pronounced without the "ct" in the artistic French way, of course.

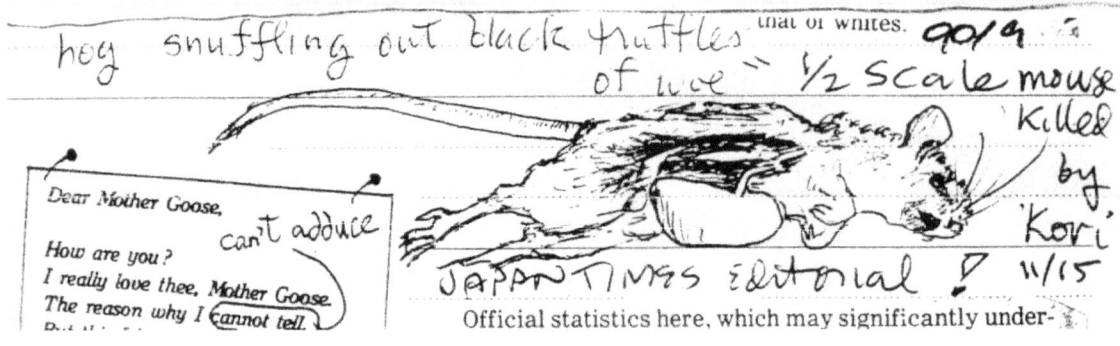

In one of my notes, I mentioned *mounting*. That was no joke. If I really knew how to do it, I would have. Imagine a gallery of your cat's kills mounted on proper-looking little plaques and hanging on your wall! But heads were not the only dead things that met my eye. Some were *not* pretty. The mouse above was killed by Kori. Above the drawing, cropped for space, are these words: *"Paglia on Dickinson: "She is a shark lured by spilled blood, a rustic hog snuffling out black truffles of woe.""* And below it, the end of an inane *Japan Times* editorial on AIDS the last line of which reads, *"However frustrating, sexual revolutionaries of both sexes must stay on guard."* I do not know if the words and clipping were fit around the drawing or vice versa but the editorial was sickenly patronizing. Yet, to be honest, that internal organ, eviscerated yet shiny and intact, was pretty in its own way. That and the pretty ear was what made me draw the gruesome picture of the poor mouse.

Then, there is the bird, I noted a strange dream. A woman dying ballad style, pining away with the lover out of sight, but her final breaths sounded like an orgasm! I wondered if some oily pizza I ate was responsible and thought of the possibility for food for pleasant dreams, like Ben Franklin's idea of food for sweet farts (in the 1990's a Japanese company actually put on sale just such an "etiquette pill"!) The note says only that I was "woken up [at] 4.30 AM Sunday by Kuroko's play." And that "it probably had fallen from nest in storm & was already dead."[pic] Unlike the adult birds, each of which I feel for, the death of the baby bird little disturbed me. What sadness I felt was for its parents. I hoped the whole nest was not lost and other chicks remained. I was able to enjoy the interesting design of the ill-fated creature:

And, I was able to wonder later: Is my little drawing, my memento, worth the death of the baby bird? I thought of Audobon shooting his subjects. Would it be best that we drew or painted all of our pet's kills to atone for the waste of life? Or, is this drawing of mine but a less obnoxious form of trophy collecting?

a true hunter's end

Although Riko was the witchiest looking cat I have ever known. You will instantly recognize her in the photo on the next page. If she was a witch, then, she was a good witch, a superb mother and aunt. Although we fed her all she wanted, she chose to spend most of her time outdoors; and judging from the walks we took together, was familiar with far more territory than common for a female cat. Indeed, she continued with me when the males (excluding Ôsama, the visiting King (pages 139-40) chickened-out and turned back home.

She probably caught as much game as all my other cats together! Usually, the only time you can *count on* a cat to catch things is when it has kittens to teach; but Riko hunted *for the sake of hunting*, year round. On July 5, 1852, Thoreau wrote in his *Journal* the following about bird song. To me, it sums up Riko's feeling for hunting perfectly.

> Some birds are poets and sing all summer. They are the true singers. Any man can write verses during the love season. We are most interested in those birds who sing for the love of the music and not of their mates; who meditate their strains, of deeper sentiment; not bobolinks, that lose their plumage, their bright colors, and their song so early.

Riko, the true hunter, disappeared in 1990. One rainy night, I came home to find an enormous brontosaurus tail of mud filling in the crevice of the valley above and wrapping part way around the apartment house. The trees that slid, still standing, down the slope looked much better (in the streetlights) than the massive ugly concrete stairs and ramp soon to be bulldozed clean. All in all, it was thrilling. No one had been hurt and I only wished I could have been there to witness the land sliding.

The next day, Riko was missing . And the next. *Riko was never seen again.* She often hunted moles in the area that collapsed. Well, maybe she dug into one to many a molehill and brought down a mountain that just happened to be slated for "development." I like to imagine she died defending her hunting preserve, though chances are she was so traumatized by the cataclysmic event that she fled to another valley.

envoi

If the cat's large eyes are not enough reason for gifts tending to come in the night, how about this: what if they choose that time the better to disturb us yet still not get whacked or have the prey taken away because they know we are slow and, perhaps, amusing to mess with when sleepy? Then, again, cats are not the only ones making noise in the wee hours of the night.

> *Dec 29-30 Couple next door doing it up good – 3rd time, that night? She, yelping like a vixen, & cat brings in [what I took to be]a mole. The incredibly loud [and fast] hyper-ventilation of the girl [if I had made a tape of it, I could be rich!] and the cat's announcement, not to mention scampering about, are making for one pandemonium of a night & throws it around room, but later discover it isn't a mole but a bird, because of unsweepable features. [all but the feathers was eaten]. Reason [for my thinking it a mole] was a real mole, a huge mama, rat-size! but saw the little tail [stubby and unique to moles] several days earlier on the day after Yoko moved [The cat was so upset by the moving that it took on a dangerously large mole?] It hid in a vest of mine left on the floor between the artificial fur and the lining – gnawed right in. I let it go, being Xmas, & cats came running [when I tossed it together with vest out the window] but already dug in [to the ground as easily as a diver breaks the water of a swimming pool] & escaped. [I think it was gravid.](notes)*

A similar dirt-diving mole killed a tree outside my window. Meg – a big-butted calico like her mother Riko – saw the mole burrow in under the tree. Unwilling to lose her "catch," she dug a dog-size foot-wide six-inch deep trench around the poor tree, which, unlike the mole, could not escape. Why did I let her do it? Because I had never seen a cat do so much digging and I thought the observation worth the life of the sickly tree. It also made me give more credance to my silly idea about her mother's death. *Digging like that was probably learned from observing her mother Riko the witch and if her mother had done the same to a tree on a crucial point on that slope, she may indeed, with a little help from the rain, have brought down the mountain.*

cat tails

Hunting as a Good Thing! The only book I have read to take an entirely positive attitude about hunting by domestic cats is Paul Corey's *Do Cats Think?* Had I read it earlier, more would be in this or the other hunting chapter. Corey is happy with hunting because he finds it an extension of the cat's natural desire to give us things and to be praised.

> Our youngest Siamese, Mao, before he was old enough to begin serious hunting, used to bring us pretty autumn leaves. Once he brought Ruth a beautiful flat stone the size of a half-dollar.

I love this example for shows without argument why the idea that cats bringing gifts are treating us like kittens is too simplistic. I have already covered the matter of praise, though indirectly, when I wrote about the need for cats to show off what they catch (pg.242-244). Desire for a reaction was implied, though it need not be praise, *per se*. Corey trained his cats to kill their prey quickly before playing with them by killing the prey himself and criticizing the cat. In fact, he noticed that criticism got results before he realized praise did. I trained my cats differently by confiscating and letting live prey go. They quickly came to learn that dead toys fared better and took care to dispatch them. For more about suburban hunting, read *the Working Cat* chapter of Corey's book.

The Cats in the Photograph are Riko the witchy huntress, Zoro (see the moustache stain) of the lightning fast paws who fought the great rat-snake and Shimo a young Tom who was to disappear.

Couple Next Door in my notes. College kids with nothing to do but do *it*. Could the girl's high-pitched, loud love-yelps have helped propel the cats out into the woods to hunt?

Are We keeping the Right Pets?
A Little Red Mouse

Christopher Smart (1722-71) witnesses for his "servant of the Living God" Jeffrey the cat. His words are are a beautiful example of what we might call Christian natural history:

> For having consider'd God and himself he will consider his neighbor. For if he meets another cat he will kiss her in kindness. For when he takes his prey he plays with it to give it a chance. For one mouse in seven escapes by his dallying. JUBILATE AGNO

the mercy/cruelty of cats

My two main mouse catchers, Kori and Mechan (a.k.a. Meg), were not merciful. They learned to bring mice inside, where there were no holes, before beginning to dally with them. Yet, with more than one cat taking turns with the prey, it was often left untended – "I thought it was *your* turn!" "*I* thought . ." – so many mice enjoyed a brief escape, but rarely for longer than a day, and usually for only a few hours.

This pitiless mother-daughter pair brought to mind another Christian statement, no.73 of how many items I forgot to note in our (the American colonies') theologian Jonathan Edwards' collection of *Images or Shadows of Divine Things*, where the "way of a cat ("a foul unclean creature" according to Levi.11.29 etc.) with a mouse" is shown to be God's perfect allegory for, or "lively emblem" of, "the way of the Devil with many wicked men."

> The cat makes a play and a sport of the poor mouse . . . . When they seem to escape, they fall into them again, and so again and again, till at length they are totally and utterly devoured by Satan.

do cats keep stock?

My cats were so casual about "losing" the mouse, and they seemed so confident, dozing off with their ears pricked up (mouse movement woke them like trip-wired clackers!) that I seriously wondered whether their intent was to stock the room with mice, as game-keepers stock ponds with trout. No, well-fed cats do not want to kill off all the mice any more than we want to run out of sport fish.

In Donald Griffin's *Animal Intelligence* there is an account of a fox, that had already eaten to his heart's content and cached a mouse, after which he caught a shrew. This,

> he carried some distance to an open roadway where he began to play with it. As Henry [1986, 136-40] described the fox's behavior in his field notes, 'the fox is leaping around, dancing about the shrew who runs over to one side of the road before the fox herds it back to the center. After 45 seconds of playing with this animal, the fox does an extraordinary thing. He picks up the shrew in his mouth, walks down the slope to where he captured the prey, and then with a toss of the head spits the shrew out directly at a small burrow. In less than a second, the shrew disappears into the hole and is out of view."

For food or fun in the future, Henry hypothesizes. I saw a killer-whale do the same with a young seal it was using as a football on a TV documentary. He or she let it go near to the shore with a flourish that seemed to say, *Now off with you! Today was fun, I'll be back to eat you later.* In Charles Darwin's *Notebook M,* we find something similar for cats:

> Fox believes cats discover bird's nests & watch them till the young are big enough to eat. – There was blackbird's nest, near hot house at Shrewsbury, which the cat was seen by Hubberley to visit daily to see how the young got on. This nest the cat could [easily reach?]
> If cats will ((ever)) eat little birds, this [would be a] most curious instance of reason & abstinence.

While I doubt we'll ever hear of a cat bright enough to invent a savings account like the dolphin that hid trash under a platform so that it could exchange the bits for fish rewards at will, I believe that cats do occasionally consider the future. This cannot be proven here. Cats do eat baby birds, but there are other possibilities. Fear of the mother blackbird. Affection for the chicks (perhaps they cheeped in a way that softened the cat's heart). Regardless, who is to say cats do not think of nature as their refrigerator and desire to keep it well stocked?

Of course, food may have nothing to do with it. The cat may want to keep its play-pen stocked with toys. Playing with little birds learning to fly would be a lot more fun than picking them out of a nest. Compared to that, even a slink would offer more fun. I can definitely point out a clear instance of what Darwin called "reason & abstinence" which points to this possibilty. I used to enjoy finger spun tops (my mother collects them), especially when I learned that by spinning them upside down on their stalks they could skitter across tatami mat that would prevent their normal use. The hum and jittery movements are irresistable to most cats, and spun rightside up or down, elicit a powerful paw whack. But, Han-chan quickly learned by trial and error how to touch moving finger-spun tops ever so gently so as not to knock them over and end the fun! He would let one brush his paw three or four times in one 30 second spin! None of my other cats learned to do this; but I think that if one cat could, it at least proves a cat *can* forsake instant gratification for a slightly longer reward.

"sinister killers at the hearthside"

The above was the title of one of Mark Brazil's *Wild Watch* columns published in the "Japan Times," the gist of which was "the domestic cat is a killer." After introducing the great English *cat kill debate* – cat-haters claiming up to 200 million birds and mammals per year are killed by pet cats, while a "procat biologist . . . eager to show the domestic cat in a friendlier, less harmful light, recalculated the death toll as merely 28 million small animals a year" – the columnist comes down hard, *real* hard on cats. At the head of the article, he warns "If you are a confirmed cat lover and wish to hear nothing but good about your feline friend, do *not* read on." Here is why:

> The saddest case of all, that I have found, relates to the arrival on Stephen's Island, New Zealand, of a lighthouse keeper with a cat. The cat discovered the previously unknown Stephen's Island wren, and systematically set about catching them all. That single cat eradicated the entire species. It is almost as if cats gained some kind of feline pleasure from learning a search image and then exercising it until that species has gone!"(June 18, 1997)

If Jeffery Smart's cat is a little too merciful, Mark Brazil's is a little too mean. If nothing else, the individual cat mentioned can claim *extenuating circumstances*. Without other cats to share one's catch with, any cat goes crazy. Showing off is the exclamation point on a cat's get-and-bring behavior. Without it, the cat had no choice but to go on and on. If only the man was not too busy tending his lights to pay the cat enough attention or, better yet, had brought a second cat, the birds might have survived.

the other side of the story

This type of thing – like the dogs that did in the last dodos – obviously should be guarded against. But bird-lovers hate cats for killing birds that are far from endangered, too. Barbara Holland gives much needed perspective on this broader issue:

> "Wildlife managers estimate that birds kill more birds than cats do. I believe it, having watched a blue jay murder a nest full of baby wrens outside my window. The wrens had successfully routed the cats from their whole end of the yard, but they were helpless against the jay."

> "Birds know more about cats than bird-lovers do. The sedentary robin, checking the grass for worms, flies only eight or ten feet when he sees the cat approaching . . ."(Ibid.)

Not that such rationality has any effect upon someone whose favorite bird is murdered by a cat, even if the cat happens to be your own. John Skelton's long and sweet masterpiece "Phyllyp Sparrowe" (1505~7) says it all. After depicting the many endearing mannerisms of the pet sparrow and the sorrow of finding him slain, *"Gyb our cat"* is treated to twenty couplets of the best cursing found in the English language. It is *too* fine – only a few words per line, with bits of Latin mixed in (early macaroni), it hops about nimbly like the bird itself! – and too touching a poem to be quoted in part, so I will not do it. (It is *also* said to be a translation from Catullus; but, if so, it is so convincingly English, that Skelton must have taken great liberty with it!)

a fine coincidence

At 6:00AM one day in 1990, my notes say a mouse was brought in and "given a sporting chance (one meter headstarts);" after which "I sleep again." I slept-in, waking shortly before noon, and went outside to study in the sun. Decadent? No. This was the way I kept comfortable in the winter without heating.

Shortly thereafter, I saw the postman climbing the hill. He brought me a letter from Jack Stamm ("minor beat poet" (his words), copywriter, translator and harpman. In it I found a rhymed translation of the ninth century Irish monk classic: *The Scholar and His Cat*, which I had requested of him only three days earlier!

> 1.
> My cat and I have different tastes,
> ergo, we go our separate ways,
> as far apart as day and night.
> His name is Pangur; he is white.
>
> 2.
> I have my pleasure out of books;
> he waits for rodents by their nooks.
> He goes his way and I go mine;
> both of us think this is just fine.

7.
We live in two-part harmony:
Each of us lets the other bee.
I have my labors, he hath his.
Our mutual ignorance is bliss.

8.
And if there be a moral here,
'tis this: Enjoy each passing year,
muster your craft, and love your cat –
and that, I do believe, is that.

I was running an experiment of sorts, asking many people to rhyme a scholar's unrhymed English translation (supplied with the terse alliteration-filled AABB end-rhymed original for reference), with one object being to learn whether the rhyme would draw the poems together – i.e. *books* leading to *nooks* – or, conversely, pull them apart by allowing the plot to follow its own rudderless reason. All of Jack's reading, mine and some others may be found in *A Dolphin In the Woods*. To continue the story, after reading Jack's letter, I went back to the mouse-stocked room for my afternoon nap. Adjusting my blanket, I was surprised to find an area full of holes. The mouse was nearby, in a fold, trembling. Mice *always* tremble like vibrators left on for life. That is why their batteries run out so quickly. The only trouble is you cannot tell if they quiver from fear (At this point [real time, first draft!] I open the window to let in Kori-chan with another mouse, which she immediately drops onto a page of a magazine used for a plate for cat food where it is immediately picked up and thrown about the room by Me-chan, who just now dug it out from the folder where I keep notes for this book, and tosses it so energetically that I fear being beaned.) or shivering from the cold. (I have put Me-chan with *that* mouse *out*.)

This mouse had reason to tremble. The lower half of its body was paralyzed, one eye bulged grotesquely and one was sunken in and sealed. Only the delicately crafted little ears and paws said this was the fine beauty we call mouse.

I stroked it gently. It nipped me hard. Luckily, no blood *was* drawn. Had it been, I probably would have turned it over to the cats. How strange, I thought to myself, a mouse this far gone rarely tries to bite *cats* – why, then, did it bite *me?* Then, I figured it out: my fingers were icy cold and almost as big as the mouse. If I were a mouse, I would bite, too! After warming my fingers thoroughly, I tried again, and sure enough the mouse did not bite me. Within an hour, it not only put up with but *liked* to be touched.

training the mouse

I can not remember the exact order of things I offered to the mouse to eat. I called around for advice and *all* of it was wrong. Even the vet who told me sunflower seeds and cabbage was *wrong.* This mouse turned out to love roast soybean powder (*kinako*) more than everything else put together, but also did not mind water sweetened with a bit of raw brown sugar, cooked rice, corn, turnip stalk, cheese or butter.

The first night, the mouse slept like a log, or rather a twig, beside me, because it was incapable of doing otherwise. When we woke in the morning the deformities had vanished! The mouse was cured of all its ailments. It was good as new! You have never seen such a pretty mouse. The rusty red-tinged hair, the delicate fairy-like features . . .

And almost as soon as it was on its feet, the mouse was performing tricks. If I scratched the *futon* or *tatami*, it would pop out of my book-pile (the books overflowed the shelves), scamper up my leg, climb out my arm and daintily eat up the food on my palm. At that time, even Han-chan could only shake hands. I had yet to teach him his panopoly of tricks. True, the fact the mouse ate a full meal every 40 minutes or so gave me leverage over him, but still the mouse was so eager to learn!

It set me thinking. *Maybe we are keeping the wrong animal.* My cats have been with me for years and how much have they learned to do? Most learned very little. Yet here was this little red mouse, a total stranger until the day before, and we were already prepared to put on an animal circus. The next day, that is exactly what we did. But that is getting ahead of the story.

"Oops, we got the wrong pet!" rhymes

There is probably a potential anthology of alternative pet rhymes out there. Here are two of them for a start:

THE CAT

You get a wife, you get a house,
Eventually you get a mouse.
You get some words regarding mice,
You get a kitty in a trice.
By two A.M., or thereabouts,
The mouse is in, the cat is out.
It dawns upon you in your cot,
The mouse is silent, the cat is not.
Instead of Pussy, says your spouse,
You should have bought another mouse.

The italics are mine. The poem is Ogden Nash, of course. Shel Silverstein suggests how to get rid of those cats:

DRATS

Can anyone lend me
Two eighty-pound rats?
I want to rid my house of cats.

His drawing in *Where the Sidewalk Ends* shows a pair of rats that weigh *at least* two-thousand eight hundred pounds (my italics).

the longest night

The second night was trying. I was determined to keep my little friend alive, but it was mid-winter so I could not force the cats to sleep out. There had already been a few close calls during the day where I had whacked cats out of pre-pounce postures. Han-chan accepted my perverted love and consented to sniff the mouse and pretend it was a kitten; but the three females could not even *look* at it without getting a bad case of the dying-to-pounce jitters.

When the mouse, half-paralyzed, stayed put on that first night, I got some sleep. But that 40-minute timer in the mouse's belly went off all night long. Now he could move.

Each time, he would pop out from wherever he snoozed and search of food. So, water pistol – a pint-sized plant sprayer – in hand, I sat up all night, feeling every bit like a body-guard.

Had the mouse's only interest been getting to the food without the cats getting to him, I could have protected him. But no, he wanted to examine the cats. So long as I was *between* him and them, it was easy to squirt a cat who was thinking about what it should not – But this youngster (any old mouse that acted like that would have died long ago) took to walking among the sleeping, or apparently sleeping cats.

I would start to doze off only to awaken just in time to snatch my friend from the doors of death. The first time, *I* caught the cat by the scruff of the neck. The second time, by its *tail*. The third time, I missed the cat but miraculously got the window closed before the cat, mouse in mouth, was out it. My slobber-covered friend was none for the worse. I was shook up. I drank strong coffee and stayed up the rest of the night.

curiosity killed the *what?*

Funny, I thought, an animal bright enough to learn a trick in a day, and sensible enough to nip me without bringing blood – I deliberately touched his back with a cold finger again to confirm that hypothesis – was dumb enough to let himself be caught time and time again by cats. Or, was this little creature simply more driven by the need to satisfy his curiosity than by anything else?

And, let me be honest, I was delighted to witness this show of innocence not yet lost and saddened to reflect on what usually happens to the curious. It happened that I had just seen a documentary where a kangaroo was killed by aborigines for coming up and "offering itself."

The emissaries of peace, the ones who are most willing to establish inter-species relations are eaten. What a shame! I'd rather we kill the ones that run away. The ones that lack curiosity and do not give a damn about us. Call me an idealist, but I would *always* reward curiousity!

how to save a mouse

Not knowing where the mouse was abducted, I dared not free it; I doubted it could survive without its family in this cold weather. The mouse needed to be put up until Spring. That morning, I chased out the cats and went next door to try to convince a high-school girl that this little red mouse was just the pet for her.

The high-school girl was not very impressed with the idea of keeping a mouse. Neither was her mother. But I explained how he learned a trick in a single day, how we spent the night, and what that meant: If you do not take him he is *as good as dead!*

I knew no teenage girl likes to be held responsible for the murder of something cute. She reluctantly agreed to meet him. He played his part perfectly, coming out *at once* when I scratched the *tatami* and did his trick. Then, I had her warm her fingers by breathing on them before petting him, and sure enough, he accepted her petting. *She was hooked.* But her mother still had to be convinced.

I bought time until the mouse's next hunger attack, by telling her all about the mouse and how to care for him . Then and only then, I had her phone her mother , who came right over. Again, the mouse responded on cue. The daughter looked at her mother as if to say, "See, I told you he was smart!"

The mother either expected the mouse to have a particularly brainy or beatutiful look or she pretended to be nonplused,

>*"Nanjya! Tada-no nezumi deshoo!* (Why, it's just an ordinary mouse!")

But, bless her heart, she let her daughter keep the mouse, who apparently did not perform so well in her room and spent the nights gnawing holes in her desk. I am sure he was frustrated, for there was nothing half so nice as my book-pile in her clean room. Within a month he reportedly left on his own.

the mouse I failed to save

I must confess. Not all my rescues were successful. A paralyzed mouse found a couple years later was given the same treatment of strokes by breath-warmed hands and electric light bulb heating – I had forgotten about that, but it is in my notes: with no heater, I had to warm up the mice by putting them in a box under a light bulb – only to leap frantically from the box (he actually bonked his head on the light-bulb) and hide in the book-pile, from where he never came out – at least not when I was looking – and could be heard chewing up a storm. Fearing the worst for my books, I finally let Me-chan, my best mouser, do as she wished. She *did*.

It would seem that this mouse got well too fast, i.e., before it had bonded with me. This, together with my experience in moving cats, tells me that it is necessary for an animal to be in a weak or dazed state for a considerable period of time if it is to adjust to new circumstances without trauma. *Getting well too fast can kill you.*

on keeping mice

One would think a creature as cute and cunning as a mouse would be a far more popular pet than it is. Only the difficulty – impossibility? – of house-breaking them and the damage done by their chiseling prevent them from being accepted pets. A cage could stop that, but it spoils half the fun by making mice captives rather than pets.

What to do? We must create dwellings that may be shared in peace. The mice might be given a hollow wall and a ceiling with connections to the outside to be used at the mouse's discretion and to the inside, depending upon our discretion. I'm thinking of something like an ant-farm, where the inside of the wall would be transparent – some one-way glass to allow the mice to feel at ease and some two-way glass for us to enjoy looking at each other. One might even incorporate a hose attachment to wash the *mouse-farm* out as needed.

There may also be cultural blocks. In China and Japan there are *mouse* rather than *cat*-burglars. One year of twelve is the Year of the Mouse and one night each year the time to celebrate their nuptials. They star in many Chinese Mother Goose rhymes (one, where a baby mouse gets stuck up a candle stick may be *the* most well known Chinese nursery poem) and are symbols of prosperity. Then again, "we" did come up with Mickey Mouse . . .

I have thought of doing a book on/of literary mice for decades: *Of Mice By Men – an international anthology of mouse tales*. I have already championed their character in public debate in Japan. *Literally.* I argued in the Asahi magazine *Aera* that, while it may be hard to *write* the character, 鼠 , it is easy to *read* and deserves to join dog 犬 and cat 猫 in the newspapers, rather than be written with phonetic syllabets ネズミ. As the Chinese once appreciated mice more than any other culture I know of, their way of writing mice *must* be on the cover of my book.

a cat and mouse paradox

During the short time I was with my red mouse, I sometimes thought the same thing I thought when visited by *tanuki:* Maybe *I* would be better off without cats. Cats offer a lot, but they sure do put a crimp in your relationship to other species. But, then again, if it weren't for my playing in the woods with the cats, the *tanuki* would not have called on me; and if it were not for my cats' hunting, I would not have known there *were* such cute mice around me. None of the neighbors I asked had ever seen one.

cat tails

My rhyme of the *The Scholar and His Cat* is far more convoluted than Jack Stamm's crisp rendition and starts with a couplet. Again, if rhyme as a game interests you, see *A Dolphin In the Woods*.

Pangur Ban, me cat, and I are brothers at heart:
Though our aims differ, there is but One Art.

how cats and tanuki interact
& the Racoon Foxes

> "The way to know if a suspicious person encountered in the mountains [wilderness] is a fox or a *tanuki*. You must peek at it through a hole in your left sleeve and if it is a *bakemono* (changeling) its true form can be seen." – from haiku poet Issa's notes (*zatsu-roku*) of folkways.

This chapter, originally titled *The Third Generation Tanuki, a new hypothesis of domestication* was several times longer. Coming back to edit it after over a decade, I can see that most, like the above quote, has nothing to do with cats and the main subject, the *tanuki,* deserve a book rather than a chapter. So I have copied the file to a new folder where it may be nourished until it grows into a book and give you just an introduction, the cat-related part and my hypothesis.

japan's weirdest folk animal

The dictionary Englishes *tanuki* as "a raccoon dog" because they have raccoon-like masks and belong to the canine family. Old Japanese prints show them with balls large enough to use as a blanket or a boat, and ceramic statuettes have them standing with a gourd of *sake*. Seeing those pots, you would not think he was *standing*, but *straddling* two big sacks of rice (doubtless for making the *sake*). Why *sake?* Because the *tanuki* makes many odd sounds as if he could be drunk, is up at night and sleeps in the day and when mating under the full moon gets so involved in brawling with his fellows that they may roll right into you (it happened to me!). Why the huge *balls?* I would guess the first potter who decided to make a *sake* jug that looked like a standing *tanuki* wanted something to fill in between the legs, and this was copied and exaggerated by graphic artists, but the common explanation is that the skin of *tanuki* balls was reputed to be the best material to put between a hammer and gold-leaf, allowing one midge of gold to be pounded into eight-mats of gild. That is to say, the size of a large room. Before long, the tanuki's balls were themselves believed to be that large! Here is my notebook description of the real thing:

> SHY as a RABBIT yet NOISY as a BEAR; COAT like a SHEEP & little skinny FOX-like LEGS; EYES beg affectionately, like a DOG; no *kitsusa* (sharpness) in glance like a *kitsune* (fox).

I assumed they had frightfully powerful claws, like a badger, because most translations call them "badgers" and they, too, live in burrows. Up close, their paws were slight, even feminine. It is one reason I believe we should call the *tanuki* a racoon *fox* rather than *dog*, but will leave that debate to another book. Here we will just call them *tanuki*.

e-zuke

The day after I pointed one out on a moonlit night to Yoko, I returned from work to find raw yams and eggplant scattered outside. Yoko was very excited to have seen the legendary animal, and though she was disappointed it did not walk on two-legs as she had imagined, she brought it equally legendary food. It, I mean *they* – there were two this time – did appear again, but only sniffed the vegetables. (Unlike many dogs, they were *not* omniverous)

That got me to thinking about why the *tanuki* visited in the first place. On that day, we had gone into the woods with the cats to play. We took along *chikuwa*, cheap fish hot-dogs with the centers drilled out. We stuck them high on tree branches and threw them down hills so the cats could enjoy working for food. The latter game was particularly thrilling as the slope was thickly bambooed – an average of one every 4-9 square meters – very steep and covered with bamboo leaves. Yoko feared I'd get them killed, and I must admit to having some qualms of conscience, but they were far outweighed by chagrin at not being able to get this slaloming event on video. I swear it was far more exciting than anything in the Olympics! The first *tanuki* must have been attracted by the smell of the *chikuwa* and followed the trail to the apartment.

They did not appear for a week or so. We went to the woods and played with the cats as before and sure enough that night they appeared and cautiously ate the *chikuwa* we left out after feeding the cats. They would not dare approach close enough to take the *chikuwa* near the window, and they made it a practice to run off ten or twenty yards before stopping to eat.

Within weeks, they were taking food ten or twenty feet from the window and only running away a few yards. Then, they settled for a safe distance of about half that, and only started if we made any quick movement or a noise. They did not mind our calling them in a soft voice. *"Tanuki! Tanuki!"* It was not long before they inched nearer to hear me better. But they were so jumpy a dropped can of cat-food or a footstep fifty yards away would scatter them so quickly you would think they exploded. Sound travels at 625 miles per hour and I would bet *tanuki* manage to keep up with it for at least the first fifty feet! Then, they slowly inch back to the area of the window. This type of thing would repeat itself once every few minutes as long as they visited. It was funny and sad.

"E-zuke," my title, is a term from Japanese primatology. It means getting a wild animal to learn to take food offered by humans. Shortly later, I learned at least one other house was on their route. I do not know how much *e-zuke* by one house or person affects that at another.

tanuki in the neighborhood

Before long, these *tanuki* were visiting almost daily and even brought their children whose existence we had ascertained from the amount of food carried away. I found they *loved* canned sardine in their jelly but only *liked* fresh sardines. On the other hand, they *went crazy* for the dark and bloody part of tuna (the cheapest animal protein in Japan. Spiced up with a lot of ginger, I, too, eat it. The *tanuki* preferred it raw. Dripping blood. Hardly the vegetarian most Japanese imagine!

It was vital for me to *prove* Tanuki existed to neighbors because their sleep-disturbing wrestling matches were being blamed on my cats, so I went out into the woods to search for one of their public restrooms, which I had heard of in a public radio documentary. Luckily, I found one right on the backbone of the hill, plump in the middle of the *kedamono-michi* or "beast-path" (as Japanese call small trails made or preserved by the four-legged kind), circular and about 4 feet in diameter, and raised up about the thickness of a deluxe pizza. I managed to drag the neighbor's fourteen year-old girl up to the site, but 50 yards from her home, and soon the entire neighborhood knew.

tanuki manners

> *[raw]egg-carrying mama tanuki [at same time] chikuwa gathering – picking up too many & losing all many times . . . [The tanuki] backs down from cat hissing [face to face only a foot apart] over food & retreats 3 or 4 yards & [and the moment the cat looks down at the food] charges noisily [paws scuffing the leaves and making a sound somewhere between a pig's grunt and a chicken's clucking] back & cat [panicking, runs away].*

I drew a picture of the first part of this. It is poor, like a cartoon of a racoon trying to smoke a whole pack of cigarettes at one time. But you really had to see it happening. It is hard enough to carry a raw chicken egg in your mouth. Imagine trying to cram in *chikuwa* fish-tubes before and behind it. You'd think she – for this was a mother – was finally ready to leave, then a stick would pop out and she'd try to pick it up and then another would drop, and this went on and on. I got to laughing so hard I can't recall what finally happened. If any animal deserved to have its paws turn into hands it was a *tanuki!*

The encounter with the cat has been described already, but is remarkable enough to warrant a repeat. *Tanuki,* singular or plural, often pretended to be afraid when a cat hissed or threatened, then, called the cat's bluff the moment its attention wavered. I can clearly recall how one *tanuki's* charge began as soon as the cat glanced my way with a *"Huh! I scared that sucker off!"* type of look. Or at least that is how *I* understood the cat's look, before she ignominiously fled. Pride commeth before flight? *Tanuki* clearly deserve their reputation as a foxy animal.

Yet, for all their clever interspecies' diplomacy, among themselves, the *tanuki* could be very rough. The ones low on the nipping order quickly learned to appreciate my pea-shooter justice and stay near for protection. And I liked them around, for they were the most *deliberately* expressive animals, other than humans, I'd ever met. Dogs and cats have ways to show us what they like or do not like; but only a *tanuki* will sniff and pick up something you give them, carry it a bit closer to you, looking you in the eye, lay it gently down, and then look at you again as if to say *"Thank you, but no thank you!"* And they thank you for *all* the food they eat. If they only glanced up at you *before* eating you could interpret their behavior as cautious; but they also look up at you as if to say *"Thank you"* when they've *finished!* They even made it a practice to hang around for a while after eating, as if rushing off too fast would be insulting to my hospitality. Or, maybe it was only that they liked to eat the beetles drawn to my desk light by the bay window for desert.

the 'third-generation tanuki'

Before returning to the relationship of cats and *tanuki*, I want to sum up my relationship with them. With the first generation, as described above, they would not come close and were terrified when I moved. But soon, they took their puppies with them on their rounds and this second generation that grew up witnessing my generosity and kindness, gradually tried to approach the window. When they got to within ten or twenty feet, their parents dashed over and pinned them to the ground using their jaws, as we would a forked stick to a snake's neck! Nothing else would hold them (*tanuki* fur is so loose that only biting an ear or the base of the tail hold them without pinning them down) and that was evidently unpleasant for the pups who let out sharp pained yelps. I noted *"even wary Mother cat's eyes express sympathy when they are disciplined."* Within a year, one of these second generation *tanuki*, a female came to my bay-window on her own almost every night and lay down on her belly with her legs sticking out frog-like behind her. Sometimes she came so quietly – or was waiting when I came home? – that I failed to notice her until I felt *watched* and looked out to see her warmly gazing at me. She was not begging for food. She just liked me, or, rather, *loved* me. When she had cubs of her own, she trusted me enough to leave them with me for a half an hour or so when she went up the hill to visit other human patrons on her route. Or another might take the kids for an hour and she would snooze under my protection. Yet, for all that, she and other second generation *tanuki* never could bring themselves to take something from my hand, or allow themselves to be petted. They, particularly this young mother, longed to be touched, but their unconscious held them back. Their hearts were mine, but their guts were still pinned to the ground by their upraising.

Her puppies, the *third generation* were not taught to fear me. When they came to the window to take food from my fingers she looked a wee bit apprehensive, but she did not stop them because she *knew* deep down in her heart that I was good. Thus, they were able to do the things their mother only wanted to do with me. They were a bit anxious about being touched on the forehead, but other than that had no hang-ups whatsoever.

So we have a sequence of rudimentary domestication: the *head*, the *heart*, and finally the *guts*. While the bring-a-pup home theory of domestication is the simplest and therefor best, I think my observation of a three generational change from wild to tame should also be taken into account by ethologists, cultural anthropologists and psychologists alike, as I believe it suggests that, in the absence of separation at, or near birth, it takes three generations to completely overcome prejudice.

cats and tanuki

So how did the cats feel about my consorting with the *tanuki* and vice versa? On the whole, the cats and *tanuki* got along *remarkably well*. A *dog* in the woods, large or small, put all of my cats into a panic. If they were on the verandah they jumped on top of the narrow ledge of the storm-shutter box despite the fact that no dog ever managed to even come close to climbing upon the verandah. Their terror did not subside after I closed the window; they darted about as if they expected the dog to burst right in! As their friend and protector, I must admit to being a bit miffed by their lack of confidence in my power. *Tanuki, on the other hand, never terrified the cats.*

Why the tremendous difference? Can it all be attributed to experience? I think not. I think it is because *most dogs – even those that turn and run when a cat stands up to them – are always chasing something*. Even running free, they strain at the metaphysical leash, panting from exertion, quivering in anticipation of attaining the object, whatever it be. Growing up with dogs, I took that energy for granted. It did not strike me as unusual until one day in (in 1995 or 1996), it hit me as a revelation while watching cartoonist Ueda Masashi leash his beagle for a walk. I suddenly felt what cats must feel: the preternatural power of dogs, the strangeness of these fearfully intense bundles of energy our weird species created. *Tanuki* may scuffle their feet in the leaves like bears and wrestle up a storm in mating season, but they do not run panting *huff! huff! huff!* through the woods in the demented, driven manner of a dog.

Still, my cats did not like to get chummy with *tanuki*. They remained at rest, confident in the knowledge that this animal was not *after them*, though they could not resist hissing at any *tanuki* that came too close (about a foot). They would occasionally hiss through the window pane, but it was less fear than resentment toward the *tanuki* moving in on their home. Cats are, after all, like the rest of us, jealous animals. That they eventually came to accept the *tanuki's* visit was largely my doing. I tried not to feed the cats until the *tanuki* appeared. This made the *tanuki* their portent for dinner. *"Come Tanuki! Meow ! Meow! We want to eat!"* The *tanuki* would have to wait a bit as I first fed the cats, but, as I have said, they were gracious diners. They patiently waited their turn. I only saw real violence that could have had serious consequences once, when a torpedo-style attack, described earlier, was launched by Kori out of the instinct of a mother with young kittens.

tanuki and cats

What about the *tanuki*? How did they feel about the cats? They put up with them; but they did not always suffer their hisses in silence. They learned to hiss right back – as I saw a crow do to Ôsama our Persian cat king. (Note: A man who raised a motherless *tanuki* and mixed his vocalizations – the most common call is somewhere between a cetacean whistle and a hen's cluck – with music to make a record, claimed an explosive hiss was part of the *tanuki's* natural repertoire. The possibility his *tanuki* learned it from a neighborhood cat was not discussed on the TV program).

The *lower-half* of this page from my newsprint notebook shows what will be described next. The tips of the snouts and tails are black but the picture was about behavior. The *upper-part* shows me investigating something my research on the Japanese banjo, made from cat-skin led me to, counting the number of tits. Because Japanese is also full of navel idiom, I also sought to precisely place it within the tits.

The *tanuki* also closely observed my relationship with the cats. The female who had a crush on me looked like she too wanted to be petted when I petted a cat, but did not seem to hold that against the cat. Whether this means that *tanuki* are less jealous than cats, or simply that they realized their position as an outsider was more precarious, so they had better be nice to my friends or face the consequences, I cannot say. They did not, however, *always* behave perfectly. When I played tug-of-war with the pups of my *tanuki* "lover" using a doll on a string, the elder *tanuki* jumped at sweet Kuro'ko-chan when she tried to join in the fun. Doubtless, they had already experienced too many glares and hisses on the part of my other less angelic cats. The game itself did not last long. One pup pulled on the doll while the other moved in at a perfect ninety degree angle to saw off the string. Cats and dogs also may attack the string, but that is usually to get at the object themself. This *teamwork* blew my mind. The pups took the doll back with them as they sometimes took my sandals and other things, mostly when they were upset with me for not coming back home before they had to leave (we were part of a route that had to be covered before dawn.) Only once the *tanuki* did more than just jump at a cat:

> *Tanuki rushed up and pinned Han-chan after Han-chan jumped out of window for piece of bloody raw tuna. Didn't know (Han-chan or me) Tanuki was out there – it happened so fast. Held (& looked like biting) Han-chan for 1-5 seconds – really long. But afterward, Han-chan had no injuries (Tanuki must have been scratched some) so Tanuki treated Han-chan like it would a rambunctious young tanuki! All for show!* (notes)

My time estimate is ridiculously broad. With my affection for Han-chan, it seemed like forever. I must have shouted and clapped my hands. Han-chan took a long time to thoroughly lick off the abundant *tanuki* slobber(!) and for a long while looked before leaping from the window.

Since I rewarded good behavior by food and praise, while I punished bad behavior on the part of the cats with a whack or a squirt of water and that on the part of the *tanuki* with shouts or soybeans shot by a peashooter, it is a bit difficult to pronounce upon their so-called nature. Like Thoreau, who lifted a woodchuck from his burrow by its tail, pulled a frog from the mouth of a snake and chased (not hunted) foxes, I am no hands-off lover of nature. It is *my* nature to interact. I hope that our interaction gives rise to enough observations otherwise missed to compensate for those made less significant by it.

cat tails

Why Mother Tanuki Must Pin Down Pups With Forked Mouth. To see the rambunctious youngsters try to body-slam food out of their mother's mouth, this human did not feel as sympathetic as his cats were to see the mother pin them down with open snout as one might a snake with a forked branch, but the mother had good reason to use that method. Though fox-like overall, the tanuki was not only raccoon in pattern but in the loose connection of hide and the rest of the body. When tanuki of equal size wrestle, they grab either the ear or the tail right where it joins the body. No other place works as the tanuki will twist right around inside that loose hide. Even the 6 x 8 inch stiff cowhide dog doll I tied to a string when first grabbed by a pup got that treatment though its proportions (long legs, thin tail, etc) were far from a tanuki's.

More details on *tanuki* may be found when and if I finish a book tentatively titled –

Balls Beyond Belief
Tanuki, the Racoon Fox of Japan

This *tanuki* helping to control the earthquake-causing catfish will not be the on the cover. I will probably use a print showing a *tanuki* taking shelter from the rain under his own balls. And I may change my title to *HAVING A BALL* as *tanuki* play alot.

Afterword

Aside from time spent minding my mom's condominium or fleeing hurricanes with her, when my main duty and pleasure was amusing her great grey cat, I have had no felinity in my life for ten years. However, there is one exception, feline behavior which I did not mention in this book that I discovered in the oddest of places: high up my wall, near the corner with another wall and the ceiling. And, odder yet, those exhibiting the behavior in question were not cats.

They were *gecko*. Approaching each other, they lashed their tails in the same slow-motion yet twitchy fashion, reflecting and showing their nerves were on hair's trigger. They also turned diagonally, sometimes even horizontally to one another while raising their backs up high off the wall to exaggerate their size. And, if that were not catty enough, they vocalized, though the clicking-of-tongue-like sound was far more minimalistic than a cat's growls. Like toms, their rivalries sometimes continued so long that the word *feud* comes to mind. Usually the one remaining by its home corner would psych out or repel the visitor. Sometimes, however, a bullying relationship developed where even the one in his or her favorite place always fled at the sight of the other. That, too, happens with cats.

After a couple years of living with gecko, I noticed that two of them, one of whom lived near the kitchen and was not adverse to ambushing and eating large cockroaches and the other, near the front window who was more apt to starve down, then gorge on plentiful smaller bugs, mostly termites on the full moon, were not just following reptilian instincts, but calculating fighters, capable of brilliant tactics. Were I but wealthy enough to have owned the video camera most people in the so-called "developed world" take for granted, I would have filmed the gecko encounters and sent them to Funny Video with instructions to turn the wall horizontal and put cat faces on the gecko, for the extent of the resemblance was truly uncanny.

One day, I saw the slightly darker, larger and, it seemed to me, more muscular galley gecko come up the wall, ignoring the "keep away!" warning of the window gecko sitting near his favorite corner. The window gecko, brave soul that he was, strutted cautiously down the wall, tail slowly whipping up his adrenaline (as some scientists say). Two feet from the ceiling, they stopped about six inches apart and the galley gecko turned sideways while rising up a bit to show the window gecko just how much larger he was and give it a last chance to flee, or avoid a fight with one whose head was as large as its own. At that instant, the window gecko leapt straight down that wall catching the shoulder and chest of the galley gecko in his jaws and evidently kicking off from the wall with his hind legs, for the two fell with a thud, or the closest thing to a thud that two small bodies can make, a foot or two out from the wall on one of the banquet tables I used for a desktop extension. After a minute or so of rolling about, the galley gecko fled to the kitchen wall while the window gecko, who did not give chase, went back, slowly to his wall, staying near the bookcase within which he had a trail to commune to his hideout in the closet.

Imagine my surprise when the galley gecko, limping horribly with one front-leg still paralyzed, worked around toward the window gecko's corner from the far wall, while making wretched-sounding clicking noises. The window gecko, noting his limping, eventually gave chase and followed the galley gecko back two thirds of the way to the kitchen, where a palmetto frond hung on the wall. Imagine my surprise when the instant the galley gecko went under the palmetto, he spun about to catch the pursuing window gecko's snout between his jaws! They stayed like that barely moving on the wall an excruciatingly long time, maybe five or ten minutes, and just before I, fearing the window gecko would lose his life, got up to separate them, the galley gecko, almost as if he was reading my mind, suddenly let go and the two went their separate ways!

It is one thing to creep up on a smaller prey, but quite another to stand up to and try to outsmart one's equal or superior. It is not the sort of thing genes alone would want us to do. I recall Loren Eiseley, the first to recognize animal dreams, not in the usual sense of the word first elaborated by Lucretius and generally accepted today, but dreaming in the sense of seeking and trying to create something ideal (what else is a burrow?), rather than merely reacting to the low-blows of reality, was so impressed by rodent intelligence that he was sure of higher intelligence evolving once again if homo sapiens did himself in (which he thought quite likely). I would go back further yet, all the way to the gecko.

I named those two Musashi and Chôjirô, after the legendary Japanese sword-fighters. If you want to learn about their rivalry, read my friend William Scott Wilson's book, *The Lone Samurai*, about the former (Bill knows he fought as a *ronin* not as a samurai, but his publisher knows the market. As a sword-fighter, Miyamoto Musashi reminds us of a gun-fighter in the Wild West, but note that his cunning, discipline – not to mention calligraphy – are on a higher plane. He had grizzly power, tanuki guile and cat speed.

I expected these gecko would eventually provide me with a saga to relate, but family circumstances demanded a move North into the woods of North Florida and, like my magical days with the cats in Japan, my nights with the gecko on Key Biscayne were suddenly over. Some day, if I am ever lucky enough to find a place to *stay*, where I can swallow the anchor and share my dreams with others until I pass away and, like that old lady on the hill, "be there still" I hope to become truly familiar with another species. I hope it might be a house-wren, for they are my favorite bird, by far; but, whatever it turns out to be – if it is to be – one thing is certain. We will enjoy each other's presence and I will discover yet more bravery, intelligence and, dare I say it, goodness.

Update. Almost three years have passed. Those circumstances – a member of the family undergoing chemo – remain. My only buddy in what has been for me, by far the longest solitary confinement of my life is a cat! A black cat with a white blaze on his chest and four white paws that only a year ago dragged a squirrel off a bird-feeder when he was so skinny you could count each vertebrate, now, maybe three times heavier, lies on the table next to me sharing the view of the bird-feeders only a foot away. Boogaboo mews sweetly like a cricket from delight to see the first birds after I fill the feeders (actually baskets); but whenever he sees the birds fight, wants so badly to jump in and referee that, tail lashing violently, he forgets himself, whacks the window, and even pushes his mug against the glass. I laugh. He hears. *Were he a white cat I think I would have seen him blush.*

Seriously. I could write another short book about this cat, who is unlike any cat I have known because he has spent most of his life with nothing but two humans and four grumpy old dogs used to killing and eating cats. He is the only cat I know who literally bounds to greet returning humans in the style of dogs, despite his usual method of moving further than fifty feet being an all-out dash. He is also the only cat I know who was so lonely for four-legged companionship that he allows a dog to push a cold nose into his you-know-what without turning about to scratch the hell out of him or her by turning it into a see-if-you-can-kiss-my-you-know-what. And he is the only cat I know who can eat dog food as fast as a dog, gulping it.

Boogie-boo, unlike Han-chan, is dangerously proud. He *will* not deviate one-inch from whatever he intended to do and pretends to be absolutely fearless of the dogs though he acts quickly when necessary to extract himself from mortal danger (brushing the snouts of two dalmations one on either side). The courage and good judgment he has demonstrated while working things out with the above-mentioned grumpy old dogs – now down to two who are insanely jealous of one another – and even becoming friends with each (though I deserve some credit, for using strategic feeding to make the dogs to think of the cat as a harbinger of food rather than an item of it) never ceases to amaze me. He still chases squirrels and keeps them away from bird feeders, for which he occasionally takes a tax though it is generally not a local bird. Call it a tourist tax. Most recently, he came in with a tiny bird, with a touch of red on top of its head far smaller than that of the ruby-crowned kinglet (a gnat-catcher) and far redder than the orange crowning one variety of warbler in the books I consulted. It had a broken neck but no feathers were messed up, so I gave him the benefit of the doubt. He might have seen it fly into a window or something. He brought me a live hawk when he was still a big kitten and when I freed the hawk, he came back with a bird in less than thirty seconds which told me how he managed to capture the hawk! I had a hard time convincing Boogie-boo to surrender the bird, but he did and she, with cardinals it is easy to tell, flew off!).

I am getting to like him more and more despite knowing that I must almost surely leave him here for he is as much a creature of place (he also loves the cows and even walks the boundaries of the 8 acre property, or, rather sprints it fifty yards at a time) as person and this is not my place: I cannot imagine living here too much longer.

Mark Twain was right. Writers who cannot stay put should *lease* cats rather than own them, not that I went looking for this one!

p.s. While working with illustrations, doing spell-checks and whatnot shitwork a penniless author-publisher cannot avoid doing, a final observation, or discovery, from Boogie-boo. As I was walking from the feed-room to the old tobacco shed where the hay bales are stacked, with a blue tarp to fill with hay, bundle and put on the back of the Baby, a massive four-year old black calf so lonely with only a mother, grandmother and unrelated auntie to relate with (no bull!) that she behaves herself and will help me carry it to the trough a hundred yards away. Anyway, twenty feet from the shed I saw a very deep narrow and perfectly conical giant mole hole – the armadillo leaves more angled, and broad-topped gouges in the earth and pointed it out to our exterminator who pawed the top slightly then stuck his fore-leg down that hole up to his shoulder. I assumed he was fishing for praise as he knows that I work hard to get him to focus on rodents and not birds. But the instant he pulled up his fore-leg, he spun about and *sat* on that hole. As I was just forming the words to praise him for at least pretending to be on duty, it took me a second to realize what was happening. Boogie-boo was doing his business! It is probably an extraordinary example of what Japanese call a *Retsu Maikeru* (*Let's Michael:* see pg. 175-7) moment, but I like to think it will turn-out to be the *Eureka!* start of a labor-saving discovery. If it turns out to be the latter, I will write more about it in the next edition. If not, not.

With gratitude to all who gave me encouragement, the cats in my life, and those who loved or put up with them.

An Impurrfect Bibliography*

Anthologies seen and recalled include *The Domestic Cat* (Serpell ed.:1988) a good source for science, either a *Celebration of Cats* (Roger Caras: 1986) or the Vintage Book of Cats (ed.Wheen: 1996) impressed me for cat literature, but I forget which. I have a fond memory of *Puss In Books* (Maria Polushkin Robbins: 1994) and think it may be the source for quotes marked "l.s.." *

Seven Noteworthy Books (you can search for others on-line)

Clutton-Brock, Juliet: *The British Museum Book of Cats Ancient and Modern*. 1988. An excellent eclectic selection of cat depictions.

Corey, Paul: *Do Cats Think? Notes of a Cat-Watcher* 1991. This book is, like Holland's, the exception, because the author creates what is in effect an exhibit of cat intelligence in action.

Hearne, Vicki: *Adam's Task* 1986. What a joy to read someone delighted in and at home with ideas, i.e., abstract things, who also observes real things so carefully and, even with occasional deconstructionism-inspired excess, is a fine literary stylist! Those who only read her articles in defense of the bulldog do not know what they are missing. Her single chapter on the cat has more of value than most entire books on cats.

Holland, Barbara: *Secrets of the Cat* 1994. One gets tired of reading stories about somebody's cats, but this book is the exception because the author is not only a fine observer but writes as beautifully as a cat moves and is a superb aphorist, which is to say she quietly turns observation into theory. When I read a NYT review of a book I shall not name, I thought the reviewer should have written, "Why publish this book when Barbara Holland's *Secrets of the Cat* is available?" Perhaps the best cat book to date.

Lorenz, Konrad: *Man Meets Dog* 1953. The chapter on the cat, like that in Vicki Hearne's book, is, by itself, worth many books. It is remarkable how clearly the greatest ethologist of the twentieth century could think and write!

Masson, Jeffrey Moussaieff: *The Nine Emotional Lives of Cats* 2002. There are generalizations someone with more years with cats might think misleading, and some readers may find his question-to-answer ratio too high, but a psychoanalyst familiar with many animals willing to go out on a limb about the feelings underlying feline behavior provides food for thought.

Michaels, Leonard: *A Cat.* 1995. A little book that probably taught me close to nothing about cats but makes many of the same observations I made so poetically that had I read this early on I might have stopped writing.

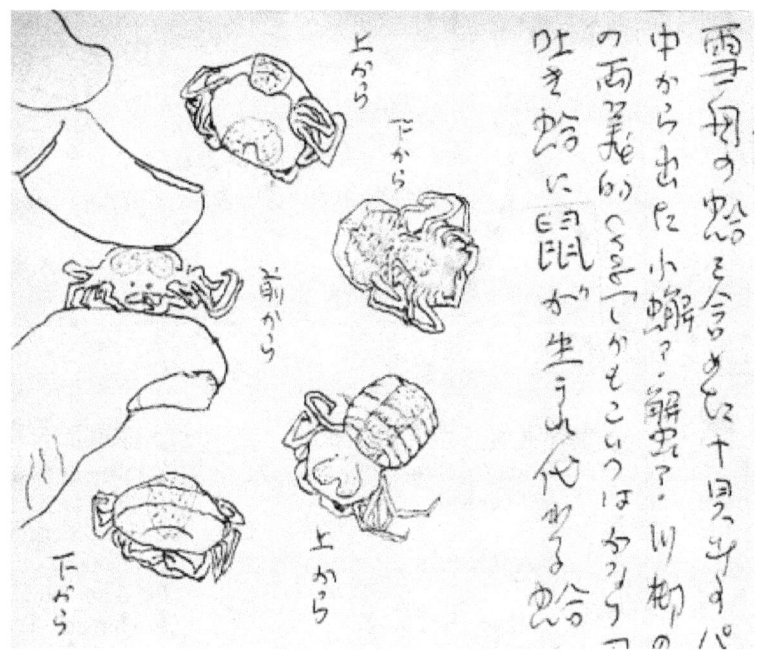

♪ To be poor and write nonfiction is to live in the basket of a leaky hot-air balloon, throwing books overboard to keep afloat. Not only is my library scattered over two continents, but what little I have here includes work with chapters cut out or chapters cut from them as it was the only way I could keep vital information with me (These were my books to cut, so librarians, please do not get the wrong idea, I feel guilty enough already, though it could not be helped). In the 80's and 90's when I was relatively settled, holding down a part-time position with a fine (but tiny and poor, itself) publisher in Japan, I assigned a letter and number to many of the hundreds of books I read that year – then, I would scribble that upon notes assigned to various books-in-progress, saving the trouble of writing down the full title information on each – but even those scrap-book journals were not on hand as I re-wrote and edited this book. Lacking a cipher, my code was worthless and my labor-saving system backfired. So, expect to find some misattribution in the text and mistaken editions here. As the book is not academic, perhaps it does not matter, but knowing how much such details matter to some, I thought, if not an apology, at least an *apologia* was in order. None of this has any relation to the tiny creature pictured above, a crab in a clam I bought for its beautiful design. Drawing cats, mostly sleeping cats, encouraged me to take on other things.

People

Index

Akhmadulina, Bella 25
Albee, Edward 248
Andersen, Hans Christian 193
Atxaga, Bernado 220

Bacon, Francis 191
Bateson Gregory 203
Bateson, Mary Catherine 203
Bateson & Turner 127
Belloc, Hillaire 129
Betsuyanagi Minoru 250
Block, Marylaine 198
Boone, Sylvia Ardyn 143,191, 219
Brazil, Mark 273-4
Brown, Thomas 32

Callenbach, Ernest 135
Caras, Roger 45,215-6,
Carpenter 46
Cavendish, Margaret 247,257
Chateaubriand 29
Chamberlain, B. H. 156
Christian natural history 271
Christina, Queen of Sweden 97
Clutton-Brock, Julie 53
Colette 99
Corey, Paul 157-8,205,270
Crompton, John 215,229,232
Cuppy, William 231-2

Darwin, Charles 17,272-3,
Darwin, Erasmus 185
Dass, Daniel 157
Descartes 143
Dickinson 148
Djikstra, Bram 130
Edwards, Jonathon 271

Edwards, Monica 107
Eiseley Loren 3
Emmet Miller 142

Fox, Michael 125-6,168-9

Gallico, Paul W. 107,116, 118,124,
Gautier, Theophile 30
Gill, Prudence 18
Gooch, Stanley 186
Gorman, James 190
Grandin, Temple 44,117,258
Griffin, Donald 272
Gray, Charlotte 154,176
Guthrie, Stewart Elliott 237

Healey, Josephine 152
Heany, Seanus 172
Hearn, Lafcadio 6
Hearne, Vicki 9,10,12,13, 40,178,181-2
Hein, Piet 245
Hemingway 153
Henry (in Griffin) 272
Holland, Barbara 39,103,116, 133,169-70,173-4,274
Hornady 149
Huxley, Aldous 155-6

Issa 101,136,165.167,176, 184,283

Kobayashi Makoto 175-7,179

Keasler, John 159
Kipling 234
Komatsu Shigeo 83-4

Kropotkin 58
Kuniyoshi 177

Langer, Susanne K. 244
Leonardo da Vinci 194
Lehmann-Haupt 45
Leyhausen, Paul 45,239,241
Liberg 168
Lorenz, Konrad 35-6,45, 147-150,153
Lucretius 26,207

Marlowe, Christopher 32
Masson, Jeffrey M. 29,38, 80,114-5,150,183-4 208,
Mclean, Paul 152
Melville 9
Michaels, Leonard 29,39,145, 152,182,195,208
Millen, Susanne 38
Miyamoto Musashi 295
Montaigne 197-8
Morris, Desmond 19,124,142, 171-2
Moyes, Patricia 132-3
Murasaki Shikibu 14

Nash, Ogden 17,250
Neckam, Alexander 85
Nollman, Jim 81

Okakura Tenshin 245-6

Paglia, Camille 147-8,151,154, 158-9,178-9,186-91,200,266

Pflugel 26
Pindar, Peter 118
Poincare, Jules Henri 176

Quintilian 151

Rahman, Haroon 157
Repplier, Agnes 29
Romanes, George 182

Scheper-Hughes, Nancy 173
Scidmore, Eliza 192
Seaton 37,248
Sharp, Joane 31
Simon, Clea 115
Skelton, John 275
Smart, Christopher 271
Soseki 14
Spence, Joseph 10
Spinka, Marek 258
Stamm, Jack 275

Sterne, Laurence 13,14
Stevenson, R. L. 22,27,148,258
Sumner, William Graham 165
Szasz, Suzanne 107

Tanizaki Junichiro 112
Theroux, Paul 129
Thomas Elizabeth M. 45,241
Thoreau 127,134-5,146,221-2, 268
Tinker Belle (Barrie) 106
Turner & Bateson 10
Turner & Meister 240-1
Twain 11

Ulmann, Liv 117
Unamuno 250-1

Vanderpost, Lauren 135
Vitton, Louis 110

Ward, Lucy Miranda 251
Warner, Charles D. 30
Watts 12,14
Webster, Barbara 176
Wilde 147
Wilson, Prof. 168
Wilson, William Scott 295
Wolcot, John => Pindar P.
Yôko (Miyata), who would have loved this book, shared four or five years with the cats and I and is mentioned in some notes.

Concept
Index

Absences 38-9
Angry looks 154-5
Anka => electric heater
Anticipating pain 145
Anti-language 133
Aodaishô (blue-boss) 225
Apes 191
Associative movement 180-1

Bad dream (must be a ~) 203-14
Basque chicken 220-1
Behavior 10-1,
Bird character 205,
~ vs snake 219
Birds as bird-killers 274
~ on rainy days 263
Biting by cat 119,150, 158-9
Bite injury to cat 137
Blanket cat-door 64
Body language 123,130-1
Bullying toms 161-2
Bullying revenge 108

Cannibalism 165
Castration 168-70,174
Cat and Mouse paradox 282
Cat defined 13
Cat haiku 61,63
Cat language 99-122
 as beautiful **185-202**
Cats as cold/selfish 29,39
   as **cruel** 246-7
   ~ **deceitful** 147-60
   ~ **face-savers** 175-84,297
   ~ good 40

~ **independent/solitary** 29, 45-6,67
~ loving 29-44
as "killers" 273-5
as mysterious 147-8
as rat-catcher 215-6
as **retriever & hunter** 216-7, 229-30
as sincere 33,40-1,182
as **sociable** 35-6,56,65,114
as snake-killer 217-8
as sympathetic 287
as teachable 41-2
as **transparent** 148-9,156-7,
as wild 153-4

Chickens as mousers 219-21
Chikuwa 257,286
Child-rearing 47-51
Cleanliness in cats 188-90, 201
Closed eyes 123-136
Cricket sound 23
Coat patterns 65,70,74
Cold cats 73
Covering food 94
Cover up 175-84, 297
Cows 191
Crossbow 97
Culling litters 172-4
Cussing body language 179

Dead mouse 265-6
Dead baby bird 267
Deaf cats 116
Death 35,36,105,232,269-70
Deceitful cats? 147-60
Definition of "cat" 13

Delicate cat 109,199-200
Delusion 137-8,142-4
Deprived cats 119
Devious cat 160
Dirty look 86
Discipline 54-5

Dog vs. Cat mind 254
Dogs 22,26-7,29,30,41,58, 147-51,153-4,157-60,162, 182-3,192,208,211-2,234,249
Dolphin 159,273
Domestication 58, 215-24
 => Third generation *tanuki*
Dreaming 1,3,181,
Dream awareness 207-8
       interpretation 210
Dull cat wake up 81
Dumb things they do 203
Dying Han-chan 35-6

Ears 196
Ecological 126
Ecotopia 135
Editing vs. forgetting 206
Egyptian 147,191,201
Electric heater 21
   (pic only) 67-9,79
Emotional single-track 106
English 117
Evil looks 155
Eye contact 126-7,133
 ~ -squeeze 132-3
Eyes 196, ~ closed 23
       ~ open 264

Faking it 175-84,297

302

False => Deceitful
Fear of cats 156
Feline reptiles 293-7
Felinese 6 => Cats language
Female-female attack 37, 51-4
Femininity & Masculinity & Cats 115-6
Feral cats 138
Ferret 203
Fleas 83-91,97
First-princessing 60
Flower torture 246
Fly-guard 91
Food 92-4
Foreleg folded 130-1
Fox 272

Gecko 293-7
Gifts of game 259
'Gregory story' 203,213
Greeks 188,201
Grooming & Love 39,44, 188-90,201
Grooves 14

Haiku (some Englished) 60, 61, 63,72-3,76-7,91,101,165, 167,176,184,197,259-60,310
Hallucination 137-8,142-4
Han-chan
  as a bed-mate 88-91
  as a male-mother 46-51
  as fastidious 93
  as hypersensitive 81-3, 92-3
  as terrorist 50-1
Hanchan's Death 105
Hanchan's Dream 1, (really dreaming) 200, sequence 204 => Bad dream (it must be a ~)

Han-chan speaks 104-5
Han-chan's tricks 41-2
Herpephobia 233-4,236
Hissing 58
Homosexual cultures 174
Homosexual mounting 162
Humans, our value to cats 37,
~ our history in a nutshell 108
Human thought 181
Human ugliness 197-8
Hunting 239-58
  a positive take 270
  & mother cats 239-40
  & hunger/nutrition 239-40
  & anxiety 240,
  & training us 241
  & bringing home 241
  & showing off 242-4
  & play 244-50
  hours 259
  birds in the rain 263
  moles 268-70

Hypershort animation 1
Ideals 3
Imaginary snow 82
Imagination as safe bet 237
Improvisation 13-4
Infanticide 172-3
Infantile 26 => neoteny
Instinct 11
Intelligence (yes)

Jaded cats 254-5
Japan 19,29,58,83-5,90, 96-7,105,112,123,137, 156,170,175-7
Japanese language 99, 112-3,117,118
Japanese New Year 259-61
Jealousy 56
Juvenile 26 =>neoteny

Kick-start sex 163-4
Kissing 129
Kitten-killing 172-4
Kneading 18-9,25
Korean language 99,117
Kôri's name 105
Kuro'ko's name 109

Landlords 140,169-70
Laughing at animal 24,182-4
Let's Michael! 175-7,
184, 297
Life value 172-3
Life as a dream 181
Lonely cats 23,25
Loss 205-7
Love to be loved 33-4
Love for the world 12
Love-drunk 32-3,34,44
Love-nibble 109
Loving look 30,32

Mad cat 106-7
Make-believe 249-51
Male covering scat 94
Male mothering 46-51
Manga 175-7
Manipulative cat 107-8
Materialism in the good sense 12,14
Medley 13
Mende people 219-20
Mental illness in cats 45-6,
Military socks 235
Mind-body 143
Mistakes by cat 175-84
Mole and mountain 268-70
Mosquitoes 90-1

Mothering skills 165-7,239
Mother's love 32,167
Mother's defense 51-4,225-9

Mouse
  -farm idea 281
  ~ in China and Japan 282
  ~ rescue 276-80
  ~ touching cold finger 279
  ~ tricks 279-80

Mouth of cat 197
Mouthfeel 240
Moving a cat 139-42
Murder by toms 171-2
Mushiness decried 134
Musical cats 106
Mysterious cats 147-8

Neoteny 17-28
Newspaper heating 72
Nomi-jigoku 85 **page 303**

Nose of a cat 195, 258
Nose of a dog 253
Nose vs eyes vs ears 251-3
Nostalgia for world 23
Nursing 18,47-8

Obedience 40-1
Observation powers 231-2
Octopussy 1
Oh-sama 139-40
Older women 163
One-string experiment 235
Overflow of emotions 179

Paling 138
Pangaea 65
Pangur Ban 275,282
Paranoia 223-8
Peashooter 55-6,142,170-1
Perception 238

Play 17,95-6,166, 244-51,284
　with prey 261-2,265-6,271-2
　stocking prey 272-3

Plum blossoms 65
Politicians 199
Posing 43,187,192
Pregnancy 32-4,44
Predation 10-1
Prey's feelings 247-8
"Pro-life" 172-2
Psychic 159
Puncture wound 137-8
Purring 105,107,113-5

Queendom 52-3
Queens 161-174

Raccoon 23-5,27
Raccoon dog => Tanuki
Racoon fox => Tanuki
Racism 96-7
Rattlesnake's rattle 225
Recognition process 238
Relative beauty 185-6
Responsible behavior 40
"Revenge" 229-30
Reverse yawn 70

Rights of words 6

Round as happy 34

Saving toilet paper 235
Saving face 175-84,297
Sea cucumber style 14
Self-control of Han-chan 273
Sex 162-5
Shere Kahn's eyes 126
Shit-licking 44,47
Shitty story 297
Showing off 242-4
Sick cats 22,27,35
Sign invention by cat 104-5
Silent meow 109-12,116, 123
Sincere response 41-2
Skink hunting 262-3
Sleep pattern 65,70
Sleeping cats 59-80
Sleeping man 89,98
Smiling eyes 128-9
Snake and cat battle 225-32
Snake intelligence 225-32
Snakes as mouse-traps 215-6
Snakes and the West 222-3
Snow, cats at play 95-6
Social intelligence 40
Sound 117
Spraying 168
Stilts 87
Stock-keeping 272-3
Straight lines 9-12
Stream of consciousness
　　　　　　　181-2

Tailless cats 156
Tails 112-3,155-6,166,201,
Tanuki 283-292
　described in brief 284
　gratitude 287
　tactical genius 286-7
　tanuki balls explanation 283
　who loved me 287-8
　& cats 286,288-91
　Tatami 87
Teaching a cat to talk 119
Technology and cat

　behavior change 67-9

Teeth and sex 163
Teenage mother 47
Territoriality 52-3,161
Think too much 82
Third-generation tanuki 283, 287-8
Thumb-sucking 18-19
Timothy Turtle 212
Tinkerbelle syndrome 107
Tinnitus 124
Toms 132. 161-174
Tonal change 99-100
Tongue-out 20-23,27,42
Tops 49,273
Toys 255-7
Tranquilizer 139-40
Trauma-reduction 206-7
Trusting cat 81

Ugliness 191-3,197-8
Universal language 101, 103, 117,118
Usania/ns 26-7,115,126

Veterinarian 22,105,138-9, 142,163,169-71
Vicarious 56
Vowels 99

Wellness 23
Whiskers 119-20,196,264
White cat 96-7
Why we do things 10-11
Wild, feelings about 154
Winter sleep pile 65-80
Wolf's eyes 135, sex 168-9
Woman's lib 129-30
Working for food 257
Worm-hunter 230

Yamami dreams 210
Yawn 114
Yawn, reverse style 70-1
Yin-yang sleep 65,75
Young toms 161

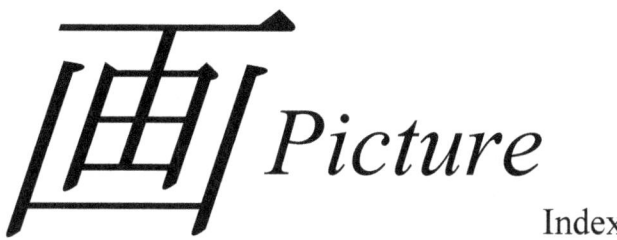

Picture Index

* Cats becoming Octopus 1
Han-chan asleep on book 3,
* Tristam Shandy plot-line 13
Ears in Spring 15,
* Tongue-out picture 21,
Raccoon 24
* Kori & Han-chan on pillow
Tongue-out close-up 42
* Han-chan & Kori Picasso 43,
Kori with ill Han-chan 35
Kori with dead Han-chan 36
Han-chan, Kori & kittens 47 (x2)
Han-chan & kittens alone 48 (x2)
Han-chan creeps like mantis 49
Han-chan jealous of kittens 49
Pea-shooting with tongue 55
* 4-cat sleep, Fall cluster 59
Kori sleeping with part of a cabbage 60
Paws by face sleeping 61
Medium temperature 3-cat cluster 62
My toes & paw-pillow 62
Curled kori 63
Blanket slit door 64
Old Han-chan sleeping 64
* Han-chan sleep-ball pangaea & plum blossoms 65
Sleep Yin-Yang 66
Heater individualism 67
Heater raft 67
Heater hidden 68 (x2)
Heater +pr 69 (x2)
* Sleep as bicycle wheel 70

Reverse yawn 70
Pike position reverse yawn 71 (x2)
Old Han under newspaper 72
Cold cats, 1 awake 1 asleep 73
Sleep ball pattern 74
Sleep pattern 2-cat 74
* Yin-yang 2-cat sleep, crisp 75
Nose-to-nose 2-cat sleep 76
* Kuro'ko & Han-chan abstract ball 77
* 3-cat ball sketch 78
3 cat ball in Issa journal 78
4-cat oblong-ball on heater 79
6-cat ball photo 79
Nose-to-paw of another 80
The Very Thought 82
* Stilts over fleas 87
Sleeping with Han-chan 89
Fly-protector on my head 91
* Cats playing with snowballs 95
* Shy cat and snowballs 96
Crossbow for hunting fleas 97
* Sleeping with cats 98
SilentMeowPicture111
Meg's whiskers 120
Han's closed eye smile & meg 123
Picasso-esque Han & Kori 124
* Han-chan foreleg fold yakuza pose 131
* Han-chan and Issa's life 136
Ohsama, the king cat 140
Mikan looking angry 154

Kick-start 164
Let's Michael cut 1,2, 177
Open-eyed Han-chan 185
Seductive Kori 187
4 takes on cleaning cat 188
Licking own butt 190
Licking paw + composed eye-closed Han-chan 193
Hunkered down smooth lines 194
Fractal weed beauty 195
eye-reflection on fogged (not "misty" as already pdf 'ed file says) window 196
Sprawling sleep "Han-chan Dreaming" & nose 200
dozing in the cold with daikon 202
Bamboo from bay-window 203
Han-chan's Dream sequence 204
Han-chan alert paw pillow 211
Sleeping tongue-out 213
Mikan retrieving chikuwa 257
New Year's present 259
Chickadee-like head 262
Riko eyes wide open 264
Mouse head 265
Eviscerated mouse 266
Dead baby bird 267
Riko, Zoro and Shimo photo 268
Cold cat does business 310

* = favorites.

(Microsoft Word tortures people trying to number pages with multiple columns!)

Curious?   Books in English by Robin D. Gill, all 100% viewable at Google Books.

Rise, Ye Sea Slugs! (1,000 *ku* re. sea cucumbers compiled & transl. from Japanese). paraverse 2003. pp 480.

"I wondered, can one really devote 480 pages to haiku on sea slugs? The answer is emphatically 'yes.' Although difficult to read from beginning to end, this book contains great learning and insight, and deserves a wide reading among specialists and non-specialists alike."

"For many of the haiku, Gill gives multiple translations as a way of showing possible interpretations. I know of no other book of English translations of haiku that goes to such lengths to explain translations, which in Gill's hands are accurate, economical, and often elegant."

"For all the eccentricities one might expect (and does find) in a book devoted entirely to Japanese haiku on the sea slug, the author is an accomplished haiku writer, a very talented and engaging critic, capable of reading with an acute understanding of culture and cultural differences."

–Thomas H. Rohlich, Professor of Japanese Language and Literature at Smith College, from *Metamorphoses: the journal of the five college faculty seminar on literary translation* (Vol. 13.1, Spring 2005).

"This single-topic tome may be our best English-language window yet into the labyrinth of Japanese haikai culture. If you have read Yasuda, Blyth, Henderson, Ueda, and Shirane, then read Gill. He will expand your mind. If you have not read those guys yet, then read Gill first. He's more fun."

– William J. Higginson, author of *Haiku World*, in Modern Haiku (volume 35.1 winter-spring 2004).

Fly-ku! (Translations of fly & fly-swatting ku, + an in-depth study of Issa's famous fly-ku, "Don't swat!") 2005

"An American scholar and poet who writes in an extemporaneous style akin to that of Jack Kerouac; thinks like Herman Hesse, Kobayashi Issa, and Lewis Carroll, all rolled into one."

– Robert D. Wilson, founder of the on-line magazine *Simply Haiku* (2005-summer). Author of *Jack-fruit*.

"Gill strikes us as no less than amazing. Why isn't he teaching at Yale, or the University of California, or Tokyo University? His references include no end of obscure Japanese lore, plus quotes and notes from such artists as Clare, Lovelace, Steinbeck, Dumont, Verdi, Satie, Blyth, Shakespeare, Emily Dickinson."

– Carlos Amantea, author of *The Blob That Ate Oaxaca* R.A.L.P.H. (Review of Art, Literature, Philosophy & History)

Not as much natural history in this wee bk. as in Rise, Ye Sea Slugs!, but a good discussion of the supposed anthropomorphic fallacy & a comparison of translations of "Don't swat/hit/kill" the fly that gives great detail on what makes "precise" translation between exotic tongues impossible.

Cherry Blossom Epiphany (Three thousand *ku+ka* on blossom-viewing, including many by Sôgi) 2007, pp.740

"It was bad old Ezra Pound, acknowledging his heavy debt to haiku in translation, who affirmed that the first rule of poetry was "Make it new." This is something Gill has done more effectively, as far as remaking haiku in English goes, than anyone else around. . . .

"One of my favorites is on p. 375, where no less than seven translations are proposed, but four of them *"sous rature,"* or _misekechi_ ['erasures shown,' literally]: in old Japanese, words crossed out in a manuscript but left legible enough that the reader can see what was discarded, and imagine why. (Publishers with accountants are not likely to tolerate this kind of haikaiesque mischief. Gill gets away with it only because he is his own publisher.) And (another reason, if needed) in his commentary Gill distances himself from the conventions of pedantry just as effectively as the haikai poets he translates departed from the venerable (and staid and eventually stuffy) traditions of classical linked verse to make something new."

– Lewis Cook, professor of Japanese literature, CUNY (in a blog at one of Gabi Greve's fine haiku *kigo* and Buddhism-related sites, in response to another's questions about my work.

"This book is exceedingly delightful – what word could be more accurate I cannot say! Here is a guide to allow every reader to play with their own translations of these poems – indeed all the important ingredients – are amply included: . . . nothing in this book is cut in stone – it is pure water, ever-flowing – and that is what is so inspiring about it, its generosity and delightful creativity!"   – s.w. at mountainandrivers.org

***

The Fifth Season (2000 *ku* on 20 New Year themes & first book of ten in the IPOOH series 2007, pp.500)

Excluding books on *surimono*, beautiful color-prints accompanied by *kyôka*, published by presses or lines of books dedicated to *art* rather than literature, the New Year, once the Original, or First Season, of the *five* seasons of haiku, has been neglected in favor of the other four by Occidental translators. *The Fifth Season* finally gives this supernatural or cosmological season – one that combines aspects of the Solstice, Christmas, New Year's, Easter, July 4th and the Once Upon a Time of Fairy Tales – its due. *This book brings the Moon back into the calendar and humans back into haiku.* As this book has sold only a dozen or two copies since being published the *In Praise of Old Haiku* saijiki project has been temporarily suspended.

***

The Woman Without a Hole and other risky themes from old Japanese poems; also _Octopussy, Dry Kidney & Blue Spots_ (about 2000 dirty *senryû* essay 30 themes 2007, pp.500)

No reviews interesting enough to quote, but one sweet fan letter from Germany:

"I normally don't annoy authors, but I simply need to tell you how happy your "woman without a hole" book made me. It's so interesting, funny and well-presented, I loved it to bits, and I don't even speak Japanese. (perhaps I should add that I translated (and published, which was kind of not easy) Lord Rochester's poetry into German; which makes me, kind of, a colleague?)   Thank you very much!"

  – Christine Wunnicke (And, reader, if you read any German, buy her translation of John Wilmot, Earl of Rochester *Der beschädigte Wüstling** and you will thank *me*. It is *charming*.   *Like mine, not for readers under 18.)

***

Mad In Translation – a thousand years of kyôka, comic poetry in the classic waka mode. 2009, 740pp. *Kyôka,* usually translated as "mad poems" or "mad-cap verse," is usually identified with and exampled by late-18c Tenmei *kyôka* in Japan (in translation, all kyôka but those on surimono have been all but ignored) but, actually, the playful B-side of *waka* has existed as long as poetry has in Japan and is found by many names, and the *kyôka* of the 16-17c deserve as much attention as the later ones, as proven by example, 3000 poems, w/ original . . . annot. biblio, bio, poet & poem index, glossary. Much 'extreme translation' here!

***

Kyôka, Japan's Comic Verse: a Mad in Translation Reader 2009. A 300-page double distillation high-proof sample of the poetry and prose, with improved translations, re-considered opinions and additional snake-legs (explanation some scholars may not need). The scattershot of two-page chapters and notes have been compounded into a score of cannonball-sized thematic chapters with just enough weight to bowl over most specialists yet, hopefully, not bore the amateur and sink a potentially broad-beamed readership.

***

Topsy-Turvy 1585 – a translation & explication of Luis Frois S.J.'s Treatise listing 611 ways Europeans & Japanese are contrary (2004/5) 14 thematic chapters, essays of the history of topsy-turvy, cultural accommodation, China vs. Japan as *the* cultural antipode. As I was well-known in Japan for books challenging antithetical cultural stereotypes by showing deep similarity within superficial difference, it was ironic but fitting that I read a book of differences. Frois wrote in Portuguese (included). In a 740pp. and 400 pp version. Find out why we sniff melons on top and Japanese on the bottom!

***

Orientalism & Occidentalism – Is the mistranslation of culture inevitable? (2004 pp280). The odd "nihonjinron" world of antithetical cultural stereotype – the author's experience in Japan, discussion of how and whether we can make sense of exotic tongues (to Japanese English and vice-versa), with especial attention to frequency of personal pronoun use vs the psychological impact and the problem of two conflicting ideas of faithful translation: maintaining word-order vs maintaining flow or connections.

***

A Dolphin In the Woods – Composite Translation, Paraversing & Distilling Prose (2009) 248 pages for $23.45! Those numbers speak of the content, a book on poetry as word play, written with the hope that people do paraverses rather than crossword puzzles, so the solutions may delight us all.

八十、九十年代の和書はすべて、ロビン・ギル（1951～）。洋書は Robin D. Gill。

古今洋和拙著大全

在日の本は、出版社が名づけた『おもしろ比較文化考』＝後に『英語はこんなにニッポン語』（筑摩文庫）、『反・日本人論』工作舎、『誤訳天国』白水社、など七冊あります。全書は、民族を分ける差異に関する先入観を反論か deconstruction した本で、書評の抜粋、ほんの少しですが。『おもしろ』の読者カードで井上ひさしは、「著者の言語力にただただ頭は下がる」と。『反・日』は松岡正剛曰く「著者のヘンリー・ソローばりの自然主義観もすばらしく・・・ハヤリのジャパン・アズ・ナンバーワン型を十冊読むよりずっと気分がいい」と。『誤訳』について佐藤良明は「陥落寸前大関互助会的なニッポン・アカデミズムに、小錦のごとき突っぱりをかましました」と。二冊の本を合わせて評した板坂元曰く「気持が良いのは、日本に淫することなく、一つの文化論を展開してゆく 。。。古い世代が良いにつけ悪いにつけ持っていた偏見に囚われていないところが特徴になっている」と。単行本以外にも、記事と連載は、朝日新聞の文化欄からアエラ迄、様々あったが。和書はすべて first+last name で出したのが大間違い。というと、同じ名前を持つ英国の神学者も和訳されて、本が混合されてしまった！で、我がことを、ネットで調べやすくなるように、必ず middle initial（つまり Dallas 略の D）を入れてください。日本の参考用目録の本ではロビン・ギルとギル・ロビンと、拙著の出番も分けている！下記は、英語で書いた本の紹介のみです。日本でもアマゾンから買えるはずだが、英訳された和文のすべて含めても安く売るために、既製の出版社を抜きに、自分の出版社 paraverse press から出すことになった。

Rise, Ye Sea Slugs!（海鼠千句）について。五大学の文芸翻訳誌、Metamorphoses 2005 春号評者＝スミスカレッジ日本語学、日本文学教授トーマス・H・ローリックの書評より

ギルの手によるその翻訳は簡潔で的をえており、しばしば優雅な味わいがある。　これほど翻訳を詳細に説明してある俳句の英訳書は、私の知る限り他に類を見ない。すでに熟練した翻訳家であり、俳人でもある（本書中百句以上が敬愚というペンネームをもつ著者の作である）著者は、芸術としての翻訳の強力な擁護者でもある。どの句にも彼の翻訳のあとに続いて、それぞれ微妙に異なる解釈のあいだを日本文学、歴史、現代の文化についての余談、さまざまな色合いの逸話、ときには暴言までが自由に往来する。（中略）文学についても日常生活についても必ず信頼でき、しばしば愉快でもある彼の日本文化観に私は舌を巻くほかなかった。なにしろ徹頭徹尾ナマコが句題の俳句を集めた本と聞けば当然期待される（事実そのとおりの）風変わりな点はともかく、著者はくろうとの俳人であり、文化と文化間の違いを機敏に理解しながらものを読むことのできる優れた才能に恵まれた魅力ある評論家である。　興味津々の本書は、広く俳句愛好家、日本文学と海洋生物の研究者、プロ，アマをとわず翻訳家のすべてに喜ばれるにちがいない。

同著について。*Modern Haiku* 現代俳句（2004 年冬春 35．1号）*Haiku World:* 1996 の著者、ウィリアム J．ヒギンソンの 5 ページにわたる書評より

一人の翻訳者として、わたしはギルの俳句翻訳に対する姿勢は刺激的で挑戦的であると思う。彼は「翻訳者の原作に対する責任」（「対応する力」＝　ロバート ダンカン）という点で、果たすべき水準をきわめて高いところまで引き上げてきているのだ。（中略）この単一季語の大著は、日本の俳句文化の迷宮への、今までで一番優れた英語の窓口であろう。（中略）もし、ヤスダやブライスや、ヘンダーソンやウエダやシラネ＊［注：過去半世紀の俳句英訳名家］を読んだことがあるなら、ギルもお読みなさい。あなたの意識を深く広く拡大させてくれるから。

そして、先の方々の著作を読んだことがないのなら、やっぱり先にギルをお読みなさい。彼のほうがずっとおもしろいから。

科学者の評 =「凄い！惚れてしまった。小柄な我が友を何年も研究してきたが、悪態をつかれるか、さもなければ忘れられた存在でしかない、と思っていた。ナマコ文学をめぐる日欧の差！悲しいかな、互いに隔てられた科学と文学には、理論においてはむろんのこと、用語上ですら、とてつもないギャップが随所にみられる。両者を深いところで見事に融合した本で、科学者も納得させる。恐れ入りました。」Alexander Kerr 博士 = Web of Life プロジェクトの海鼠科担当、独語の海鼠研究（古典）の英訳、環境進化論の研究に従事する気鋭の生物学者。James Cook 大学属。

Fly-ku!（蝿句）について。オンライン句誌 Simply Haiku 創立者かつ編集者ロバート・D・ウイルソンの書評より

書きぶりはジャック・ケルアック流即興を思わせ、ものの考え方はヘルマン・ヘッセ、小林一茶、ルイス・キャロル、このすべてを丸めて一つにしたような本なのだ。。。

Cherry Blossom Epiphany: The Poetry and Philosophy of a Flowering Tree 桜・花見三千古句、歌も百二百ほどある 2007 年。NYU＋コロンビア大にも教える、わが最も厳しい批判もする教授が、この本で、小生を、Ezra Pound 以来の、原文を自分のものにする翻訳（上記の英文参照）できたと。

The Fifth Season: Poetry for the Re-creation of the World とは、欧米で見逃れてきた新年部句、二千句ほど英訳。ブライスすら、殆ど相手しなかったが、書評の少なさを考慮すれば、自然より文化が中心なる俳句の英語紹介は無理だったかもしれない。

The Woman Without a Hole 又は、***Octopussy, Dry Kidney & Blue Spots.*** とは、エッチな川柳二千首を題毎に分けて紹介。書評という書評はないが、学者の論文には既に二階の言及あり、わが大好きな英国の詩人の独訳をした方から「普通著者を邪魔しないが、穴無し女のご著作はどんなに幸せ　にさせてくれたかをのべなければならなかった。後は、上記（英語のままで）にある。独語読める方は、Christine Wunnicke の John Wilmot, Earl of Rochester Der beschädigte Wüstling を見ていただければ。

A Dolphin In the Woods – Composite Translation, Paraversing & Distilling Prose (2009)。複数訳と脚韻礼賛といってもいいから、日本語ばかり読みうる方にとって無理であろうが、Google Books で 100%見えるから、ご自分で見てください。書名は、ホーラス（Horace）より。想像力を使いすぎて、森林に海豚、又大海に猪も現れてしまう、という警告に学んで。本全体の主張は、言葉遊びしたければ、皆と分け合える遊びをしなさい、ということである。

Mad In Translation – a thousand years of kyôka, comic poetry in the classic waka mode. 2009, 740 頁. とは狂歌を三千首の英訳。原文もあり、天明よりも見逃されてきた 16-17 世紀に力入れた。柳瀬がジョイスを和訳すれば、日本はわいわいしたが、米国は翻訳を考える基盤がないから、本書の翻訳文化上の重要性が認められる迄は、数十年もかかるはず。***Kyôka, Japan's Comic Verse: a Mad in Translation Reader*** 2009.前者の 300 頁略版。テマ毎になってわかりやすい。

Topsy-Turvy 1585 – a translation & explication of Luis Frois S.J.'s Treatise listing 611 ways Europeans & Japanese are contrary (2004/5) 740 頁。イエス会のフロイスの、ヨロッパ人とその文化と日本のそれ、611 項目まで対照する Tratado の全英訳＋長い解説＋対照文化人類学の小史。欧米の対極として、中国対日本。解釈を半分まで縮む Short Version もある。

Orientalism & Occidentalism – Is the mistranslation of culture inevitable? (2004 pp280). 拙著の反・日本人論（つまり白黒通念の解体なる）一連の本の要略を英米人向きに、一応、と。

In case you read on-line or a jacketed library copy,
here is the *back-cover* picture:

No cat likes being watched doing its business. Yet Han-chan did it just outside the bay-window because snow was on the ground and he hated the cold. I was curious. The insert-like drawing shows him hunkered down over a small felt-covered electric heater. One of the haiku may be Englished: *"When nature calls in the winter my old cat – a straight out and back."* And a *senryû* becomes *"The old cat – the world without is only number one and number two."*

The old cat does not shoot the breeze when nature calls in the winter.

your cat tails〜

www.ingramcontent.com/pod-product-compliance
Lightning Source LLC
Chambersburg PA
CBHW080423230426
43662CB00015B/2198